Any But Ordinary

I began the first of my many lives in 1911, a Continental born in London, with Bavarian, Hungarian gipsy, Italian and Swedish grandparents. I grew up in Hampstead, wanting to be English but with the various national characteristics of my grandparents still very much on display. The resulting turbulent family life often resembled grand opera ...

From pioneering stints as a woman decorator and occupational therapist, to solo travels in exotic and far-flung locations, from canal boat to camper van, Cambridge to Cottesloe, the lives and adventures of Cécile Marguerite Gabrielle Dorward have been anything but ordinary.

Cécile, 1940 version, meets Cécile 2000.

Anything But Ordinary
The Nine Lives of Cécile

Cécile Dorward and Ron Davidson

FREMANTLE ARTS CENTRE PRESS

Prologue

I am eighty-nine and, having been brought up in the sexual Dark Ages, it is only recently that I have been able to use the word penis. I knew that if I were to work on my story, I needed to be able to deal with sex without shame or embarrassment. So I implemented my own program of psychological desensitisation, starting with the 1963 *Concise Oxford Dictionary*. I read:

Penis — copulatory organ of male animal (L.= tail, penis).

I went to my local library to check a more recent (1993) edition of the *Oxford* and found, to my disappointment, the same prim definition. I talked with the librarian about this but he was more interested in my enthusiasm at being able to articulate the P word for the first time than in its definition. Obviously he thought I was very strange. That night I rang my friends and extended the deconditioning process: they knew I was strange. Soon I was ready for my writing task.

Please don't think I was working on another *Fanny Hill, Memoirs of a Woman of Pleasure* — although naturally I have had my pleasurable moments. My story focuses on a chance meeting with and continuing love for Alan Dorward, a philosopher from Cambridge, twenty years my senior, and a former student of Bertrand Russell and G E Moore. Alan was a considerable thinker while I was virtually unschooled, but we delighted in sharing matters of the mind. He was like a god to me — though not in bed. This left me with problems with my body, which I dealt with as best I could. Intermittently.

When Alan died in 1956, I began travelling and forgetting. I taught occupational therapy at Royal Perth Hospital, and made increasingly longer and more adventurous journeys out of Perth by car. These culminated in a twenty-six year odyssey, roaming the world at the wheel, mainly of a Land Rover. I covered a comprehensive mileage in my van as my age increased from fifty-eight to eighty-four. I ate breakfasts of egg and bacon in bed, and drank gin and tonics at dusk; in between I drove and met hundreds, no thousands of people. I was called the Mother of all Hippies by youth in the Middle East, and the World's Oldest Hippy in newspaper stories. I travelled much as they did except that I had no interest in drugs.

Meanwhile, I repressed my memories about Alan and my feelings for him. This worked for forty years until Ron Davidson, a writer and psychologist, arrived on my doorstep and offered to work with me on this book. We agreed that this would be, in theatre terms, a two-hander. I would write of my specific memories of my experiences and responses to them, whilst he would draw the parts together and help provide context and detail of people, places and times. But it became more complicated than that. He reminded me of Alan, the one man I still loved and my protector: yet he began uncovering things I thought I'd managed to forget. Then on my eighty-seventh birthday I exploded, and the protective lid I'd clamped over memories of my married life was blasted away ...

Life One
A Continental in London

A Cocktail of Nations

I began the first of my many lives in 1911, a Continental born in London, with Bavarian, Hungarian gipsy, Italian and Swedish grandparents. Most of them also carried a significant overlay of French culture. I grew up in Hampstead, wanting to be English but with the various national characteristics of my grandparents still very much on display. The resulting turbulent family life often resembled grand opera.

I was in London because of events which occurred in Paris in 1870. That was when the Franco-Prussian war arrived at the outskirts of Paris. My father's father, Georg Schmidt, had gone to Paris as a youth after running away from his parents' farm near the Black Forest in south-western Bavaria. The urge to escape the constraints of rural life came while he was sheltering under a bridge during a thunderstorm. By the time the rain had stopped Georg had conjured up a grand vision of his future material success. Paris, then in a period of peace and brilliance between times of revolution and war, was the city where he thought he could best realise his ambitions. He never returned to the farm but instead headed west.

Georg Schmidt soon had himself apprenticed to Revillon

Frères of Paris, furriers to the aristocrats of Europe and Britain, and worked with them until 1870. Then, with the Prussian army encircling Paris, he decided there was no place in this city for a German. He departed for London with a Hungarian associate, Peter Csomor, and together they set up as furriers just behind Oxford Circus. They were able to offer a reliable service to their English customers while their Paris counterparts, with their city under siege, were having trouble getting skins in and finished garments out. Schmidt and Csomor prospered. Soon Peter Csomor could send for his sister, Julie, to keep house for the pair. This prosaic arrangement became a romantic one: Julie married Georg and became my paternal grandmother.

My grandfather grew rich. He moved to a large house in Islington, a northern metropolitan London borough. As with many of those who had recently moved into the middle class, Georg Schmidt took particular pride in his possessions. He was able to retire at forty-six and devote much of his time to the month-by-month adjustments to the artificial climate necessary for his large conservatories to produce fine grapes, peaches and pineapples. Dinner guests could admire a superb pineapple which seemed to be a permanent feature of his table decorations. They must have wondered why the pineapple, a symbol of hospitality, was never cut and offered around, but I imagine this happened after the visitors had left, and the fruit was eaten by the family.

Georg and Julie produced a daughter, Emily, and two sons, George and Gustave. My father, Gustave, grew up as an Englishman in this very Continental household. He attended the school founded by the Worshipful Company of Haberdashers, as the ancient livery guilds switched their interest from industrial regulation to sponsoring educational and scientific institutions. Scholarships provided at these schools were seen by the liverymen, who were often religious Nonconformists, as a return for their material success. Gustave rode horses in Epping Forest, and he occasionally fell off. One such mishap reshaped his delicately moulded nose into what he called a beak. Gustave also acquired an appropriate brand of middle-class English, but one spiced with occasional Hungarian and Bavarian phrases. He achieved a high point of financial and social recognition at twenty-eight with a seat on the London Stock Exchange. To be accepted for this honour, one had to be a British subject, be re-elected each year and have a wife who was not engaged in business. Gustave became rich — for a while.

The Prussian assault on Paris — in a war largely provoked by the French — and the accompanying turmoil that engulfed the city in 1870, also drove my mother's branch of the family to London. My grandmother was Italian. I know that her father, Luigi Isler, eloped from Rome to Paris with a young aristocratic woman but details of that marriage and what happened to his wife have defied family investigation. I do know that Luigi was a celebrated carver of cameos: the Victoria and Albert Museum in London still displays some of his work. I had his cameo of Menelaus, the husband of Helen of Troy, which is now in the Art Gallery of Western Australia.

In Paris, Luigi created delicate cameos from striated onyx to enhance the bosoms of the wealthiest women of Europe. He was also a sculptor of larger works during the surge of artistic display which marked the Second Empire in France. He had two daughters, Charlotte and Pauline, who attended a Paris convent, sponsored — and protected — by the resolute Empress Eugénie, wife of Napoleon III. There were also two sons.

Paris became a desperate place in which to live as communal rioting followed the Prussian siege. My great-aunt Pauline told me, with particular anti-Prussian fervour, how there was almost no food in the city. Cats were on the menus of middle-class restaurants, while a multitude of rats was hunted by the poor in their search for meat. The trees of the Champs-Elysées were cut down and burnt for firewood. The political disorder brought the Second Empire to an end, and caused Napoleon III and Empress Eugénie to flee to Britain. Luigi left Paris before the Empress brought the convent school's nuns and its students with her to Chiselhurst in Surrey. One of those children was my grandmother Charlotte; another my great-aunt Pauline. One of the sons, Camillo, came too. Luigi established his studio in the garden of his house near the London Zoo, and became a Freeman of the City of London, 'for his works of art', and a Freeman of the Worshipful Company of Turners. He died in 1884, aged seventy-one.

The fourth of my grandparents was Hugo Björkman, a Swede who lived in Britain where he traded in timber. He married Charlotte and they produced two children. One was dark and Italian-looking like her mother; the other was fair and looked Swedish like her father. The dark one, Marie Louise, was to become my mother. Marie Louise and Gustave met: they almost had to. Many members of foreign families in London knew each other, as did most of those with an involvement in art. The pair were destined to meet on both counts. But, more importantly, my father was classed as a 'desirable match' because of his money, just when my mother's prospects for independence had taken a severe knock. She was an operatic contralto and her sister, Gabrielle, a soprano. They seemed likely to become an opera company's delight: sisters, dark and fair, contralto and soprano; both highly talented. Then their career prospects were abruptly ended because of the rivalry between the opera management and their teacher. This rivalry resulted in each sister being failed unfairly, by one-quarter of a mark, in the final exam which could have launched their careers. The rebuff sent the family in search of 'men with prospects'. They decided on my father as Marie Louise's future husband. His parents were apparently enthusiastic as well.

When Gustave and Marie Louise married in 1902 it was an occasion for grand dressing by the family members. This was recorded in big studio photographs incorporating many potted palms and a number of big hats. The stolid faces in the photograph hide a number of tensions. Marie Louise did not love

Gustave Schmidt marries Marie Louise Bjorkman in 1902. Cécile's Hungarian grandmother, Julie Schmidt, is on the extreme left of the middle row and her paternal grandfather, Georg Schmidt, on the left of the top row. On the right of the top row is Hugo Bjorkman, Cécile's maternal grandfather. His wife Charlotte is immediately below him.

Gustave and resented the fact that her fate was to be an arranged marriage rather than a glittering career in opera. Her own family was ambivalent about the match: they were strongly pro-French and disliked Gustave's Bavarian heritage. My great-aunt made her dislike clear when she described to me her last days in Paris under Prussian siege. But obviously the family hadn't been able to bring off a match incorporating both apparent financial security and an appropriate national heritage. My grandparents and their friends, none of whom spoke unaccented English, apparently opted for French as the lingua franca for the festivities.

The three children of the union appeared at five-yearly intervals: my sister in 1906, myself in 1911, and my brother in 1916. My sister was christened Madeleine, my brother Raymond, and I was Cécile Marguerite Gabrielle. The name Cécile came from my mother's closest friend. Marguerite was a widow who lived alone near us. Her walls were covered from ceiling to floor with paintings. I spent more than a little time lying on my stomach so that I could look at the paintings near the floor, which probably taught me to look long and well at pictures. Gabrielle was my mother's sister, and we called her Tante Gaby.

The reason for the long breaks between births at a time when intervals between pregnancies tended to be brief was never mentioned. I do know that the basis for restraint was not economic. When I arrived my family was enjoying comfortable times, financially if not emotionally. I had a French wet nurse which meant that not only had I no English blood in me but no English milk either. I also had a nurse, Dora, who wore a striped cotton uniform with a starched white apron over the top. I can remember the smell of starch as I buried my face in the apron to signal the end of one of the fierce tantrums which I could readily produce. The tantrums often began when my parents went out, leaving me in the cot under the care of the nurse. I would give the cot a heavy shaking before all passion was spent. My gesture of surrender would not, however, save me from one of Dora's

Baby Cécile with nurse Dora and sister Madeleine.

13

stern smackings. Dora came with us on our frequent family vacations to Dinard, a small French town on the north-western coast whose stark beauty, warm climate, and good bathing made it popular with English holiday makers. Dora insisted that I wear a large white bow whenever I went out.

Suddenly and traumatically, my father lost his money in a share trading disaster around 1915. Apparently a client was unable to meet the cost of a big package of shares and my father had to do so himself. He found this impossible and was declared a bankrupt. We had to shift from our house in Maida Vale to a less desirable apartment in Finchley Road, Hampstead. It was large enough, but two floors up, and above a decorator's shop. The entrance took us past a row of often unemptied bins, smelling with the refuse from surrounding businesses. My parents managed to keep much of their furniture, porcelain and glassware, to provide a rather grand interior which contrasted with the commercial activities outside.

My first vaguely coherent memories are of life in London early in the 1914–18 war. I was aged about three or four and being held in the arms of Eileen, our maid, outside our home. She was watching a German Zeppelin, probably about two hundred metres long, floating silently overhead. I was not yet afraid of them, but did sense that the adults around me were. The air raid threat had not been great early in the war. It was more of a nuisance: Londoners resented the effrontery of an enemy that dared to breach Britain's long-standing immunity from attack from Europe.

The feelings of vulnerability and impotence increased over the following two years. Zeppelins improved, there were more of them, and the tactics of their crews switched towards creating civilian terror. Also, biplanes with extensive wingspans were increasingly being used for raids. I remember electric signs on lamp posts flashing TAKE COVER whenever a raid was expected. Similar signs were conveyed through residential areas on large black cars driven by policemen. At night I was starting to be frightened by the noise of anti-aircraft guns on Hampstead Heath, as they tried to puncture the ponderous bags of hydrogen drifting overhead. The Zeppelins looked like giant glistening sausages when reflected in the beams of searchlights probing upwards from sites all over London. The guns were ineffective. There were not enough of them and the Zeppelins were too high. The same went for the small fighter planes which tried to intercept them.

More frightening for me were the prayers for protection being proffered noisily by Eileen while we cowered in the passageway of the house, supposedly to reduce the possibility of being hit by flying glass. Next morning Eileen would take my sister and me, and later my brother in his pram, to view nearby damage. I have one vivid memory from these inspection tours: a house sliced in half from top to bottom: a bed teetered on the edge of the shattered upstairs flooring with a Union Jack acting as a defiant bedcover, and a teddy bear perched on top of all that.

When the war ended, our neighbours hung Union Jacks on wooden poles from their windows, but it was the French *tricolore* which my mother hung from our front window. She was French in so many ways, but she also admired the English. She said they were very clever in not wasting time on emotional displays, and that this had allowed them to concentrate on winning the war.

I didn't realise the cruel toll the war was taking on Eileen's family. By November 1918, all four of her brothers had been killed in France. Eileen made a point of going to see her bereft mother on Wednesday or Sunday afternoons when she was free, between three and ten o'clock. That was the only free time she had. Eileen's mother lived in Kilburn, a working class area not far from Hampstead. Sometimes I went with Eileen and we returned by six o'clock. From the top deck of the bus I could look out at the dwellings of the poor, and peer down into the dark basements. There were urchins — that's what my mother called them — playing in the gutters. Whole families seemed to be living in every room: I wondered how they could survive.

There was a dairy near where Eileen's mother lived, which had a metal cow's head on the door. I liked to be sent out with a jug to get the milk. I'd slide a penny into the cow's head and milk squirted into the jug. These journeys also gave me the opportunity to explore. I noticed the houses were poorly kept, the gutters dirty, and the streets unswept: in Hampstead there were always men in the streets sweeping, and shovelling up the droppings of passing horses.

When I returned with the milk, Eileen's gentle mother would show us to the table which was in the kitchen. In winter it was dark there by four o'clock so the gas lamp would be lit. I loved the noise it made and particularly the real flames, rather than the silent incandescence of our electric light bulbs. We were served tea, with a dish of scones and a small bowl of butter. But there was no butter knife so I watched to see what the others did, which was to use whatever knife they had. I didn't know how I could butter my scones as I had been instructed by both my mother and my aunt never to use anything but a butter knife to transfer butter from the dish to my plate. I solved the dilemma by choosing a biscuit.

At five or six years of age I was sent to Louise Haycock's school. Louise Haycock and the two other Haycock sisters lived in a tall house not far from our own. Hers was no ordinary school with desks and a playground and lots of children. I remember that we sat around a dining table in a half basement which opened onto a walled garden. Miss Haycock, short and neat, was the sole teacher. I started by learning to write my name. I knew I had been christened Cécile Marguerite Gabrielle Schmidt. My Christian names were not my problem. However, the surname, Schmidt, was suddenly replaced by the commonplace Smith. I did not understand the effects of the 1914–18 war. Some newspapers carried headlines like MEN AND WOMEN TORN OPEN AND ROASTED ALIVE and supplied the extra information that the victims had been eaten. Not surprisingly the owners of foreign businesses made a point of specifying their origins, if they were not German. There were signs like RUSSIAN OWNER painted on the walls so that passers-by would not think they were German.

My father, Gustave Albert Michael Schmidt, felt he had to disguise his obvious German origins, and made the simplest change of names, by anglicising Schmidt to Smith. That had the advantage of costing nothing. The more affluent Uncle George, who was a lawyer, paid a deed poll fee and became George Martin. We thought Martin sounded much more imposing than the commonplace Smith.

At six I could read and write. Around that time, Miss Haycock set everyone a poem which had to be recited the next morning. I was so frightened that I wet my knickers while waiting for my turn. I was sent off to Louise Haycock's sister Miss Edith, who gave me a pair of her own copious knickers to wear home. Later we had lessons on the Old Testament, British Empire history, arithmetic, spelling, and grammar, with a particular emphasis on parsing and analysis and the use of correct pronouns. I still cannot listen to someone saying 'It's me' without wincing.

I was about twelve when a special mathematics teacher was brought in for two terms. Just as I began to get interested in maths that teacher left. Miss Haycock also made a point of teaching us Latin and French when we were relatively young. I, who had grown up hearing the real thing, sniggered as her English accent pervaded her French. Over my years with Miss Haycock, enrolments ranged from twelve down to six pupils, both girls and boys.

One thing that didn't change was the content of the lessons: I studied the same material, year after year, for the last four or five years. There was only one desk, which was reserved for the most senior pupil. I sat there for longer than was good for me, which was until I was sixteen. However, it was not all bad as Miss Haycock introduced me to Lewis Carroll's *Alice in Wonderland* and *Through the Looking Glass*, both of which I read many times.

I made a few friends, mainly boys from Miss Haycock's school.

The boys seemed to like my impulsive ways, particularly when we were out on scooters. I talked a lot and loudly, but I also wanted to be restrained like the English students. One of my friends was Sidney who was ten when I was eight. We pushed our scooters up the long hills of Hampstead Heath then raced down the steep streets to Finchley Road. We had no brakes. Slowing a scooter meant placing one's shoe against the back wheel or dragging it on the footpath. Sometimes we went to Regent's Park where, more than once, we saw Queen Mary as she passed us in her carriage on Queen Mary Drive.

Another boy, Robert, often stopped outside our house and rang the bell on his bike. I would stand on the footrest attached to the rear axle and we rode rapidly around the Heath. When I was ten I got my own bike. Ernest, another boy from my school, lived in a large house through which travelled the most wonderful Hornby train set. I remember that Ernest had only one hand and had trouble operating the train set. He needed the help of a friend like me. After playing, we would have what was called nursery tea, with slices of white bread covered with brown sugar and served by the maid. I rarely saw Ernest's parents even though I spent considerable time at his house. That was not unusual in the early twenties when upper and middle class parents saw their children only at set times.

I regularly went with some of my friends to a picture theatre at nearby Golders Green for the Saturday matinee, where we saw silent films like *The Kid* starring Charlie Chaplin. On the way we passed the house where the Russian prima ballerina Anna Pavlova lived, and the Hippodrome, the large theatre where my mother took us to see her dance.

While we played, work went on around us. We saw single horses and pairs of horses pulling large loads of coal up the steep streets around Hampstead Heath. They sweated even in winter. The drivers would allow them, complete with cart and load, to cool off by crossing the pond on the Heath, near Jack Straw's Castle. This was very exciting, particularly when we were sailing little boats on the same pond. Our boats would bob up and down on the horses' bow waves.

There was a darker side to my childhood, which I have only recently allowed myself to remember. When I was seven or eight I looked considerably older. My cousin,

A carthorse cooling off in Hampstead's White Pond while 'the urchins' parade in the foreground.

who was seven years older than I, began to target me for what I recognise now as sexual abuse. He and his sister introduced Madeleine and me to a game called Hares and Hounds. The game began with us splitting into two groups: the Hares would hide and the Hounds would try to find them. Invariably, I'd find myself hiding with my male cousin and with him making fumbling moves towards me with his penis exposed. I tried not to look at it; and if I did, accidentally, I felt ashamed. I was too ashamed even to pray for help.

Maude, our temporary maid, warned me about my cousin, and attempted to give me my first lesson in the facts of life, as they were called then. I dismissed her warning as mere 'servants' talk'. Sex as detailed by Maude seemed too unlikely an event for her cautions to be taken seriously. Maude claimed to practise such manoeuvres each week in a London park on her day off, but I did not believe that either. The abuse by my cousin continued but I think I managed to keep him at bay.

By the time I was twelve I was ready to leave Miss Haycock's school. I had been frittering away the early years of my teens repeating primary subjects with Miss Haycock. I wanted to move on to a school like the one my sister attended, and learn what were admittedly scaled-down versions of mathematics and science, as taught to some girls in the twenties. My sister went to a Catholic boarding school, then art school at St John's Wood. Whenever I said goodbye to Madeleine at the station as she headed back to boarding school, both of us were in tears. I wanted to go to a school like hers, and once even tried to hide on the train. My sister wanted to stay home, although I could never understand why.

I realised any move to another school would be difficult financially. My father's only income came from a row of workers' cottages in Hornsey, about ten kilometres from central London. My cautious grandfather had purchased the cottages as a secure legacy for his grandchildren. My father and Uncle George were trustees and could use the rent money during their lifetimes. My father collected these rents each week. It was his only job, and he saw it as demeaning. It made him very angry and, on rent days, he fumed over the record books on his desk in the dining room. My father claimed he had only enough money to finance one of us at a major school at any one time. But I always seemed to be forgotten. It was my brother Raymond, not I, who went off to boarding school when Madeleine finished.

Lunch as Grand Opera

We called our father Dink. I can't imagine why. It certainly didn't reflect his unpredictable temper which helped produce almost daily rows at the dinner table. These were often about, of all things, the German origins of the British royal family. Dink, despite his name change, was pro-German on a range of apparently trivial issues. I remember German names like Battenberg being tossed across the table with increasing ferocity by my father to reinforce some point concerning the genealogy of the Windsors. Nationality was teamed with art or music as the basis of further disputes. I used to think my father started the family arguments but soon realised my mother did her bit with provocative tactics like delaying the arrival of meals when Dink was in a hurry.

My parents were similar in other ways. Both were tall, and handsome. Both dressed well, although my mother often had to make her own clothes. On occasional happy moments they sang operatic arias together. Dink and my mother were also evenly matched in the daily arguments, both having considerable enthusiasm for insults. My mother's favourite was to accuse my father of being of 'peasant stock'; my father's response to this was a mocking laugh.

Arguments followed a fairly set ritual. My mother would be at one end of the table and my father at the other. The maid also sat at the table — we were a Continental family. After five minutes of shouting at one another, my mother would grab the carving knife and flourish it at Dink. The shouting would become even louder. Finally, my father's rage would build up to a point where he performed a ritualised cathartic response. This involved gathering up all the knives and the silver forks and spoons from the table in a single sweep of his extended arm. He then took the cutlery to the landing and dropped it over the banister. Then peace. Dink would resume his seat at the head of the table and talk rationally about some issue in art or Egyptology, both of which interested him intensely. My mother might question whether we should continue to use special fish knives and forks now that we knew Queen Mary had barred them from the palace. Our long-suffering maid quietly gathered the cutlery from the stairs, dusted it off, and returned it to the table. Time for dessert. All part of the protocol of lunch with the Smith family.

I remember with horror what was possibly our most spectacular family row. Though my sister Madeleine was more introverted and intense than I was, this did not prevent her from being occasionally outgoing and violent in family arguments. On one occasion she rose, picked up a crystal wine glass and smashed it on Dink's head. Then all the furies were let loose. Dink shouted even louder than usual, then moaned when he discovered blood spurting from a cut in his cheek. He decided he was dying. Madeleine, far from being appalled by what she had done, leapt on him and tried to strangle him with his tie. My mother was too busy trying to pull the belligerents apart to make her customary adversarial contribution.

I felt sure someone would be badly hurt, so I pelted down the road to get the doctor. I rang the surgery bell and knocked on the door frantically. The maid arrived to say the doctor was out. Back I raced to see what mayhem had ensured in the previous ten minutes. Anti-climax. All was quiet. The intense passion had passed. The maid had cleared the table.

These violent episodes were really sideshows which reflected the dynamics between members of our turbulent family. The cast included my mother — artistic, musical, tall, elegantly dressed, a person who had never loved my father. She came to loathe him when he lost his money. She now had neither love nor money. She withdrew from any intimate links with Dink, then from Madeleine and me. We did not believe Raymond had any needs. He was a boy. My mother made one attempt to escape, by going to France and taking Madeleine with her. Madeleine was too young to know whether our mother met anyone there. But she did remember the terrible encounter on a French beach after Dink had indefatigably hunted them down. Others on the beach feared physical violence and called the *gendarmerie*. Mother returned home.

Dink, the other principal in the family cast, thought he ranked not too far below the top stratum of the middle class, but lacked both the money and the English background to sustain that position. He had held a prestigious position on the most influential stock exchange in the world. Now, as a bankrupt, he was unemployable for any job he wanted to do. My mother locked him out of her bedroom and, when he broke down the door on one occasion, she installed my sister and, occasionally, my sister and me in her bed, as protectors against the possibility of Dink's nocturnal assaults. This left my little brother, Raymond, to sleep in the same room as the maid.

I had a quite different personality from that of my sister. I enjoyed most of the things I did, and left no doubt about my dislike of the others. Madeleine was generally unhappy with everything about her life. Not surprisingly, she took my mother's side in the family altercations: she had been observing them for longer than I had and understood them better. She understood that my mother left her bedroom door broken and ajar as a reminder of an earlier attack, when Dink sought what he called his conjugal rights, whatever they were.

23

Madeleine was the eldest and that was important in those times. She was regarded as cleverer than I and was therefore getting a better education. She was also seen as more talented artistically, and more attractive physically. But, despite being given these advantages, Madeleine hated Dink. She told me how this loathing was reinforced when he came home very late for lunch one day to find the table cleared, and Madeleine sitting there with her drawings. Dink picked up her work and threw it in a waste-paper basket, then stamped on it. His foot stuck in the basket, making him even more furious.

Eventually, when she was fifteen, the hatred developed to a point where Madeleine attempted suicide after an encounter with our father. I came home one day to find the house seemingly empty. But something felt wrong. Without thinking, I raced up to Madeleine's room and found her with a suicide note written, and clutching a container of lysol cleaning fluid. I emptied the bottle into a bucket, and destroyed the letter without reading it. Then I prayed that God would put things right and stayed with her for some hours in case He did not.

Madeleine went back to her more direct — rather than psychological — action against Dink. She was particularly active on my mother's birthdays when my father tried to kiss my mother. Madeleine, with a little help from me, would shepherd him away. This was a serious matter. We thought that a kiss between adults must be the ultimate sexual act, and were determined not to let it happen.

When I was seven I told my sister that our mother had placed a steel plate in front of her heart to protect herself from her situation generally, but particularly to rebuff any emotional demands I might make of her. I needed affection but knew my mother would not provide it. Madeleine agreed about my mother but it didn't worry her as much: her needs were different.

After many failed attempts at getting past the metaphorical steel plate, I began cultivating substitute mothers among older women who lived in our neighbourhood. My most successful 'mother' was Mrs Brand, who became very important to me when I was ten or eleven. She must have been in her forties; she was warm and welcoming, and almost every day I went to her house and told her about my life. We hugged intensely. This was what I needed my mother to do — receive my emotional outpourings. I imagine my mother felt jealous about this friendship even though she was unable to accept my effusions.

One afternoon, as I returned from Miss Haycock's school, Madeleine was waiting for me some distance from our home. 'Your friend has just died,' she said. I was shattered. I'd had no warning that Mrs Brand was dying of throat cancer. She had been the only person that I could really talk to. I retreated to our public library rather than going straight home. I discovered Charlotte Brontë's *Jane Eyre,* and her hero, Mr Rochester. He became my romantic ideal; he would be able to handle my emotional overflow. But before I could finish the book my mother discovered it. She decided it was too advanced for a twelve-year-old and sent it back to the library. Over the next five years, such stories of loss were repeated, with my substitute mothers either dying or moving from the neighbourhood; and my romantic icons crumbling, as books were snatched away. I worried that everyone and everything I depended on would be destroyed. I did not want this to happen to my velveteen rabbit who until then came to bed with me. In future I would not be dependent on him — or anyone. When I was fourteen I flung him into a corner under the bed and left him there.

Another of my problems as I entered adolescence was that I was born in England, lived in England, thought of myself as English middle class, but had little close contact with English people of the middle classes. My family was largely made up of artists; and artists seemed to be a no-class class. I had no English 'blood' either.

Our only visitors were the exotic remnants of my grandparents' Continental generation. Tante Sichel, the mother of my godmother, Cécile, wasn't a real *tante*. She came every

Sunday for lunch. Tante Cathelin, who frequently took us on her painting trips in Kew Gardens or Golders Hill Park, arrived later in the afternoon to make up the fourth hand for a game of bridge. We always greeted these ladies in French and with ritualistic kisses on both cheeks. This was something I disliked. It seemed so false. I used to wonder why the French flaunted emotions they didn't feel, and the English hid emotions they did. Predictably, the games of bridge ended in pandemonium, with shouted accusations of cheating all round. An amicable cup of tea and delicious *mille-feuilles* followed.

Portrait of Cécile, aged eleven, by Adele Martin.

Most of our visitors were artists. One of these was Aunt Adele, the wife of my father's brother George. She was from the United States but I noted with approval that she did not have an American accent. She was one of a number of artists who painted my portrait: the difference with Aunt Adele's was that hers was accepted for exhibition by the Paris Salon. I was delighted when she gave me the painting as a wedding present, and I still examine that distant gaze and wonder what it told Aunt Adele.

These constant visits

by Continentals to our home meant that we lacked English role models. My sister and I acted out characters from European grand opera, with frequent gesticulation and writhing and groaning on the carpet, in one death scene after another. We'd be accompanied by Caruso arias on the wind-up gramophone. Even mundane tasks like darning socks were given a special flourish as needles were plunged through the fabric and the thread taken up with a wild waving of hands and arms. It was not surprising that when I did meet English people it was a battle to keep a lid on this sort of flamboyance.

I was at an age when girls invited their friends home for a meal, but I couldn't take that risk with the small number of friends I knew. I had heard that some English behaved badly at home, but I knew they could not behave like we did.

The major meeting place for members of my mother's side of our family was *Speranza*, a large house at Bognor, a resort and convalescence centre ninety-five kilometres out of London on the Sussex coast. The house featured the mandatory conservatories and a fine garden which was tended by two gardeners, the very English Herbert, who was always called 'Erbaire', and Tippet. Our great-uncle Camillo, whose wife Rose had died many years before, went to *Speranza* at weekends. He was an engineer whose company provided much of the plant for the London water supply. The turnstiles we passed through at the London Zoo also carried a large brass plate announcing Uncle Cam's firm had constructed them. We felt a sense of ownership whenever we saw that sign.

My mother's mother, Bonne-maman, and my great aunt, Tante Pauline, lived there permanently. When I was six I discovered to my amazement that the three were brother and sisters. To someone of my age they seemed too old to have brothers and sisters.

The ritual of a visit to *Speranza* would start on Friday when Uncle Cam collected us in his Peugeot then later a chauffeur-

Bom and Tante Pauline.

driven blue Buick, and we headed for the sea. On those journeys I badly wanted to stop to pick the buttercups which flowered in the fields, right up to the edge of the road. But I was not game to ask. Once we were at *Speranza* our lives became more foreign than usual. French manners ruled. Tante Pauline saw to that. She also reminded us we could call great-uncle Camillo 'Uncle Cam' but we were not to call Bonne-maman 'Bom' — which of course we did. We slept in *Speranza*'s office and telephone room, where we would hear Bom ordering the week's supplies. We wondered how the shopkeepers could decode the order, which always included *'bananes'*.

Bom became anxious whenever we were preparing to leave for the beach. 'Don't go to the water to sunk,' she'd warn us. But we'd go anyhow. We'd climb into the bathing machine, and be towed by horse into the deeper water for discreet swimming. Come Sunday, Uncle Cam would give me a half-crown piece to take to church to put in the collection plate: I used to substitute it with a penny. One Sunday I absent-mindedly dropped my half-crown into the plate, then had to chase the collector to the back of the church to make the swap. Sunday was also the day on which Bonne-maman and Tante hired an open carriage and trotted in state along the Promenade. They were on their way to visit Madame Bhorringer for afternoon tea. Madame Bhorringer was the wife of a jeweller and I can remember her prodigious bosom which was almost covered with jewellery. Along the way the horse would lift its tail and splatter the roadway. I watched with interest but no one said a word about it.

The less pleasant aspect of these weekends was that my abusive cousin often came along and insisted that we play a more rural version of Hares and Hounds. I remember being trapped in a smelly pigsty somewhere on the periphery of Bognor. My cousin had exposed himself and was trying to corner me. I was getting stronger and rebuffed him vigorously. I do remember that I had no idea what this thing, of which I caught an unintentional glance, might be. My cousin said, without prompting, that I too would grow one when I was older, and I made subsequent examinations to see if this was the case. Dr Freud would have found all of this highly significant, and there is no doubt the ten years over which my cousin pursued me left its mark in terms of my later behaviour towards men. Certainly, I never wanted to be beholden to them. I would never make the first move. Perhaps that also was the protocol of the times, but I had spent ten years protecting myself from such overtures. I became exceedingly choosy. At the time, however, my one hope was that no one would find out about my cousin and me. I felt what he was doing was wrong but couldn't imagine why; also that somehow I, too, was culpable. I waited for the day when I would be big enough to fight off my cousin and this abuse would stop. I never thought of telling my mother until many years later.

My father was not always the violent, temperamental, and physically abusive person who could throw a beer bottle at my mother, or push our maid off a chair at the dinner table. Dink could also be gentle, loving, and very, very funny; just as he could be highly neurotic in his attention-seeking and quest for status. This makes him seem a very fragmented personality. Probably he was, although the fragmentary nature of my seventy-five-year-old memories may contribute to this impression.

Dink used to take us on long walks over the Heath and on to

Highgate and the Ponds where eighteenth-century road makers had dug their gravel. Occasionally, we'd stop at a certain historic pub where Dink would have a beer, then confront a resident cat with the most extraordinary cat-like screeching. This amazed both the cat and other hotel customers. Then we'd eat the lunch which we carried in our rucksacks. I liked having a rucksack on my shoulders. It made me feel I was really going somewhere — and perhaps not coming back. But we always did. Sometimes we would catch a train for fifteen kilometres in any direction and saunter back a station or two before returning by train. A steam locomotive would be involved in many things we did. Dink loved them.

It was no surprise that, when the General Strike hit Britain in 1926, my father was particularly excited. The strike was a time for the middle classes to come forward to do industrial tasks. Tens of thousands of volunteers helped load food trains and sometimes drove them, organised a milk pool, set up a special constabulary, and helped Royal Naval ratings secure the power stations. Genteel ladies tended the large horses used on the Great Western Railways delivery wagons. The die was cast for Dink. If he couldn't be a locomotive driver he'd be a train conductor. He walked proudly down the platform of Euston Station, locking carriages with a special key once they were full. I'm sure he was saddened when the strike ended and he had to return his distinctive cap. Dink, however, brought off a major coup. He managed to purloin his special key as a souvenir of an exciting six weeks. Whenever we travelled by train on our treks, Dink locked the door once we were inside. We travelled like royalty. Outside the masses wrenched at the immovable handle. We also travelled anxiously. We were afraid the conductor would discover how Dink locked the carriage doors and uproar would follow. But that never happened.

When Madeleine was at boarding school, Dink decided my brother and I should learn to paddle a canoe. We went to Regent's Park Lake by bus. My father always said to the conductor, 'One and two halves,' and I used to wait apprehensively for the argument to begin, because I was tall for my age and looked older than fourteen. Even when I was fifteen, my father refused to pay the adult fare for me. Everyone would look at us when

Raymond, Madeleine and Cécile at Bognor.

he started shouting at the conductor. If there was no argument originally, my father managed to generate one and attract attention. Finally, we refused to travel with him. We became skilled at leaping off the moving bus, and he was carried away gesticulating and shouting. When we arrived at the lake on the next bus he was there to greet us — lovingly. Then we got in a hire canoe and learned to paddle to Dink's stentorian instructions. He taught a Canadian style of canoeing with both paddles entering the water from the same side of the canoe. 'Anyone can paddle with the paddles on either side,' he'd explain when I asked the obvious question.

Once my mother came with us but she seemed more interested in a group of barefoot children playing with toy boats at the edge of the lake. 'Who are they?' I asked her. My mother said off-handedly: 'Keep away from them. They're urchins.' She made them seem like members of another species. They were not like us.

Other family activities were more cultural. Even when we were quite young we made frequent visits to London's many art galleries, the Victoria and Albert Museum, and the British Museum where Dink always found the mummies in the Egyptian section fascinating. We were also taken to inspect the remnants of Roman roads in St Albans. My mother was very fond of theatre and dance, and we went with her to see Anna Pavlova in the *Dying Swan* and Sir Johnston Forbes-Robertson in *Hamlet*. She also liked to take us shopping but even this became an educational tour. My mother had a good eye for line and architecture. Her favourite thoroughfare was Regent Street and she made us stand outside the Swan and Edgar store to study how the ongoing redevelopment with its modern shopfronts and bigger shops was destroying the elegant curve of the street.

My mother loved London for its parks and streets, and shops. She made sure that we grew up appreciating what we saw around us, including the city's art. When it came to appreciating the artistic efforts of her children, however, my mother was a disappointment. She had been raised in the tradition of the Muses, those goddesses who presided over musical and artistic enterprise. This meant that whenever I produced something that seemed really good she'd only say, 'Well, the Muses are at work today.'

I was a Catholic and that fact would eventually set off a series of dramatic events. But my indoctrination into the church was fairly haphazard. Dink insisted all of us should practise the faith, but left the supervision to our maid, Eileen. Each Sunday morning she led us to a small church at the top of the hill at Holly Bush for the 9.30 Mass. We always stepped through the church door just as the bell stopped ringing. We were breathless, and breakfastless if we were going to communion. Fasting from midnight was a requirement for communion. Before communion we would go to confession. I'd have to recount to the priest all my transgressions — being mean to my sister and brother, stealing my mother's biscuits and, ironically, being rude to my father. It was a very venial list as sins go but enough to focus my daily prayers, which I said under Eileen's supervision. 'Help me

God, to be good,' I requested. Prayer became more serious as gradually I became a committed Catholic. The priests constantly warned us about the threat of both Hell and Purgatory. Even with my limited repertoire of sins, Purgatory seemed a real threat.

At home my brother Raymond and I discovered a more adventurous way of entertaining ourselves than touring places of culture and roaming the Heath. Our iron fire-escape led up to a flat roof four storeys above the ground. My mother would never climb the fire escape, so we felt we had free rein up there. We found we could tumble over the brick walls which separated adjoining houses, which meant we could run across a dozen roofs, then watch the steam locomotives passing beneath us at the end of the street. We went quietly on the trip out but stamped our boots on the way back to frighten the residents below. An old man on the opposite side of the road would impotently wave his fist at us as we raced past. We smiled at him, but we were lucky we did not fall and break our necks. I imagine some of our neighbours would not have worried too much if we had.

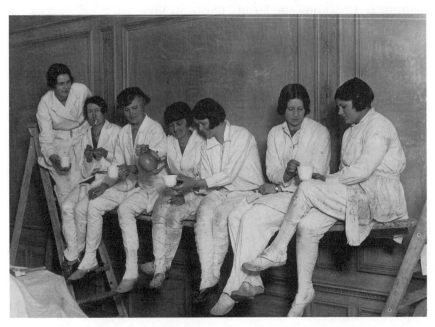

Morning tea with the Women Decorators. From left: Smiffy (Cécile), Miss Almack (a business partner), Bruce, Miss Quin (a partner), Crysell, Stansell (Hilary), and Boxill.

Life Two
Not Just Decorative

Not Just Men's Work

In adolescence I sought recreations more solitary than family outings with Dink, more tranquil than running on neighbours' roofs, and found myself involved in an important feminist project.

Most Wednesday afternoons I rowed alone on the artificial lake in Regent's Park, the site of Dink's earlier complicated canoeing lessons. Some mornings I rowed out and had breakfast with a friend. Along the way to the lake I sometimes stopped on the one-hundred-year-old Macclesfield Bridge over the Regent's Canal, and watched the canal boats, loaded with coal, passing quietly beneath. I imagined standing at the tiller of a craft like that but never thought that, twenty-five years later, I would be — and passing under the same bridge. On the way home I often explored the nearby streets.

One day I turned into Baker Street, and walked past the house where Sherlock Holmes had 'lived'. Then into Upper Baker Street. My attention was drawn to a sign which would change my life. I can still visualise it. The border was blue, as was the lettering, set on a green background — 'Women Decorators'. In the window were displays of wallpaper and curtain material, and photographs of girls in smart white uniforms hanging wallpaper, and mixing paints and applying them to doors and window frames.

I was fascinated as I had become interested in suffrage and other equality issues. I went inside on an impulse and was met by a Canadian, Mrs Goodhugh. I asked if I could join her company. She asked just two questions: How old are you? and Why do you want to leave school? I told her I was sixteen, and I had learned all that I could be taught at my school, and that there was no prospect of my moving on to another. I wanted to be able to earn a wage and not be dependent on my family. The dependence of my mother on whatever cash Dink would part with was at the back of my mind.

My answers apparently satisfied Mrs Goodhugh. She said I could take a year's course for fifty pounds, and would be paid ten shillings a week over the second six months. I was ecstatic. I had enough of my own money to pay for the course. Uncle Cam was now dead and had left his grand-nieces one hundred pounds each. The big question was whether my mother would allow it. She had firm ideas about what work was suitable for women. Sixteen-year-old girls painting houses would not fit comfortably with such ideas. So before I left the shop, I asked if my mother could come to see how nice it would be for me to enrol and learn a skill. My mother exploded when I told her my plan: 'You'd be doing not just men's work but workmen's work.' Still, she eventually agreed to examine the shop, and the cool competence of Mrs Goodhugh won her over. She also took comfort from the fact that, even if we were doing workmen's work, at least I wouldn't be working with workmen.

Soon I was leaving home for my first day at work. My mother had made me the white overalls cut to a special pattern, a very smart jacket styled on a riding coat, and breeches with gaiters and lots of buttons. Standard trousers were unacceptable, even for women doing workmen's work. I spent the first weeks at the back of the shop learning how to mix paints, clean brushes, prepare woodwork for varnishing and, most exciting of all, how to paper a ceiling. Painting was no easy task in those days, before plastic paints with multiple colour formulas made it something any fool could do. When the principals decided I had learned enough to be useful, I was sent on jobs to prepare surfaces for the more expert women to finish with paint, wallpaper or a favourite finish, Eggshell Flat Varnish which was made by Thos. Parsons and Sons Limited. It was very exciting to be doing men's work, but I'm not sure I ever asked myself why.

We usually worked in fairly high class homes, often owned by friends of our four principals. Despite the apparent importance of their contacts to the business, the principals still told us we had to do a better job than the men so that Women Decorators would be recommended to other house owners. Our principals were not just well-connected feminists making a point about equality of employment opportunities across genders, but also hard-working ones. They provided estimates, gave expert advice, and did much of the actual decorating, as well as teaching 'apprentices' like me. The house owners typically wanted us to create the 'modern look'. To achieve this we used lots of stippling and shading to establish a particular mood for a room, rather than emphasising architectural features like arches and columns. Wallpaper was also making a comeback after the reaction against Victorian excesses.

I loved wallpapering because of the skill required to hang each piece so that it matched perfectly the pattern of its neighbour. To achieve this on a ceiling was just that much harder, and just that much more enjoyable. It was pleasing to finish a wall or ceiling, step away and view a surface apparently without seams.

Kathleen Boxill, who started at Women Decorators before I arrived there and remained a friend for the next seventy-one years, was similarly devoted to wallpapering.

When we stopped for lunch, we ate our sandwiches and were given tea by a maid from the house in which we were working. We sat around, proud of the paint and putty under our fingernails, and discussed current topics. We talked about the place of women in Britain and in decorating; about the arts, politics, and even religion, as well as less elevated topics, such as how we had entertained ourselves the previous evening. It was 1928 and, after forty years of activism, universal suffrage for those aged twenty-one and over had finally passed into British law. There was an atmosphere of excitement wherever we went. One of the women decorators wanted to know what I thought of being able to vote soon. I had to admit I had some time to wait. I was then only just seventeen.

At the time I was enthused by current events involving women's rights, but did not comprehend all of the more subtle issues of feminism which Women Decorators sought to emphasise. The principals were not just interested in political equality for women through the Suffrage Act, but social and economic equality as well. Women Decorators had been established to allow women to work at what was categorised as 'men's work'. We talked about this often at lunch times. But at sixteen I was more thrilled at the prospect of working at the top of a tall ladder than engaging in an ideological debate. The other decorators wanted to know what I thought — and took my thoughts seriously. This had never happened to me before. It was also the first time I had heard quiet discussion of issues, rather than impassioned argument. I wondered whether this was the restrained English way which my mother talked about, and resolved to practise keeping my instinctive reactions to myself, and to try to think before speaking. These were not inconsiderable aims. They went against my upbringing and the family's operatic mode of expression.

I was the tallest and youngest of the decorators so I was

usually sent up the tall ladder, which we called the Giraffe. Up there I was in a world of my own. When I came across three ladybirds spending the winter on the top of a window frame, I could leave their area unpainted and the ladybirds undisturbed. No one would ever know, at least for some time. One morning, in a large and lofty room, two of my colleagues were scraping off old wallpaper. They were having an interesting conversation. I was on the other side of the room on the tall ladder. I leant away from the wall and started to make a clever comment. It remained unfinished. The ladder toppled away from the wall, I dropped the bucket, and followed it to the floor. I saw the shocked faces as I descended. Amazingly, I broke no bones and little harm was done. It was just fortunate that the bucket contained water and not paint.

That afternoon I got a message to go back to the shop. I expected a routine transfer to another job. Mrs Goodhugh was waiting. She said women decorators not only had to be better decorators than men as she'd told me before, but also safer than men. She suggested I should go back to school 'to play tennis'. To play tennis, indeed! I didn't understand that for 'play tennis' I should read 'grow up'. I'd assumed that, because I was paying Women Decorators, I didn't need to do too much actual work for the group. I begged for another chance. I promised to change my ways and work like a beaver. The principals gave me a reprieve but refused to guarantee my ten shillings a week until I showed more responsibility.

I apparently responded adequately to the warning. While I was still seventeen, I was in charge of a job, and had two trainees to instruct. These were very heady times for the decorators. We dashed about to different parts of London by tube, bus and on foot, seeking the shortest routes that would get us to our houses so that we had time to change into our elaborate work clothes by eight o'clock. There were other excitements. Occasionally, a man standing beside me in the crowded bus would push his elbow against my side. I'd feel the sustained pressure and reciprocate, without looking at his face. It felt quite exhilarating but I had no idea what it might signify.

The sole man in Women Decorators trailed forlornly behind us on our way to work, bearing the paints, planks and ladders piled on a large barrow, which at times he had to push two or three kilometres. Sometimes we'd forget an important piece of equipment and I'd have to take a taxi back to the shop to pick it up. I'd feel very important doing that. I felt equally conceited when a cool mood was required for a room and I was brought in to do my speciality — painting tasteful clouds on ceilings. I'd use clusters of real clouds passing the window as my models, but they tended to be blown from view before I had finished painting them and I completed the scene from memory. Sometimes my fine work would be obscured by clouds of smoke inside the room. There were no restrictions on our smoking at the workplace; in fact smoking was considered smart for young women in the late twenties; also, cigarettes cost only sixpence a packet. We wanted to work like workmen even to the point of smoking on the job.

The two trainees assigned to me were Dorothy, Lady Balfour of Burleigh, and Hilary, the daughter of a building contractor from Taunton in Somerset. Lady Balfour, who was in her early forties, was a prominent feminist advocate of equality between the sexes in employment and other areas. She was married to Lord Balfour, a prominent banker who had come to the issue of absolute equality for men and women in paid employment through membership of the Open Door Council. Lord Balfour was also a passionate advocate of improved public housing. He had been known to pass around, at black-tie dinners, a matchbox. When diners opened the box they found a bed bug, dramatically indicating that people were forced to sleep with such creatures, sometimes in properties these diners either owned or controlled

Hilary, my other apprentice, was a year or two older than I was, and unaccustomed to the ways of a big city. She wished to experience these ways, but also to prepare herself for decorating the houses her father built around Somerset. I taught Lady Balfour and Hilary how to put together compounds to fill cracks in walls and apply graining to painted wood; how to achieve a glass-like finish on mahogany panels by rubbing with pumice powder; how to wash a wall, stain wood, mix paints, and erect scaffolding and heavy ladders.

Lady Balfour wore breeches and gaiters like the rest of us, and we looked as if we were dressed for riding rather than painting, papering and polishing. She told me to call her 'Bruce', her husband's family name. The family traced its origins back to the fourteenth century Scottish king, Robert I, 'the Bruce'. Bruce called me 'Smiffy'. There wasn't a Lady, a Mrs, or a Miss amongst the women decorators. Bruce brought sandwiches and took part in our discussions — with a considerable degree of hand-waving I was pleased to notice — and emphasised the importance of what we were doing, but also raised many more mundane topics. She seemed to enjoy being away from the ideological spotlight.

Until recently, Dorothy Bruce had been secretary of the feminist umbrella group, the National Union of Societies for Equal Citizenship. She supported the philosophy of Lady Rhondda's Six Point Group which wanted legislative, economic and social reforms to 'secure an equality of liberties, status and opportunities between men and women.' The president of NUSEC, Eleanor Rathbone, argued on the other hand that women could never attain equality unless their special needs as mothers and their economic dependence within the family were addressed.

In 1927 Dorothy Bruce was one of the leaders of a group of women who resigned from the National Union after narrowly losing a vote over the inclusion on the agenda of industrial protection measures designed to keep women out of harsh areas of employment like mining, heavy and dangerous operations, and night shifts, which also happened to offer higher rates of pay. Bruce and the other equality feminists saw this 'protection' as a form of negative discrimination. They sought absolute equality of opportunity, and the extension of any protection which might be required to both men and women.

Eleanor Rathbone and her supporters claimed that opponents like Dorothy Bruce could not know what it was like to work in male dominated and often physically demanding and dirty jobs: the working class women knew. The claim was wrong in the case of Bruce, although her early life had been conventionally upper middle class. Her parents, Richard and Louise Done, liked to travel and they took their daughter with them. This didn't help her progress at school. On a trip to the south coast of France, the family met the vivacious French comedy actress Gabrielle Réjane, and Dorothy travelled with her and her daughter for several years. When a principal left and the understudy was ill, Dorothy Done made her stage debut.

She was living in Paris when World War One erupted, and wrote to the British Red Cross, seeking to join and offering her help. They took too long to answer, so she joined the French Red Cross. Her job was to collect the seriously wounded from railway carriages where they might have been lying for two days, and prepare them for the operating theatre. This meant cutting away uniforms and washing bodies which had been dreadfully mutilated by bullets, high explosives and shrapnel. Soon she was summoned to work in the operating theatres beside tyrannical, tantrum-prone surgeons. She certainly knew how unpleasant a job could be.

After the 1927 NUSEC defeat, Bruce tired of argument about feminist philosophy: she liked doing things rather than debating ideology. She began the six-month course with Woman Decorators so she would be equipped to set up her own firm, and be able to advance equality of employment in a practical way.

Once I was earning money my mother decreed that I was old enough to go out with my sister in the evenings. We queued for cheap seats in the pit or gallery of the major theatres, saw all the Shaw plays, and many of the best actors — all at two shillings a show. I also assumed with Hilary the teaching role that Dink and my mother had taken with my sister and me. I took her to the theatres: to the opera at Covent Garden, and to Dink's favourite, the Old Vic. At weekends I retraced with Hilary my tracks through the Royal Academy, the Tate, and other Kensington art galleries. I began to realise how lucky I was to have been raised by parents who made sure that we took advantage of the fact that we lived in a very civilised city.

When Hilary and I started queuing at five for seats in the gods at Covent Garden, theatre workers would bring us chairs to help make our long wait more comfortable. We'd take a third chair for Bruce who wanted to be with us but always had other things to do before joining us in the queue. We felt she was one of us and we were very proud to have her sit with us.

My friendship with Hilary was not just about going to the opera and plays, and viewing paintings. We were also enthusiastic ice skaters and toured the local rinks which were just becoming popular — and smart. The Hilary and Cécile team attracted some attention as we swept around the rink in our 1920s version of Torville and Dean.

Next I joined the Studio Club. The club took its name from the magazine *The Studio*, which claimed to inform 'those of fine taste' on issues of art and decoration. It was, it claimed,

> the firm supporter of every fresh and honest effort to get away from the curse of plagiarism in domestic architecture, from the curse of effete ideals in painting and in sculpture, and from the curse of imitative repetition in design and handicrafts.

My mother had many friends among artists, in particular Ludovici, an old suitor of my grandmother and the brother of Tante Cathelin. He had a studio on the canal at Maida Vale. My mother joined the club so that she could attend lectures there by Ludo and other artists, and to view their exhibitions. She thought membership would be good for my education. So it proved, although not quite in the way she had envisaged.

The Studio Club was situated in a basement just off Piccadilly Circus. It was a place where artistic people gathered and demonstrated their faith in the magazine's ideals. At the time I joined, members were outraged that Jacob Epstein's statue of Rima in Hyde Park had been splashed with red paint by someone who obviously was not a person of fine taste. On reaching the club I always ran down the stairs, through a small anteroom where tables were strewn with art magazines, then into the large exhibition space which incorporated a dance floor and restaurant. There was also a small bar with a barman who knew everyone but made a special point of talking to me. The crowd was generally young, although not as young as I. (Louise Haycock rides again!) At seventeen, I was the youngest member. We danced the Charleston, or in a simple smoochy style to a single piano. Sometimes there was a drummer as well.

The club was a major education for me. I still found English behaviour a mystery, but was able to make some attempt to adjust. I knew I had a deep booming voice so I tried to restrain it when I was in the club. I knew I waved my arms and hands in the Continental manner, so I restrained them also. Despite this restraint I attracted the attention of many members, including an ageing artist who sat me on his knee — whenever my mother wasn't watching — and secretly explored my thighs. I was too naive to see this as significant. I also encountered several young men, some of whom were said to be very handsome but, after my experiences with my handsome cousin, that was a term I would be reticent to use about any young man. Even the tall youth who owned and raced an MG sports car failed to qualify. I was allowed to go motoring with him into the country, although only in the afternoons, never at night. I loved to be at the club. Whenever I was there, I had a feeling something special was about to happen to me. And it did.

Encounter with a Tall Stranger

I'd had a typically exuberant evening at the Studio Club. I ran up the stairs and out to the pavement — and into a cloudburst. I retreated under cover to watch for my bus. While I was waiting a man came up the stairs from the club. I had not spoken to him before but surprised myself by saying: 'It's teeming out there. I hope you've got a mackintosh.' He passed me his black walking stick (with an elegant gold band), and asked me in a voice which was educated English with a Scottish underlay, to hold it while he put on his overcoat. Then he said: 'Let me take you home? I'll call a taxi.'

I thought of my house with its embarrassing rubbish bins lining the entrance and said: 'Oh no, thank you. I'm catching a bus. And here it is.' I dashed for the bus without looking back. Then I realised the tall stranger was right behind me; then sitting next to me on the upper deck of the bus. He said he had seen me in the club and asked a friend to give him an introduction, but I had disappeared too quickly for this to happen. The bus conductor came around to collect our fares. The stranger asked how much my fare was and paid for a four-penny ticket. I breathed more easily when he took a penny ticket for himself.

For a penny ticket he obviously wouldn't be seeing me home. The secret of the rubbish bins was safe — for a while at least.

As the stranger was about to leave the bus, he took a slim silver cardcase from his waistcoat pocket and extracted a card which he handed to me. He said he would like to see me again, wrote down my name and phone number, and was gone. I glanced at the card. It read: 'Alan Dorward MA, Don, Trinity College, Cambridge.' This was mystifying. I knew about Trinity College, Cambridge, but what could a don be? Someone religious? Or Spanish, perhaps?

I had plenty to reflect on during the rest of the trip. Here was a man who was different from any man I'd ever met; one of the rare men taller than I; a man with a walking stick and silver card case; a mature man who must know all about the world I wanted to comprehend. Would he be my Mr Rochester? And I Jane? Would he be able to accommodate my need for affection? Would he have his own problems, his own equivalent of Mr Rochester's mad wife? I couldn't know the answers to any of these questions, as I had spoken to him for less than five minutes.

I ran home from the bus stop to show my mother the card. She could tell me what a don was — a head, fellow or tutor of a university college. She sent Dink next morning to the public library to discover more about Alan Dorward. Dink soon returned with the awesome news that there was an Alan Dorward in *Who's Who*. He was twice my age and had recently been appointed Professor of Philosophy at Liverpool University. He must have given me an old Cambridge card by mistake; or perhaps this was a pointer that, psychologically, Trinity College, Cambridge would always be his academic home.

The following evening Alan rang to ask if he could take me to dinner that Friday. I said I couldn't go, as I would have to pack for a trip I was to take that weekend. My mother, who had been listening from the next room, intervened: 'Of course you can go. I'll do your packing.' I relayed the message and we decided to meet at the Studio Club. It was not like my mother to facilitate my social life. Normally she railed about me 'wearing myself out'. Now she was clearly being swept along by the mixture of awe and excitement generated over the previous twenty-four hours.

And so we met again. Alan suggested dinner in Soho. I said boldly I was not at all interested in being shut up in a small Soho restaurant. It had been a beautiful sunny day and I suggested we go to Richmond, by the river, with its charming woods.

On the train, I took time to study my Mr Rochester in some detail. He was about three inches taller than I was which made him six foot one and a half inches. He carried his slim frame in an upright but easy manner. His long face was split up by black-rimmed glasses which gave him a bookish look; which was appropriate. Unlike me, he spoke only when he had something to say. But at the same time he clearly liked to take the opportunity to tell me things. When he did he often provided a restrained emphasis to his comments by steepling his long slender fingers and looking at me over them. The other characteristic I noted was that he never had anything bad to say about anyone.

I soon felt brave enough to ask lots of questions about what Alan did, and where, and how often he came to London, although I already knew some of the answers because of Dink's research. I discovered from his comments to me, and later from his diaries and writing, that he was born in the historic Scottish border town of Melrose, and grew up at nearby Galashiels where his father owned a mill which produced Scottish tweed. He had been an academic star from an early age and won a number of scholarships which eventually took him to Edinburgh University, then, in 1910, to Cambridge, as the winner of the prestigious Ferguson Award. Here he encountered Bertrand Russell, the eminent philosopher and mathematician and strident advocate of radical social and political causes, as well as the commonsense approach to philosophy of G E Moore. While his colleagues argued about the essence of identity Moore would say: 'This is a chair, I can see it's a chair ...'

Russell at his intellectual peak had in 1903 written *The Principles of Mathematics* in which he demonstrated that mathematics was reducible to logic. When Alan Dorward first met him, Russell had, with A N Whitehead, converted this idea into a formal system in the classical text *Principia Mathematica*, and was about to return to the problems of general philosophy. He was also conducting, largely by letter, his first major and most emotionally extravagant affair. The object of his obsession was Lady Ottoline Morrell. Lady Ottoline was tall and striking, and had become famous for her salon, where she entertained a wide circle of literary figures including Virginia Woolf, T S Eliot, D H Lawrence and Aldous Huxley. Russell's mind clearly entertained Ottoline although she took some convincing about the merits of his short scrawny body.

Bertrand Russell, 1910.

Russell had noted Alan Dorward, as this letter shows:

My Dearest
After posting my letter to you, I saw North and Burns and Dorward and Geach, and talked to each of them about how well they had done in their Tripos; then I lectured to Wittgenstein: then I had Sanger to dinner, I love him very much; then an enormous crowd at my evening — I was very full of wit and kept them in fits of laughter. I have hardly ever been more gay.

The young Alan Dorward.

Alan had pleasant memories of his first years at Cambridge when he attended these Russell evenings, known as crushes. His diaries record afternoons spent punting on the River Cam, and considerable attention being paid to the Edwardian pastime of flirting. There were 'outrageous flirtations on the tennis court' with young women whose names were always prefixed with Miss: 'I certainly get plenty of encouragement from Miss Bell; I think she is one of the most accomplished flirts I know.' He also wrote a slightly precious mini-essay *On Flirtation*:

> I never really fall in love now; I consciously work in order to deceive myself into believing that I am, for the pleasure it gives me, and the material it provides me for reflection on myself. More accurately there are several motives. (1) The pure sex-motive, which I suppose lies at the root …

When he wrote this I was three months old, and we would not meet for another eighteen years.

In his diaries were comments on academic arguments with friends at Trinity, which extended late into the night; notes on probability lectures from Maynard Keynes; games of hockey and tennis; and black moods which overtook him from time to time. He joined the Fabians and spent time with one of their most prominent members, the poet Rupert Brooke, a 'charming man', then, later, 'somewhat conceited'. He wrote papers and came 'to dread Bertrand Russell and other fierce critics.' He spent time with a member of the eminent Scots family, Beveridge, and wondered 'whether I will ever be at ease with the English.'

Academic issues were noted: 'I get more and more dissatisfied with Moore's *Principia* [*Ethica*], without being able to lay my finger on a definite error.' He also wrote in 1911:

> the question of joining the Officer Training Corps is causing me much heart searching. On the one hand I feel it is my duty to join it, on the other the knowledge that it would take up much time … There is also my timidity in starting anything out of my own line, which is really study. This applies also to hockey but I can stop hockey whenever I like … Very unwillingly I think I will have to join.

That was written on a Friday. On the Saturday he wrote: 'I have now veered round and almost decided not to join. My constitutional indolence has conquered.'

Alan volunteered for active service in 1914 but was rejected because of a chest problem. On the train to Richmond he told me, with some pain, of the white feathers he attracted from London women while working with the War Office. He gave little indication of the long-term effect that might have had on him. I discovered also that he had a fine taste in music and in French literature, although his spoken French wasn't great — about my level. I told him about my Continental origins, my grandparents and my mother, but I didn't mention Dink. Also, apprehensively,

I told him I was a Catholic, and a believing one. Already I felt this would become a problem for us.

We walked from the station to a Richmond hotel near the Thames. Alan went to the bar, probably a bad omen which, in my enthusiasm, I failed to notice. So I went on my own for a joyful walk along the river bank toward the Royal Botanical Gardens at Kew — and lost my balance. Instinctively, I clutched at the air behind me hoping to grab an overhanging branch. Instead, a hand grasped mine as I was about to fall into the water. It was Alan's. He had at that moment come down the trail looking for me. We hugged each other and I knew I would love him for as long as I lived.

Alan and I decided that we would write to one another regularly. His letters reflected the British intellectual's delight in word play. His first letter to me contained a riddle in verse:

Can you tell me why
A Hypocrite's eye
Can better descry
Than you or I
On how many toes
A pussy cat goes

The answer came in the next letter:

A man of deceit
Can best counterfeit
And so I suppose
Can best count 'er toes

I was delighted that my professor of philosophy seemed to find this nonsense as amusing as I did. This was a very important point in our relationship: Alan was attracted to me for my unusual sense of humour — not, as some must have been suggesting, for future prospects with my young body. There was another important moment when I discovered Alan was as fond of animals as I was, and of animal jokes.

Over the next year Alan spent more and more of the university vacations in London. This represented a continuing learning experience for me, and probably for him, too. He took me to the finest restaurants; we went to the theatre and concerts where I sat in the best seats rather than in the gods; and I even absorbed what subtleties may be associated with very dry sherry — a considerable step from my earliest experience with alcohol which had come when Dink gave us sugar cubes dipped in liqueur. I felt that at nineteen I was becoming a confident young woman rather than an enthusiastic girl, and gradually began to realise that Alan loved me.

Alice in Cambridge

Alan had to return to Cambridge University from Liverpool as an external examiner for the Tripos exams which determined students' honours grades. He rang and said: 'Come down to Cambridge. I'll meet you at the station.' I covered my tracks with Dink then caught the train.

Alan had booked himself into the Blue Boar while, very properly, he took me to stay with the Moores. I was moving into the celebrity set. G E Moore's great work, *Principia Ethica*, seemed to be the Bloomsbury group's guiding light. Group members like Virginia and Leonard Woolf, Lytton Strachey and Maynard Keynes, said they sat at his feet. Keynes, the celebrated economist and writer, called Moore's writing 'the beginning of a new renaissance'. Russell simply called him 'a genius'.

Moore — he was always Moore to his colleagues — organised a dinner while I was in Cambridge. I sat, not at his feet like a member of the Bloomsbury set, but on his right as guest-of-honour. It was a daunting occasion. Some of Britain's best brains were assembled around the table: and there I was, virtually unschooled. Moreover, I still hadn't really been exposed to English manners, or English anything much.

Moore was a delight and, in many ways like Alan. He brought me into the conversation with a simple question. He asked what I thought of Scotland, knowing that I had just been there to meet Alan's father (his mother died many years before). I said it was interesting to see those nice big hills. I added, without really thinking about the source, 'the hills one sees around London, you'd think they were valleys by comparison.' I was horrified. Even before getting the last words out I knew I'd just quoted loosely from Lewis Carroll's *Through the Looking Glass*, which everyone knew was a children's book. I didn't know it was also the philosophers' book *par excellence*. I waited for the sneers; instead there was admiration. Everyone knew what I was quoting. It made a considerable impression, particularly when coupled with a knowledge of my lack of formal education. 'A breath of fresh air,' one philosopher said. I had passed my first exam with honours.

Oliver Strachey, G E Moore, Maynard Keynes.

Alan explained a lot about the philosophical world and its politics over the next year. There had been a central event in his life when he applied for a position at Trinity in 1915. He had written to Bertrand Russell from St Andrews University where he was teaching, asking for a reference. In his letter, Alan mentioned in passing that he could see from his window a number of clergymen burning what seemed to be one of Russell's anti-war pamphlets. He heard one of them suggesting the task should have been carried out by a 'common hangman'. Russell replied in small neat handwriting:

> Dear Dorward
> I have already given Broad a testimonial, which I had sent off before I got your letter. I don't know whether this makes a difficulty. Didn't I give you a testimonial before? If so would it do to say that you are using it with my permission? I rather doubt whether a recommendation by such a wicked person as I seem to be would carry much weight. Probably what was burnt by the reverend gentleman was my article in the International Journal of Ethics, which was more shocking than my U.D.C. pamphlet, since I went so far as to associate myself with some very shocking opinions emitted by an Agitator in the Sermon on the Mount ...

Russell was about to be — determined to be, in fact — gaoled for writing anti-conscription material: and Alan did not get the fellowship. It was a rejection which I suspect had already set the seeds of his, and my, later problems.

As I became more familiar with the business of philosophy, Alan told me of the arrival in Russell's group of the tempestuous Austrian, Ludwig Wittgenstein. When Wittgenstein, the engineer and soon-to-be-great philosopher of logic and language, arrived in the Cambridge group in 1913, Russell told Alan he thought the newcomer's comments were 'silly'. He soon decided, however, that Wittgenstein was saying something important about language and changed his tune. Alan, who was for Russell 'a sombre Scot, quiet but rather able', had a temperament well suited to maintain a strong personal bond over the years with the sometimes manic, more often depressive, genius who was Wittgenstein.

All of this was a great learning experience for someone who

knew almost nothing about anything. Alan introduced me to increasingly complex philosophical topics and I also listened to him talking with other academics. He seemed to relish being presented with me, the original *tabula rasa*. He seemed to know I was eager to learn and instructed me in many things directly. Other times I seemed to be taking in knowledge about the world by a process of osmosis. There was, however, one subject we edged away from — religion. I knew the current crop of philosophers tended to be sceptical about religion. Moore had begun a lecture with: 'In the beginning was Material; and Material begat the Devil; and the Devil begat God'; and there was no doubt that Russell's position was one of hostility. Alan was less sure about religion. As a student he flirted with joining the Cambridge atheist group, the Heretics. He wrote in his diary at the time: 'Religion is a thing I could never do without. But there is hardly one of the dogmas of the church that I accept.'

Not surprisingly, my Catholic faith became less secure under Alan's influence. For the first time I realised there were religions other than Catholicism, with very different beliefs and no pope. Sometimes I defended myself from the barrage of rational argument from Alan by going back to my early beliefs. I wondered if this attractive man, who seemed to know everything and to meet my every need, was an agent of the Devil, sent to tempt me into giving up the church. I feared the Devil might be moving me closer to damnation. I was still very much a Catholic of my times.

A terrible tension built up between us, even though we still hadn't discussed marriage. Eventually, I had the guts to put the problem into words, and chose the least romantic spot in romantic Richmond to deliver them. We were standing beside the Richmond railway bridge, with trains passing constantly and belching soot into the air. I asked Alan whether he was trying to say that he wished to marry me but NOT in a Catholic church. Exactly, he said. He also clearly appreciated my unusual choice of venue. The problem was out in the open and we both felt much better because of that. We gave ourselves a week to think things over.

I knew Alan wouldn't change his views about my church — and I didn't want him to change. It was my decision. I tried praying to God for an answer, but realised I was really asking God to give me the strength to give up my religion. I should have been asking for help to reject this man who had become my guide, my love and my life.

Finally, the strength came to me to sit down and write to Alan to tell him I had chosen the church. The fear of retribution had won. Alan had lost. I wrote because I knew I would weaken if I had to reject him face to face. Soon, I was wondering about the effect my rejection would have on him. After all, he was much older than I was, and did not have as much time in which to recover from the rebuff. I was very miserable and my attempts at rationalisation only increased my misery. I wrote another letter, which predictably started with: 'If it is not too late, I think I would like to change my mind. I've decided I would rather live with you even if it means I have to go to Hell when I die.' Alan replied that it wasn't too late; it would never have been too late; and that he was delighted that I'd changed my mind.

We became engaged when I was nineteen and a half — but without a public announcement. Alan gave me an engagement watch rather than a ring as I was sure I would forget to remove a ring every time I returned home. I was not prepared to confront Dink with an engagement just yet. Dink found out anyhow, and the intensity of family rows increased. He told me no daughter of his would be married in a registry office. My mother provoked further heat by belittling the role of religion in anyone's life. The two shouted at each other continually. I listened sadly but contributed little. After a series of awful debates Dink seemed to win. I was sentenced to house arrest, and had to give up work until 'you come to your senses.' I suspect that Dink was most worried that my actions would result in his going to Hell.

I was allowed out of the house to talk with a priest at St

Joseph's in Highgate about my dilemma. My father's behaviour was becoming so unpredictable that my mother thought it best for me to be smuggled out of the house and into a waiting taxi, even though the meeting had been organised by Dink himself. He probably saw it as a last chance to save both his soul and some sort of relationship with me. My mother came along with me, and we were ushered into a small waiting room. Then a young Irish Jesuit arrived and asked me to tell him my troubles. I said they flowed from my engagement to Alan Dorward. He knew about Alan's standing in moral philosophy, which was nice.

I told the priest how I had prayed earnestly for help; how I knew I was being tempted by the Devil; and had written a letter to Alan saying I had decided to choose the church. Then I burst into uncontrolled sobbing and couldn't say another word. The priest thought I had said all I had to say, and that the meeting had come to a satisfactory conclusion. He patted me on the head and recommended that I should seek the support of the Virgin Mary by quietly saying five Hail Marys. He then went to tell my mother what he interpreted as good news. I had no opportunity to tell him about my second letter.

I sat, quiet and alone, and pondered my position. I was nearly twenty years old, and had spent almost two years talking about the world with a professor of philosophy. But my knowledge of intimate issues was about that of today's children of age eight or ten: very basic indeed. I was about to pray to the Virgin Mary, but had no idea what a virgin might be. I recited my Hail Marys: 'And blessed is the fruit of thy womb, Jesus.' What could that mean? I didn't even know what a womb was, let alone what its fruit might be.

During this time of melodrama at my home, Bruce finished her training. She left Women Decorators to set up her own operation under the name 'Bruce, decorator', centred on a shop and equipment store on Bayswater Road. She asked Hilary and me to join her group. We were very flattered and naturally accepted.

We were to be her top decorators. The four Women Decorators principals did not seem to mind when we resigned. While a new group of women doing men's work would mean more competition it also signified that the push for equality of opportunity in the decorating industry was gathering momentum.

There were three other members of Bruce's foundation group, and we arrived at Bayswater Road for our first day wearing trousers — but without the gaiters. Fashions had changed. We soon had a highly skilled woman electrician named Bunker. That was even more unusual than a woman decorator, but I seem to remember that we higher status decorators looked down a little on Bunker who was 'just an electrician'; and probably working class as well. I discovered that Bunker remained a friend of Bruce in later years and often visited her at Brucefield, wearing her mack.

I'm not sure if the class system operated when it came to signing up houses for decoration. Bruce certainly won contracts for some large and classy houses, but that was most probably due to word-of-mouth, that most effective means of seeking jobs by trades people. She also competed strongly with male decorators on price and quality of work. Bruce advertised with posters featuring a spider which began, 'May I walk into your Parlour and redecorate it?' This was followed by some special offers on price for work done 'in the quiet season'.

May I walk into your Parlour

and re-decorate it?

This is the best time for redecorating. Then you can enjoy a clean and pretty house in Spring and Summer, instead of having the painters in at the pleasantest time of the year.

Moreover it is cheaper to have the work done now, in the quiet season. Prices always rise when there is a rush of work.

BRUCE

3 Wellington Terrace, Bayswater Road, W.2

The first house I did for Bruce was owned by Sir Ernest Somebody-or-other, a prominent surgeon from nearby Harley Street and, like many London houses, it was narrow and very tall. Sir Ernest's aged mother lived on the top floor. No sooner would we fix the Giraffe in place up the staircase — and that was a tricky thing to do — than here comes the old girl. I had to get the ladders down so she would have a clear path. Then up went the ladders again. And down ...

Another problem was the large wooden panels running up that staircase. I had to tell Bruce that Sir Ernest would be well advised to have the panels painted because we'd never be able to achieve a professional finish with sanding and polishing. Bruce relayed to Sir Ernest the advice of her eighteen-year-old expert. He agreed.

We also worked on the large house of Viscount Buckmaster in Pembroke Terrace. Stanley Buckmaster had been Lord Chancellor with the Asquith government and was a powerful advocate for progressive ideas like divorce law reform. This may have been a point of contact with Bruce. We were at Lord Buckmaster's house for months as we redecorated from attic to basement. It was all great fun. We used to joke with Bruce that she must be receiving a continual payment from the law lord, as we always seemed to be at his house. But of course money was not the point. All of those with Bruce were left in no doubt about what the point was — equality of opportunity in paid employment.

Sometimes we went to country houses and lived in either the houses themselves or in lodgings in the village. Work here, like all the work we did with Bruce, was great fun.

Wherever we worked a sign announcing 'Bruce' was erected outside, featuring the family symbol of the legendary persistent spider dangling from the roof of Robert the Bruce's cave. Beneath the spider logo was printed 'Copyright', in small letters. Bruce was a skilled decorator with a particular aptitude for stippling, and continued to work on the job. She was also very practical but increasingly left Hilary and me to organise the day-to-day tasks

Dorothy Bruce, Lady Balfour of Burleigh

while she did the hiring, the quotes, and saw people. She also had her sixth child while we were with her.

At about this time, she and Lord Balfour bought three adjoining houses in Kensington for their growing family and, naturally, Hilary and I were organised to redecorate them. We sometimes lived in one house while working on the others. Bruce was nursing her fifth child, George, while we were working on the house. I had never thought about how babies were fed before that. I also got to know her children then. I'd always enjoyed playing with children.

After about a year the fun stopped when I was forced to leave Bruce. Dink placed me under house arrest for becoming engaged. Bruce's firm closed some three or four years later. As the depression deepened she found the taunts of the unemployed — that she was taking a job they could have filled — difficult to bear. They were in no mood to discuss equality of opportunity. Bruce packed away her signs and paraphernalia and drew down the curtain on Bruce, Decorator.

Meanwhile, I began making plans for a secret — a sort of secret — wedding. Alan and I had decided to wait until I was twenty-one, then marry in the Haverstock Hill Registry Office. We couldn't risk asking Dink to sign a special permission form or having the bans posted where he might see them. We just had to wait.

My plans for the wedding day were detailed and duplicitous. I provided Alan with only the barest details. I was not sure how he would react to all these machinations designed to deceive Dink. In general, he demanded everything be judged against the criterion of absolute truth: the wedding arrangements did not seem to meet that criterion but he raised no objections.

My mother knew of my plans and was determined not to be done out of a wedding reception. She persuaded her sister, my Tante Gaby, to invite a small group of friends and relations to her house. My brown chiffon wedding dress was waiting for me there along with a cake and a number of presents. My mother's people didn't mind Dink being excluded as none were on speaking terms with him anyway.

Dink the train enthusiast represented a problem for me. He liked to go to Paddington Station to see me off or to wave to me as the train went past a crossing near our home. I would lean out the window and wave back. It felt good: no one else on the train had someone to wave to them. Dink was a man of contradictions which I may not have appreciated at the time.

I told Dink I was going to stay with Hilary in Somerset. I did not want him coming to the station or waving at a train I would not be aboard. If he insisted on coming to the station I knew I could catch the Somerset train, get off at Reading, and still get to the registry office on time. However, Dink decided to stay at home when I told him the train would be crowded and I might not get a window seat, and would therefore be unable to wave.

I changed at Tante Gaby's. While there I felt I had to confess to my mother about my cousin and the games of Hares and Hounds. She said she didn't believe me. Then she said she couldn't understand why I'd waited so long to tell her. Then my mother, my sister and I went to the registry office. We met Alan who was with his father, his brother Stewart, and Hugh Meredith, a friend who was professor of economic history at Queen's University, Belfast. Hugh was to be best man. In less than half an hour the marriage ceremony was over. I was now the wife of a professor. I had gained, or so I thought, not just a husband, but a father, an emotional support, and a teacher. I was clearer about what I expected of a father and a teacher than of a husband.

Alan and I spent the night at a hotel in Sussex, then went to Paris for our honeymoon. I had gone into our first night together with no idea of what to expect: I had never heard of an orgasm, for instance. I remember being pleased that Alan had managed to put his pyjamas on without displaying his body parts; and likewise me. I remember turning off the light. I remember the darkness. I remember the feeling that an act rich in symbolism had taken place. But the physical details have gone. I wonder now whether the marriage was in fact consummated during the honeymoon. Or not until very much later.

While we were in Paris Alan wrote to Dink. It was a difficult letter, as he did not want Dink to get any more angry than was absolutely necessary. He failed in this, as my father got very angry and had a minor stroke.

Life Three
The Professor's Wife

An Eagle Has Swept Down on Our Nest

It was a Tuesday, three weeks after our wedding, and I was sitting in the wood-panelled drawing room of our three-storey Georgian house in Liverpool, unwrapping presents and waiting for the doorbell to ring. Tuesday and Thursday mornings were the times I had nominated to be at home so that I could be 'called on', as newcomers were, by the wives of equal or superior ranking academic staff at Liverpool University. For me that meant a small number of visitors. Only the vice chancellor's wife was a superior, and there was only a limited number of professors and consequently professors' wives.

Then the bell rang and our maid, in black dress and lacy white apron and bonnet, came in with a silver tray bearing three cards. One was larger than the others and indicated that Elizabeth Hetherington MA, the wife of the vice chancellor, had ascended the imposing marble steps leading up from a street of Georgian residences, and was waiting to see me. The other two cards were from the vice chancellor, Hector Hetherington. Obviously, it was felt that only the lady of the house could be interested in the woman's card, while both the resident male and female would want the man's.

Over tea Mrs Hetherington instructed me in the complexities of 'calling' while her eyes scanned the floor littered with wrapping paper. Her eyes said there was a place where a professor's wife should unwrap presents — and it was not in the drawing room. Her tongue said nothing of the sort. Instead, I was asked what I thought of Liverpool. 'Isn't it marvellous. I absolutely love it,' I enthused.

I am almost ashamed to write about this ritualistic calling — even sixty-seven years on. It sounds so awful. It did, however, provide me with an opportunity to meet a number of women and

The young wife of the Professor.

to choose those I wanted to meet again. Flora Stephenson was one of the first wives on whom I called soon after I arrived in Liverpool in 1932. Flora's husband, Gordon, had just been appointed to the university's school of architecture, which was eager to have someone from the atelier of Charles Edouard Jeanneret (Le Corbusier) lecturing to its senior students. My calling was the start of a forty-seven year friendship with Flora while my friendship with Gordon extended over sixty-five years.

The slightly gushing comment to Mrs Hetherington about loving Liverpool was not altogether untrue, even though when in London I had disparaged residents of the maritime and commercial city as being provincial, rather too driven by money and of dubious artistic taste. I loved moving about the city in the role of the young wife of a relatively young professor (professors were normally at least fifty). I loved the attention we generated: we were judged to be a 'fine looking couple' and were very much centre stage wherever we went. I was, however, still rather impulsive when viewed against this constrained society. At twenty-one I was closer in age and in behaviour to the guests' offspring than to the guests themselves. I learned to rely on Alan, the quiet Scot, to provide feedback as to how appropriately I was performing in a particular situation. The feedback came from his facial expressions, and particularly from his eyes, whenever I began waving my hands.

Liverpool itself seemed to be nicer than I was afraid it might be; much nicer. I loved its Victorian and Edwardian buildings and those which one commentator described as having 'a touch of magnificence'. Liverpool also had a version of the Studio Club, of which I was automatically a member. I truly loved it all, but particularly the port area. There, massive stone Victorian and Edwardian warehouses advertised the city's success in maritime commerce which in the last century included slave trading and, the century before, piracy. There were frequent ferry boats which, for tuppence, took me across the expansive Mersey Estuary. Some ferries carried cars and wagons while, deep below the surface, engineers worked to complete the new tunnel.

I spent hours around the Albert Dock warehouses where ships could load and unload directly from and into the warehouses, as they were built right on the edge of the water. I watched teams of Clydesdales send up sparks from the cobbled streets as they backed their heavily loaded drays onto a ferry, so they could get under way quickly on reaching the other side of the river. I travelled with them to watch the unloading. All of this was fascinating. It was all new to me. So was the elevator railway which provided a stunning view as it circled the docklands. We didn't have anything like that in London. Nor had there been the varied social mix in a particular area, which was a characteristic of Liverpool. The impressive, fifty-year-old red brick university, with its accompanying Georgian mansions housing philosophy and other smaller departments, was surrounded by a maze of mean streets where women wore black shawls over their heads and beaten looks on their faces, and where the children had no shoes even when walking on snow-covered streets.

The statistics say that the Liverpool I was exploring had some of the worst slums in the country. More than 80,000 people still lived two or more to a room, while in the poorest ward almost half the houses had at least four families per house. The mansions of the wealthy merchants of the eighteenth century were now crowded with the present-day poor. The social significance of all this was largely lost on me at first, although I did notice the Corporation of Liverpool, which controlled the borough, was engaged in large public housing projects close to the city centre. Gordon Stephenson had worked with the Corporation planning some of the newer housing estates before coming to the university.

Sadly, I had to do most of my sight-seeing by myself. Alan stayed in his large book-lined study, thinking about mysterious topics such as whether it was possible to define 'good' without reference to good things; whether objects continued to exist when no one was around to view them; the Greeks; and where the theories of Freud and Watson would take psychotherapy. I didn't realise it at the time, but Alan was giving me an appreciation of what he later termed the 'exquisite joy of being alone', an experience which came to motivate my later life when I was on the road. At times I would run in to tell him of some particularly interesting discovery I'd made at the port, and he would tell me gently that I had interrupted 'a complex train of thought'. I suggested that he should follow the lead of doctors who used a red light to indicate when they were available to receive patients. Alan could have such a light to indicate he was not thinking and was open to receive my latest enthusiasm. We both laughed. Our love was made up of little things like this rather than explosions of passion.

The fear that my father would take the three hundred and fifty kilometre trip north-west from London to confront us about our wedding motivated me to spend more time touring the port and less at home. Dink hadn't lost his zest for disruption, and I didn't want to be at home without Alan when he arrived. If this did happen, I planned to escape through the back door, while the maid was instructed to show Dink into a particular chair facing away from the back door, call Alan home, then serve tea. Later I would enter, accompanied by my protector.

Dink, however, never arrived. Instead, he wrote letters to the vice chancellor and to the Catholic Archbishop of Liverpool, Dr Downey. We knew of these because my mother found drafts in Dink's dressing-gown pockets and sent them to us. He told the vice chancellor that Alan was a dangerous character and should not be allowed near students. However, he saved his best for Dr Downey: 'An eagle has swept down on our nest of doves and carried one away.'

Soon an unfortunate young priest arrived from the Archbishop's office and asked to see our wedding certificate. Naturally I refused and, in the process, turned on an angry performance, worthy of a daughter of Dink.

Alan intervened and advised me to get the certificate, which I did. The priest satisfied himself that a wedding, however unsatisfactory to him, had taken place, then left in a hurry. I was surprised to find that I was starting to obey as well as love and honour my husband of only a few months. I had always treasured my independence, but I didn't feel I had compromised it by revering Alan in the way I did.

I had ample time for jaunts and entertainment in my early days in Liverpool. These were good times for the middle classes.

I had a maid, who changed uniforms for different duties at different times of the day. If I even wanted the blinds drawn I'd ring for her. She also did the routine cooking and serving, and I could order anything I wanted by telephone; it would be delivered by errand boys who could be seen moving through the street all day. If a major meal was planned I could call on Nora, who lived in the basement, beneath the rather grand entry hall of our house, with her caretaker husband. Nora was a cook and she came upstairs to prepare the food and then wait in the kitchen for me to push a bell, hidden under the dining table, to summon the next course.

Nora was the embodiment of everyone's stereotype of a cook. She was bulky, noisy and decidedly non-deferential. She was also rather bold in the way she probed for information about the lady-of-the-house's more intimate activities. In the midst of preparing one of our typical, but not very adventurous, five-course dinners — soup, fish, roast, dessert, savouries — she noted that I was still not pregnant and asked how that could be. I might have told her the truth: that Alan and I had sex so infrequently that the probability of pregnancy was virtually nil. But I said nothing as the flood of supposedly authoritative advice submerged me: 'It's not good for men to wear things on their selves. It's better to stick things inside of yourself.' She then told me about vaginal caps, but I didn't have any idea what these might be like.

Obviously, Nora had decided I was so young and so stupid that I needed her help, and she was right, of course. She also informed me, without prompting, that the butcher's errand-boy 'plays with 'is self.' That night my husband had to wear the teacher's hat as he, no doubt gently, answered my very basic inquiries about that day's information. I can't remember the details of his answers but I do know that this was the only time in twenty-eight years that we ever talked about sex. He spoke just as he would have on any academic topic, complete with templed fingers, giving no clue as to what his personal feelings were on what, for him, must have been a troublesome subject.

When I had my twenty-second birthday we had a special dinner to which, for some reason, two bishops were invited. Again, it reveals how young I was and that I still had no idea how to behave with English people when I was the wife of a professor. I had been given a joke box containing six metal sheets which, when thrown to the ground, created the sound of a tray of plates or cutlery being dropped. I remembered asking Alan, quite seriously, if I could throw them down as a joke during my dinner. Alan had become accustomed to my crazy behaviour. It would upset the parlour maid, he warned. I realised that was true. He didn't criticise me, but showed me how to behave without ever making me feel stupid.

Part of my role as a professor's wife had me attending Alan's public lectures and radio broadcasts; the radio was becoming increasingly popular as a way of taking controversial issues into the home. Alan could talk on a wide range of contemporary topics, like the Italian invasion of Abyssinia; the Spanish Civil War and its implications for peace in the rest of Europe; what the psychologies of Sigmund Freud and of John Broadus Watson had to say about the human condition and its potential for change; and whether a completely tolerant society was possible — or even desirable. Concerning absolute tolerance, Alan surprised his audience by arguing that it wouldn't be much of a society where the citizens held their beliefs so loosely that they could accommodate each other's beliefs and behaviour without aggravation.

Alan's many comments on world events were based solely on newspaper reports. He was presenting nothing new but his mind was so clear that his arguments were compelling. His approach to European politics was uncompromising in terms of the need for intervention: Churchill without hyperbole. When Alan spoke about psychology, however, he brought real scholarship to bear. Psychology was still subsumed within philosophy at Liverpool, and at most British universities at that time, so that Alan was really a professor of psychology as well.

The middle classes were becoming interested in popular psychologists like the charismatic American, J B Watson. He had asserted that the proper subject of psychology was behaviour — not the mind. For him, there might as well be no mind. Mind, like behaviour, could be just a collection of conditioned reflexes. However, United States authorities had decided that Watson's study of human emotional responses, where he and his research assistant acted as both subject and experimenter, was more sexual than scientific. Watson was thrown out of university life and now in the thirties provided behaviourist solutions to life's problems in articles in newspapers and magazines. Give him ten healthy babies and he'd turn out any sort of person nominated, he claimed.

Alan provided public expositions on Watson and on the more popular intellectual movement, psychoanalysis, based on Sigmund Freud's notion that human behaviour is activated and directed largely by dark irrational forces which are set in place in early life and are normally beyond conscious access. The public equated these with sex, and showed considerable interest at a time when the sexual freedoms the middle classes had begun to enjoy in the twenties were being wound back. Freud was quoted to support the idea that this winding back might not be healthy.

I remember the night Alan was in the BBC studio to lecture on Freud to members of the Wireless Study Circle. He received national press attention by arguing that the hypothesis of a subconscious mind was not the only one which might reasonably fit the facts. He provided as an example 'repressed memory', then the centrepiece of psychotherapy and still a controversial public issue today. He said a simpler explanation would be that the resurfacing of these memories resulted from an interaction between the conscious mind and the brain. Perceived events triggered memory processes in the brain and the previously lost memory resurfaced. This didn't seem to have much relevance for me — but that was to change much later.

Alan finished his analysis with the suggestion to Dr Freud that he had tackled psychological science from the wrong end.

Instead of stating facts and then proceeding to develop a hypothesis, Freud had stated his theory first, then sought the facts which supported it. These had been garnered from the seemingly extensive neurotic population of Vienna. It all seemed so straightforward and drew a strong popular response from the considerable audience listening at home on their 'wirelesses'.

With some famous exceptions, university staff in Britain in the thirties and forties tended not to overwork. Alan was not one of the exceptions. Once the three-month summer break or the shorter term break began, we were off until the first day of the next term. The moist air of Britain's west coast triggered Alan's chest problems, so we often headed for the clearer air of Scotland. We usually travelled by train, leaving Liverpool's Exchange Station with our maid, two cats, and a parrot. The station staff came to know us and gave all of us, but the cocky, good seats. Cocky rode in the guard's van.

We stayed at Birken, a large house on the outskirts of Galashiels where Alan's mother and father had lived. Alan grew up here: family photographs show a small boy in a kilt develop into a tall student with a Cambridge scarf swung casually around his neck. Alan's mother had been dead for some years, and his father died not long after we started visiting.

Next door was Grantley, a larger house with a driveway sweeping up to a distinctively rounded front door, sculpted from the trunk of a large oak. In the entry hall was an elaborate chandelier. Alan's mother Ella, who married James Dorward, moved into Birken after growing up in Grantley. His aunt, Marjorie, still lived in Grantley with her daughter Frances. Marjorie had trained in dance and drama with Sybille Olivier, Laurence's sister. When they went out for afternoon tea after training, young Larry sometimes came along, playing a schoolboy and eating cream cakes. Marjorie was emotional and flamboyant in contrast with the austere religious ambience which predominated in the town. We got on well.

I enjoyed these holidays. I walked up the hills at the back of Birken and along the river banks, and tramped all day over the beautiful lowlands. The heather grew on the higher ground. Alan stayed at home, or went with his brother Stewart to the local pub; his

The view of Galashiels from Gala Hill.

'delicate state of health' frequently kept him in bed. From there he liked to play draughts with young Frances and contrived to lose while ostensibly trying to win.

Meanwhile, I was becoming accustomed to my own company and increasingly liking it. But not completely. I frequently felt edgy and unhappy, and at first I did not recognise the origins of these feelings. I must have been a late developer in terms of a clearly defined sexuality. Later these burgeoning feelings began to obtrude on my consciousness as sexual fantasies. While out walking I sometimes entertained the thought that a man would appear and proceed to seduce me behind a rustic stone wall or in the woods.

I was feeling quite excited during one of these fantasies when a flesh-and-blood man did appear from behind just such a wall and approached across the heather. I increased my walking pace. The man drew closer and the only way I could have avoided him was to run. But that was the last thing I would have done. I was very proud. So I stopped and faced my Scottish Heathcliff, who was now running towards me with his arms extended. Soon we were face to face. The man was a beekeeper, and simply wanted me to tie the sleeves of his coat to stop the bees from flying up and stinging his arms. He pointed to the distant stone wall behind which he said he kept his hives.

When Alan's father died his brother Stewart stayed on in the house and he and Alan shared the cost of keeping it going. We could invite my mother, my sister Madeleine, and various friends.

When Madeleine, then in her late twenties, arrived I was shocked to see how much slower she had become in everything she did. It was obvious the strain of being the only offspring left at home and without support, while the two parents argued continually, was now slowly killing her. She had finished with art school but had an afternoon job in an antique shop. When she came to Birken she brought an easel and paints. She did a few sketches but was obviously not really interested in what she was doing. Later I discovered she had been seeking psychological help at Middlesex Hospital. There she was asked to re-live her early life, which was horrendous enough, but this was done without any support between sessions. The damage had been done and her life couldn't be retrieved. When she died of pneumonia soon after I cried, but they were tears for her unhappy life, not for the ending of it.

On holidays I felt warm and loving towards Alan by day. We cuddled a lot. At night I felt unhappy and was clearly sexually frustrated, but that was a term I did not know then. This frustration became particularly evident on a summer holiday in Devonshire. We slept in single beds at home, but there were none available at our hotel so we were forced into a double. By day we cycled around the countryside, and each night for three weeks I lay with Alan, side by side in the double bed, waiting for something to happen. It must happen eventually, I told myself. But I was wrong. I noted the neat bow on the cord holding up his pyjamas. What would happen if I pulled the cord? I was too proud to do it, or even to touch him. I thought: 'If you want me, you can tell me about it.' But he never did. My tenet that, when it came to men and sex, I would never make the first move was being formulated.

A Time of Revelation

The frequent trips we took to Europe during the summer breaks often proved to be times of revelation — but none more so than the first, which centred on Austria. This was when Alan's drinking problem was revealed to me.

We had stopped overnight at Basle on the way to Innsbruck and Alan was openly angry and upset. He stalked out alone after dinner, returned late, and woke very late the next morning. This was quite unlike the calm man I knew as my husband, who seemed to relish our regular evening activities of playing cards or reading to each other. We were only halfway through Thackeray's *Vanity Fair* which we both loved. Was there another woman? It didn't seem likely.

Next day we moved on to Innsbruck. It was raining when we checked in to the small timber guest house with balconies attached to each bedroom. I woke early and saw that the rain had cleared. The sky was now a stunningly deep blue and there was snow on the mountain tops. I wanted Alan to get out of bed to share the enchanting view. But he would not move. The snow had melted before he surfaced. Meanwhile, I had in my naive way been thinking back to the recent occasions when Alan had been so out of sorts and looked for a common factor. I noted he had been drinking a lot of wine on the nights in question. My hypothesis about the impact of his drinking was confirmed when we continued on by train to stay with Alan's uncle at Wolfgangsee. Alan and his uncle went out most mornings for their schnapps and punctuated the day and night similarly. Alan seldom wanted to do much else.

I spent a lot of time alone in a rowing boat on the beautiful lake. I could see, and envied, the people of my own age cavorting vigorously on the shore. I became depressed. I wondered what I'd got myself into. And why. From time to time I thought about escaping by turning over the fragile craft and drowning. But I quickly realised the family love of melodrama was taking hold. There was no way I could be in danger of drowning and not start swimming. Besides, I didn't want to end my life with Alan: it was still too interesting. And I would be a poor sort of person to give up on my marriage in its first year.

Instead of suicide, I decided I would ask Alan about his drinking, just as I had raised the earlier question of 'marriage but not in the Catholic Church' near the railway bridge at Richmond. When I did, Alan was, as always, wonderfully reasonable. Yes, he knew he drank too much, but then he had never tried to hide his drinking from me. I realised that I had never seen anyone seriously affected by alcohol and did not know how to recognise the signs. Alan said we had agreed to accept one another as we were, which was true.

Alan told me he had started drinking seriously many years before, when he took up an appointment at the Queen's University, Belfast. The move from Cambridge and his celebrated colleagues to provincial Northern Ireland was a shock.

Then came Alan's later move to Liverpool, and further shocks for someone who was in the business of abstract thinking. The biographer of James Chadwick, who, like Alan, moved from Cambridge to a chair at Liverpool University, pointed to part of

Alan's problem with his elegantly expressed comparison of the two cities:

As cities, Cambridge and Liverpool were complete opposites. Cambridge was quiet, cold, aloof and inward looking: Liverpool vibrant, teeming with raucous dockers and sailors, 'England's threshold to the ends of the earth'. Cambridge traded in ideas: Liverpool traded in soap.

James Chadwick handled the change easily and won the 1935 Nobel Prize for Physics, indicating that Alan's problems had many causes.

As the excitement of the first two or three years of marriage wore off I became increasingly miserable about my lack-of-sex problem, although I was unsure what one should expect in a marriage. I had no point of reference and decided I should try to find out. I consulted a psychologist who also happened to be a friend. During the interview I told him I wasn't getting much sex; that Alan was capable of performing, occasionally at least, despite his drinking, but was unwilling; and that I was becoming more and more unhappy. The psychologist's advice was elliptical: 'If you lost a leg in an accident and couldn't get around you'd do something about it, wouldn't you? Like getting a substitute leg.' I agreed. Of course I would. Then I waited for some more precise instructions. But the psychologist merely smiled and waved me out the door.

Relief was soon at hand in the form of Edgar, Alan's stylish friend who taught mathematics at the University of Cairo. He was much older than I but younger than Alan. He came to stay with us over a summer break in the mid-thirties when I was in my mid-twenties. We started touring the circuit of dockland attractions I'd discovered earlier. I thought it was great to be travelling around Liverpool with my man — or rather a man. Edgar had one defect — he was not quite as tall as I was, and I

Cécile and the 1927 Morris two-seater.

liked men who were taller. But he was dark and handsome and shared my love of music; in particular, the noble simplicity of Johann Sebastian Bach. We played Bach on our fine, wind-up gramophone.

At this time Alan and I had just acquired our first and only car, and all three of us went touring in Scotland. You could buy a car for one hundred pounds. Ours was a 1927 Morris two-seater with an open top — and it cost us very little. We had been garaging it for a friend in return for a small fee. This debt totalled twelve pounds when our friend generously signed the car over to us. Apart from car trips together, we all went sailing during the holidays. I could feel a considerable attraction in the air whenever Edgar and I were together. I had no idea where this might lead. No one had ever told me that sexual intercourse was something married couples expected to do regularly; and some unmarried people likewise.

It thus came as a surprise to me when we were returning home by taxi from the docks and Edgar moved towards me: 'I love you … I must make love with you … We can be discreet so Alan need never know …' He said this and a lot more, seemingly without taking a breath. He was also kissing me enthusiastically.

Edgar's proposition was not unappealing so, when Alan talked about taking a sea trip to Norway, I did nothing to discourage him. I excused myself on the grounds that I'd probably be seasick. I knew I was about to play a dangerous game, given the censorious attitudes of the time. If word of this got around Liverpool I would be ostracised, but that only made the prospect of a furtive meeting all the more exciting. I arranged to meet Edgar for a week at a hotel outside London. Then both he and Alan left for different destinations and I waited at home, decidedly eager.

My preparations for this adventure were detailed. I even labelled my case 'Mrs E. Brown' so that the hotel-keeper would not be suspicious of

Cécile (right) beside Edgar, boating with friends on Stranford Loch.

the validity of my marital status with Edgar. On the way to my assignation I was met at the station by my mother. There were a tense few seconds as the porter paused with my case, displaying the label bearing my new identity before my mother, then placed it on another train. I never knew whether she saw it. She said nothing — but then she wouldn't.

At the hotel with Edgar there was none of Alan's reticence about taking advantage of the double bed. Edgar knew what he was about. I was a rapid learner and apparently responded appropriately. If I were a modern writer this is the point where I'd provide a step-by-step account of our illicit congress, embroidered with 'ripe and fecund' words. But I can't remember the details and won't make them up. What I can remember is buying a brass food-warmer from a cockney street vendor during an afternoon with Edgar at Petticoat Lane, and finally leaving the hotel after a delightful week, unusually satisfied, but with my love for Alan undiminished. I hadn't given him a thought over the previous seven days.

I felt a little proud of myself. I had solved my own version of the body-mind problem which in another form has intrigued philosophers for centuries. Alan and I were in love, and that involved our minds. Edgar served an increasingly intrusive bodily need. I did not love him in any way unless one thinks of love as sexual excitement, intense and obsessive, as some psychologists came to do some years later. What I hadn't figured on was that Edgar worked in Cairo, and consequently our meetings would be tantalisingly infrequent.

When Alan returned from his sea voyage nothing had changed between us. I bought him a welcome home present for the walled garden — two tortoises in a brown paper bag. I left them on Alan's desk. When he returned from his eleven o'clock lecture, and a few drinks afterwards at the Liverpool Racquet Club, a nearby 'club for gentlemen', we met in Alan's study. I noticed he carried his notes for his next lecture, on 'worry', written on Racquet Club notepaper. Psychology was intruding into his philosophy courses. He also carried an outline for his first year philosophy course, again on Racquet Club notepaper. He'd obviously been there for some time.

His eyes drifted to the parcel, which moved — but naturally only slowly. He looked away; then back again. There was another movement. He must have thought the pre-lunch drinks were affecting his perception, and he hurried upstairs for lunch. Afterwards, he was sufficiently fortified to take a look inside the bag, and we both laughed and laughed. Our minds and quirky senses of humour had not been affected by my recent physical diversion.

Tortoises were not the only animals to star in our eccentric domestic interactions. I thought a great deal about what an attractive animal the giraffe was: what an elegant head it had and such melting eyes and long lashes. I began idly to ponder what it would be like to have one as a pet and how it might be fitted into our three-storey home. I thought it would be wonderful to have my friends ushered into the drawing room to be met by such a charming neck and head.

'Why are you looking up and down at the ceiling and floor?'

Alan asked a little apprehensively.

'I'm working out how many holes I'd need to cut in the ceilings to bring a giraffe into the house as my pet. I must have its head in the drawing room so the guests can see its lovely eyes,' I replied with appropriate gravity.

Alan said a giraffe would fit easily on the ground floor and there was no need to modify the house. We left it at that. Months later we went to the Regent's Park Zoological Gardens to see which of us was correct. We approached the tall fence surrounding the giraffe enclosure. I saw three elegant but alarmingly short giraffes. They were scarcely much taller than we were. I was crestfallen.

Alan and Cécile Dorward on the road to Scotland.

'They are quite tall, but they would certainly fit into my study,' Alan said kindly. No holes would be necessary in the ceiling. Then, from the giraffe house came two far taller giraffes, and we agreed their heads would reach up into the drawing room and that we would need to cut a hole in the ceiling. Then we threw ourselves into each other's arms. We both liked cuddling.

Unusual Animals

As a result of being a professor's wife, and particularly Alan's wife, I met a number of other unusual animals — of the human intellectual kind. They stayed at the house or visited regularly or occasionally. They were people I would normally never have met, and they and their discussions helped me develop my understanding of issues. I became involved in some complex topics — with Alan's help. We were so close that he seemed to know what I was thinking before I had said much and helped put that information into words for me.

One of the first of these intellectual superstars to visit was Aldous Huxley, a member of the celebrated scientific family, whose near-blindness had forced him out of science and into writing. He had an extraordinarily inventive mind which readily produced, from the twenties to the fifties, a string of best-selling novels.

When I met him, he had just written the enduring classic *Brave New World*, an attack on the psychological doctrine of behaviourism and its progenitor, J B Watson. This was 1932 and Huxley had probably earlier called on Alan's expertise in behaviourism to provide some of the psychological foundations of the book. Another of Alan's friends, J B S Haldane, the spectacular physiologist, geneticist, mathematician, writer, and communist activist, had contributed to *Brave New World* through his development of the notion of ectogenesis, whereby a human foetus might grow outside the mother's womb. This was central to Huxley's allegorical story where science takes over at the expense of humanity.

Both Haldane and Alan grew up in Scotland and were later together at Cambridge. Haldane left Cambridge to go to a professorial chair at University College, London, at about the same time Alan went to Liverpool. He was big, bushy-browed, brilliant, brusque, and oh so clumsy. He did not have a science degree but combined the scientific worlds of mathematics, genetics and physiology with ease and distinction. As the war approached, he was providing statistical predictions on the human casualties likely to be generated by the German bombing of Britain. He was an expert on gases and explosives.

Haldane came to Liverpool as part of an investigation into the sinking of the Royal Naval submarine *Thetis*, on its first sea trials off Liverpool. It went down carrying a number of civilians who had built her, as well as naval personnel. Liverpool became a tortured city. It was public knowledge that almost one hundred men were slowly dying as the carbon dioxide levels rose. No one could do anything about it. In the street, friends couldn't even bring themselves to look each other in the eye when they passed. It was all too horrible and we didn't want to share the experience. This was where JBS moved in. He had been engaged by the trade unions, who had nineteen members on board, to investigate the tragedy. He did it in a characteristically reckless manner, spending much of his time in a diving bell recording the effects of increasing carbon dioxide levels on his decision-making and movement control. He was sometimes seriously affected when he left the bell.

Perhaps that is why he shambled through our entry hall and knocked over the fire extinguisher so that its contents squirted everywhere. Haldane picked up the extinguisher and ran into the street, spraying foam over astonished pedestrians as he went. Then he spotted our two beds of glorious black tulips in full bloom. 'Don't spray THEM,' Alan shouted as he tried to step between the tulips and the spray. It was hopeless. The tulips withered as the foam settled on them. Alan knew this was not an isolated incident of eccentricity. Haldane had decided — and it might again have been while visiting Liverpool University — that people thought he was a lunatic so he should occasionally behave like one. He went into the tearoom and, noticing one cup was chipped, smashed all the intact cups against one wall while academics in the room took shelter.

If Haldane was hulking, dark, balding, irascible, and apparently certain about most things, another of our visitors, Olaf Stapledon, was the opposite: trim, blond, boyish, peaceful, and in a state of constant ambivalence. They were alike only in their multifaceted interests, and their vigorous promotion of causes of the political left. Haldane was a Cambridge convert to communism and chaired the editorial board of the *Daily Worker*; Olaf's support for Marxism was less emphatic, less total.

These were, however, political labels in which I had only a passing interest. While I was getting myself involved in a wide range of progressive good works in Liverpool I was driven by no political ideology. I was the wife of a professor and, by and large, that was what professors' wives did. Noblesse oblige — in the beginning at least.

Olaf Stapledon was a published poet and a good philosopher who could have found a place in a British university — but he didn't, apart from occasional appearances in Alan's department as a participant in a prestigious seminar series and as a guest lecturer. Instead, he tutored with the Workers' Education Association and toured Liverpool teaching literature, history and political theory to dock workers, artisans and other trade unionists. When World War One started he found himself emotionally positioned somewhere between a combatant and a pacifist. He became a non-combatant participant and spent three years driving a Quaker ambulance in France, dodging shells and picking up the dead and wounded.

Stapledon wrote *A Modern Theory of Ethics*. He claimed it linked 'ethics to cosmology and the climactic discussion of the relation of moral theory to ecstacy.' Not surprisingly it puzzled and angered professional reviewers. It was wild, Olaf admitted, and it wasn't going to make him famous. Fame came in 1930 with his seminal science fiction novel *Last and First Men*, which chronicled the history of the next two billion years using a telepathic observer as narrator. Prescient themes included the takeover of the world's cultures by America. Other books followed. H G Wells, Russell and Virginia Woolf were ecstatic about his imagination and his rigorous presentation.

Alan spent many afternoons in his study with Olaf talking philosophy. Olaf's biographer, Robert Crossley, said Olaf did 'not warm to' Alan. Alan would not have appreciated the wildness of Olaf's mind. But they certainly spent long sessions together, discussing the unstable world order and social issues such as Olaf's belief in the democratisation of British higher education. Alan lacked Olaf's optimism on such topics.

Meanwhile, I talked in my area — the drawing room — with Olaf's wife, Agnes. We certainly warmed to each other and became lifelong friends. We talked about more mundane matters: that is, if you consider mundane a courtship by way of censored letters between Olaf, a field ambulance driver in France, aged thirty, and his sixteen-year-old cousin, Agnes Miller, in Sydney. I remember thinking the Stapledons had a rather more open and robust approach to sex than we did.

Night Blitzes

I knew the times were changing when I attended a lecture on the European crisis at the Liverpool Wives Club, just as the Spanish Civil War flared in 1936. Alan was the speaker and his message was, as always, clear: there would be a bigger war soon and the country had better prepare for it. The response was also clear and considerably hostile. It was as though Alan was advocating, or even stirring up, war with Germany. Women who normally made a point of socialising now passed on the other side of the street; some former associates never spoke to me again.

Alan became a public figure as a result of his speeches on the war. He also wrote many letters to the *Liverpool Post*, attacking what he saw as the unreality of pacifism in the face of increasing German aggression. Letter writing became for him almost a displacement activity, substituting for the need to write the significant philosophical thesis the academic community had been expecting from him for the previous twenty years. This public role put Alan in conflict with Olaf Stapledon. Olaf was advocating a 'zone of peace' in Europe, which made him the target of a number of Alan's newspaper articles. What's the point of a zone of peace when the aggressors won't join? he inquired pointedly, adding that Olaf's politics displayed the 'creative imagination' of his science fiction masterpiece, *Last and First Men*. Olaf had been in many philosophical debates with Alan and observed that the current newspaper controversy was 'not the first time his diabolical intelligence triumphed over my (approximately) divine innocence.' There were rumours that Alan was the anonymous author of a series of letters attacking views like Olaf's, which appeared in the *Post* under the pen name *Ignotus* (Latin=unknown). Staff at Liverpool University discussed who *Ignotus* might be: he wrote like an academic. No one found out, and the editor of the *Liverpool Post*, who lived across the street, ended the controversy by refusing to publish any more of the *Ignotus* letters, which had been appearing at the rate of two or three a week. I knew nothing about this and I would not have asked even if I had. We never asked such questions of each other.

As war edged closer, Liverpool's social life continued relatively undisturbed. While their employers were at concerts at the Philharmonic, chauffeurs warmed themselves around charcoal burners at their own club nearby, waiting for the performance to end. Later, there would be animated chat in the foyer as the audience waited for the commissionaires to announce the arrival of their cars. I enjoyed going to these concerts in evening dress and usually was invited to sit in the box of the Booth family who owned a major shipping line. I liked to see others dressed for the occasion as well but my pleasure in this was marred: I had taken on some of my mother's censorious French attitudes about dress. Among the glittering women a number of bare arms extended from georgettes and taffetas. Like my mother, I thought arms should be covered.

I went home as I had come, by taxi, and usually alone. Alan and I were living almost bachelor lives in public though we were still close at home. I wished he would come to concerts with me. Music had originally been one of the facets of our strong mutual attraction. But each time I became sad about Alan's absences I remembered our original pact that independence in all matters would be central to our marriage. When his absence became a talking point in the foyer, I said he was busy, or ill, or not at all interested in the program on offer.

Liverpool also had a thriving repertory theatre, and there were many parties and dinners. Alan came to the plays, parties and dinners more frequently than to the concerts. Whenever he appeared his generous social graces were apparent. He never acted like a heavy drinker. His performance was so convincing I could hope that, just perhaps, only I knew about his problem. I would not discover until much later that I was very wrong about this.

At university banquets the old aristocracy was represented by the charismatic chancellor, the Earl of Derby, in academic robes which covered most of his large frame and his wheelchair, sitting at the top table with the financial bigwigs like the Hobhouses of the Blue Funnel Line.

Liverpool was the home of a number of progressive social reform movements which gradually attracted my attention. One of these was the Victoria Settlement, which was started in 1897 as part of the University Settlements movement, when staff and students were encouraged into depressed areas of major cities as part of a scheme to better understand the causes of poverty and its social effects and, hopefully, to modify them. In the case of the Victoria Settlement, activity was directed towards the causes of women and children.

The Settlement received great support from Eleanor Rathbone, who became the Independent parliamentary member for the Combined Universities. Rathbone, who had been at odds with Bruce in the twenties, was an advocate of family allowances, universal suffrage, extension of the legal rights of widows, and a lift in the general quality of life for women.

She had returned to Liverpool from Oxford University in 1897, intending to pursue problems in pure philosophy. These did not retain her interest long in a city beset with such massive social and religious problems. She wanted the Settlement buildings to be 'an oasis of peace and tranquillity' in an area where the streets of Irish Catholics and poor Protestants intersected. Any meetings of the religions could lead to violent clashes. 'The gootters were full of blood,' one old woman once told me, adding that some street intersections had been divided by barbed wire to keep the warring religions apart.

When I became involved in the late thirties, the shipping and university wives did much of the organising and raising of finance, but there was also strong community involvement. The staff and student residential component was not as important as it had once been. The Settlement was the home for a number of women's medical services and for community groups. I started with the Young Wives' Club which met once a week. Here young women brought their babies and young children, and knitted, or took part in some group project like making slippers. On my first day, as I served the young wives cups of tea — a task to which I was not particularly accustomed — I heard a young mother ask, 'Oose wee-weed?' I could hardly believe my ears. I'd never heard that said before. I was interested to see that the mother mopped up the puddle. I thought how fortunate it was the Settlement did not have carpets.

I had not been on a committee before but was impressed with the operation of the Victoria Settlement, and the democratic way each of the several groups organised its affairs. I was more accustomed to hierarchical systems. My Australian experience, which would modify such views, was still twenty years away. In time, I was invited to join the Executive Committee of the Settlement. I was much younger than other executive members, and was asked to attend the congresses run by the young women's groups. The young women were most impressive. They came from simple backgrounds but stood and delivered their message, quite unfazed by the scope and Victorian grandeur of the Albert Hall, where they met.

I was also secretary of Liverpool Inter-aid, a group which helped Jewish children in the late thirties. The chairman was Mary Mott, calm, intelligent, and thirty years older than I. I found in her not just a mentor who could tell me how to run meetings —

'No meeting should run for more than forty-five minutes' — but a major re-shaper of my life and personality. She built up my self-esteem, and came to accept my emotional overflow in a way which had been beyond my mother and beyond Alan. She helped me — at twenty-eight years of age in 1939 — to grow up. I seemed to need the help of much older people to do that.

Mary Mott became the most significant of 'the mothers I never had'. I found that, almost daily, I was driving the Morris two-seater through the Mersey tunnel to talk with her. When rationing dried up my petrol supply, I rode my motor-powered bicycle across. The toll collectors commented on my frequent crossings: 'Out courting again, eh, lass?' I'd smile and mutter to myself: 'Out courting a mother, more like it.' At Mary's house, appropriately named Hope Lodge, I sat on the floor in front of the fire, my back against her chair. We talked: mainly I talked.

I told Mary about my mother and the steel plate which protected her heart from my overflow of feeling; and how, because of his drinking, frequent illness and constrained manner, Alan was not able to accept this overflow either. I talked about my sexual frustration and the occasional encounters with Edgar. Mary said little during my revelations, but I came away transformed. On warm days we walked, and Mary took my arm. Now I wonder whether Alan thought Mary and I were in a sexual relationship rather than an intense friendship between an older and younger woman.

Mary had read mathematics at Cambridge at the turn of the century, a time when women were not classified as full members of the university. Consequently, when the results of the Cambridge Tripos (Honours) exam in mathematics for 1903 were posted, she was ranked 'equal to eleventh'; to the eleventh man, that is. She was disappointed with that ranking, and with mathematics generally. She moved to research in physics at the Cavendish Laboratory. She married another researcher, Francis Mott, and they raised a future Nobel Prize winner in physics, Nevill Mott. After her Cambridge experience, it was not surprising that Mary Mott became a prominent advocate for women's causes: votes for women; family planning, against particularly virulent opposition; and improved housing in a city where so many families lived in slum cellars. Early in 1939 she added to her list of advocacies the plight of women and children in Hitler's Germany.

The task of Liverpool Inter-aid was to find foster homes for children with Jewish fathers but not Jewish mothers, so they could escape Nazi persecution. These were children who were falling through the safety nets being set up world-wide by Jewish organisations. Because they did not have Jewish mothers they were not classified as Jews by Orthodox groups, and did not get priority when foster homes in Britain and America were being offered. In Germany, however, children with a single Jewish parent or even a grandparent were being persecuted. We were doing the best we could to find secure homes for them. We received heart-rending letters from parents desperate to get their children out of Germany. These letters, which were translated by a German friend, and the news coming out of Germany, alerted us to the need for speed as I visited prospective guardians. Where possible, I carried a picture of the child in question; I looked for suitable schools nearby, and did the extensive paperwork involved.

Eventually, the first group of Liverpool Inter-aid children arrived at the vast Lime Street Station. A number of us were there to meet them. The younger children had their names and destinations pinned to their clothing. On the platform, the new guardians found their children and moved off with them. One young girl, aged about six, with a bag over her shoulder and wearing a dark peaked cap, stood alone on the platform, unclaimed but looking surprisingly unperturbed. I studied her label and saw that she was Irma Amschenowski; and a clerical error. She should have been met by the Liverpool Jewish group, which would have taken her to a practising Jewish family. I was not much use in sorting out the problem. Despite my family background, I did not speak German. However, we did have a housekeeper who was a refugee from Germany, and there was a small Jewish school just around the

Cécile and Irma Amschenowski.

corner from our house. So I took Irma home with me.

Seven years earlier I had begged a God I had already rejected to not let me have any children. I had wanted a child, but knew even then that Alan's drinking would make it impossible. I already knew that he needed constant support from me to survive. I liked providing that support because I loved him. But I felt I would not be able to provide the necessary support for both him and a child. Now at twenty-eight I had a child in the house but felt no urge to change my plea. However, if Irma had been a baby I'm sure my reaction would have been quite different. Instead, I contacted a non-Jewish family, with a son about the same age as Irma, who had applied for a Christian child with Jewish connections. I felt no emotion as she left and settled in well at her new home. So well, in fact, that when she was taken to the practising Jewish family that had requested her originally Irma went very much against her will. She cried continually; she wouldn't eat; she wouldn't come out of her room. Eventually, she won and was returned to the first family.

The new security for some of our children was short-lived. War was declared in September 1939. There were immediate fears that Germany would invade Liverpool from the Republic of Ireland. The fears grew and soon Liverpool was declared a 'protected area'. That protection included installing barbed wire a very great distance along the banks of the Mersey, and removing aliens from the area. Those of our children who were sixteen or over were classified as aliens and transferred to the care of the Manchester Committee of Inter-aid. Government officials thought Manchester less in need of protection. Our housekeeper was also moved away from the port area. Some of our neighbours must have known that she was German. They may have feared she could have been a contact for invading forces, and lodged an official complaint. The fact that she was Jewish and had come to Britain to avoid the Germans did not seem to matter.

Next a man came to our house to demand that we take in the two majolica lions from our balcony. Many of our neighbours, he said, believed the lions were a signal to an invader that we were pro-German. I was very anxious and asked Cecily Leadley Brown, who had been the treasurer of Liverpool Inter-aid, what I should do. She was a leading barrister and very British. I had in fact first met her under a floor mat during a game of charades when she was playing a bear. She had become a major influence on my life. She convinced me that I had nothing to fear from the authorities, and that I should leave the lions where they were. However, Alan persuaded me to allay a confrontation by bringing our lions indoors.

Liverpool became a port at war from the first day of hostilities. The liner *Athenia* was torpedoed just hours outside the port and 131 passengers died. It was expected that Liverpool, because of its port, would be the second major target for German bombers after London. But for nine months there was only a phoney war. People hurried to complete what they thought would stand as significant accomplishments; possibly their last.

My friend Marjorie Holford was an artist. She wanted to paint a portrait and asked me to sit for her. After a number of sessions Marjorie began worrying about a lack of balance in the background. At this point, Bill Holford, professor of architecture at the university and later the designer of the Perth Narrows Bridge, came down the stairs with an elaborate wall mirror. This completed the picture. The Mona Lisa smirk captured in the portrait came from thinking about a recent house visit by my doctor. He chose the moment when he was rubbing a greasy ointment into my face, to treat an outbreak of urticaria which had raised unsightly blotches, to say that he loved me. I did not reciprocate in any way but the bizarre nature of the incident was enough to keep me amused during the portrait sitting. Other friends conjured up their own significant events and set about completing them.

The phoney war ended for Liverpool late in August 1940, when the Luftwaffe sent over one hundred bombers from northern France to drop high explosive bombs and thousands of incendiary devices on the port and surrounding residential areas. A similar contingent of bombers attacked the Mersey area over each of the following three nights. The sequence was always the same: air raid sirens, the brilliant white flash of the pathfinders' flares, the thump of high explosives, and finally the red flames as the monumental port-side buildings burned. Sometimes they were still burning when the bombers came over the next night because the poor water supply in the city hindered the fire-fighters.

Meanwhile the Victoria Settlement, which was started as 'an oasis of peace', was under severe pressure as sources of financial support were withdrawing. Some did not like the autocratic ways of the current warden. Eventually, the executive asked me to relay the depressing news to her that there was only money to finance the Settlement for another eight months. The rationale for choosing me as the messenger was that I had known the warden for the shortest time, and should therefore be able to do the sacking with the least pain for all. I went to the Settlement to relay the message. The warden and I sat about a foot apart, across a chess table covered with green baize. I placed my hands flat on the table and said, rather portentously: 'I have something really not all that pleasant to say to you, and to explain to you.' I was under pressure and that was not my crispest sentence. I then told her of the time limit on funds with which to pay her salary.

I felt very sad about the likely closure of the Settlement. I decided that if there was no money to pay a warden I'd run the place myself with the help of groups like the Girls' Club and the Boys' Club, both of which were extremely well organised. And I'd raise the money needed to do it. I told the executive of my plans. 'Fools rush in where ...' said one member. And she was probably right. I also allowed myself to wonder about some of the wealthy members of the executive, and the thinness of their excuses for withdrawing funds just when they seemed most needed.

The following Sunday I set off on my bike with a list of potential donors. Lord Woolton was at the top of the list. As Frederick James Marquis, he had been warden at the Liverpool University Settlement for men, and became a successful businessman before entering the House of Lords. He was Minister for Food when I rode up the driveway to his substantial house, parked my bike against one of its columns, and was greeted by him in the hall. He wore what was reputed to be his only tie, a bright red one, to demonstrate to any doubter that he was still a Fabian socialist. 'If people know you're donating, others will follow,' I told him. I secured his donation, and used his example to obtain pledges from the others on my list.

The second line I used when seeking donations was: 'We look after our people before they are born; and we go to their funerals after they've died.' Which was true. Liverpool was doing many progressive things which later became common practice. One was to build up a network of midwives to assist home births; another to organise ante-natal classes. Since I was also a member of the Ladies Committee of the Liverpool Maternity Hospital and the hospital held its pre-natal classes in the Settlement hall, I had a double reason for wanting to keep the Victoria Settlement going.

At the other end of the life cycle, in my role as warden giving comfort to the bereaved, I was sometimes invited to view pensioner members or their husbands laid out at home in their coffins. I had never seen a dead person before but, as warden, I soon came to see plenty. The first was a husband. The coffin was open in the front room of a terrace house when I arrived, wearing a special black coat and matching accessories. However, the widow had more interesting things to show me and took me upstairs to the bedroom. 'Look at me wee. There's red in it,' she said, pointing to the chamber pot with an intriguing fabric cushioning around its rim. There seemed to be blood in the pot. I took care not to recoil as I recommended a visit to her doctor.

I loved all the women attending the Settlement, including the young mothers and the mothers-to-be, but I particularly loved the strong faces of my tough old pensioners. They seemed to like me, although I'm sure there was an element of the English class system at work here. They knew I was a professor's wife. That seemed to be important for them.

I was impressed with the way my pensioners withstood with nonchalance and good humour the hail of incendiary bombs which fell night after night. The incendiaries were designed to destroy the vast cargo warehouses and other installations along the docks, but also to terrify the Liverpudlians living in the dock area and further out. If my pensioners were any guide the latter may have been the more difficult of the two tasks: 'Oh, we had a sinnery right down our chimley and me 'usband picked up a shoovel and carried it outside.'

Outside the Liverpool Settlement.

Each time my pensioners visited the Settlement they deposited sixpence as a down payment on their holidays. The Settlement met some of the cost and everyone said they 'luved the olerdees.' They roared with laughter as a bus took us to a guest house in

Wales, with me coming along as warden. We'd arrive mid-afternoon and soon begin preparing vegetables for dinner. There was a lot of chat about life in Liverpool at the turn of the century. One of the holiday group, May, told me of catching conger eels in the Mersey and bringing them home for breakfast; and how they were so fresh they kept jumping from the frying pan 'even when 'e's coot oop.' I listened while working over a potato with a peeler. There would be very little potato left by the time I'd finished with it. One of the pensioners took pity on me. 'You shouldn't be doing that,' she observed correctly, and took the peeler from me, and the remnants of my potato. After a week in the guest house I'd had enough. I'd even been comprehensively out-talked. I'd ring Alan and ask him to come down and book the best room in the best hotel for a quiet weekend.

Back in Liverpool the raids continued. One night in March 1941, 340 bombers from the Luftwaffe formations dropped 300 tons of bombs and 64,000 incendiary devices. They were back again the following evening. Some of their bombs carried a time fuse so they didn't explode immediately. Others mysteriously failed to explode at all. Either way nearby streets had to be cleared of residents, and the Public Assistance Committee (PAC) provided the Settlement with forty camp beds so that those without shelter could sleep in the Settlement basement. Our people said they felt safer at the Settlement than at home, even though figures showed that Everton, where the Settlement was located, scored as great a concentration of bombs as did the docks themselves. They were no safer with us than at home. But they felt safer. 'I've not had me corsets off in a week,' said one woman who had been afraid to undress because she never knew when a raid would occur and did not wish to be caught without her corsets. At the Settlement she felt safe enough to take them off and relax.

Nightmare

The intensity of the air raids increased. I was asked to take on an additional job. It involved checking the safety of makeshift shelters being used by the new homeless, and writing reports to the PAC. They had a number of people sleeping on double mattresses fitted into the horse-boxes in the underground stables used for the Clydesdales working around the docks. We were on the second level down and could hear — between the thump of bombs — the horses clumping nervously on the floor above. My report to the PAC said that a direct hit would send the horses crashing onto the people below; also that the toilet and washing facilities were desperately inadequate. But no one worried too much about all of this. The most important thing for them was to be together; the next was to stay dry.

During the heaviest bombing the magnificent domed Customs House was set ablaze. Residents of Percy Street gathered on a small piece of raised ground to watch the terrible display. Our neighbours from either side of number twenty-eight were there too. We had lived there for almost ten years but we still didn't 'know' them. They were 'ordinary people'. We'd rarely spoken to them. What could we talk about? This problem was solved as another wave of bombers came on its way. The alarm sounded and we broke up and ran to our respective houses.

During raids I spent much of my time at the Settlement. I was very busy but in moments of self-indulgence I marvelled at the changes in me which two years at the

Damage to the railway after a bombing raid on Liverpool.

Settlement during a war had wrought. I had started as the young wife of a professor of philosophy, a woman who lacked confidence in her ability. Now I felt I could help a large number of people with a wide variety of problems. Under Mary Mott's guidance and under the continuing influence of Alan and the wise, no-nonsense approach of Leadley Brown, I had grown up.

Other changes, unfortunately more temporary ones, were also taking place. One night while sleeping in our basement during a particularly severe raid, Alan's fear seemed to be transformed into sexual excitement; or perhaps he thought he would never do this again. I don't know which but we made love with enthusiasm.

Alan supported my wardenship, and spent considerable time with me at the Settlement. I appreciated his support but also wished he was away writing his great treatise. All he'd say about this was: 'There's enough ink been spilled already without my adding to it.' He did, at least, keep in touch with his old colleagues from philosophy's glory days at Cambridge, particularly with G E Moore.

I have one of Moore's letters in which he writes, in spidery hand, to 'Dear Dorward', his friend of thirty years: 'I'm glad you saw Wittgenstein. I think you are quite right that he has changed hardly at all from what he was in 1912.' This was when Russell described the gangling Austrian as 'teetering between genius and madness' and prescribed a physical cure for his depression, which included keeping a supply of biscuits handy for him to eat at night. Moore tells of lunch with Bertrand (by then Earl) Russell and 'his new wife' Patricia. He noted Russell was 'very little changed except that his hair is now quite white.'

At the time of writing the letter, Moore was incensed at 'the way he [Russell] was treated.' Russell had been driven out of City College in New York, following a successful appeal to a judge to end his appointment to teach logic and mathematics to male students. It was claimed *inter alia* that he was an alien atheist and an exponent of free love. In court, he had been called 'lecherous, libidinous, lustful, venerous, erotomaniac, aphrodisiac, irreverent, narrow-minded, untruthful, and bereft of moral fibre.' American youth needed to be protected from this 'ape of genius, the devil's minister of men': Bertrand Russell at seventy!

Our friends the Chadwicks were also in America, although nothing was said about why they were there. Aileen would write to say they were well and include some information about the girls while her husband James worked secretly on the Manhattan Project which would produce the atomic bomb.

By 1942, after more than two years of war and work, I was nothing more than a bag of bones. My skin was covered with a rash and mentally I was at the end of my tether. I worried about Alan's drinking. Friends said the Settlement work was exhausting me and that I should take a break. But I knew it was only those old women who stopped me from going mad. I remembered only recently one really tragic moment. It happened in our bedroom where our single beds were arranged in a T configuration: Alan's ran along one wall and mine down the centre of the room. I saw Alan leaving his bed and apparently heading across for mine, but he collapsed on the floor before reaching it. I helped him back to his own bed. I never thought of helping him to *my* bed.

One day things got worse, much worse. I was at home and we were eating breakfast. Alan was reading the mail. 'There's some bad news,' he said bleakly, 'Edgar is dead.' I can't remember what he said next and I'm not sure that I ever discovered the cause of death. I looked at the pair of Roman vases on the table which Edgar had given us for a wedding present. I wanted to cry. But that wouldn't have been appropriate. Instead, we sat grim faced, like characters from a Noel Coward patriot play, and dealt with the dreadful news in a very British way.

The impact of Edgar's death, the months of bombing, and worry about Alan, left me feeling I did not want to go on: that I couldn't go on. I wanted to commit suicide; but I wasn't sure how to do it. I decided to throw myself into one of the nearest docks. After a thirty-minute walk I was staring at the water. It was dark, oily and disgusting. I couldn't jump into that. So I turned and began to walk slowly and sadly back up the hill. I heard the unmistakable steps of a young police officer who was almost beside me. I was nearly home before he spoke. 'Are you all right now Madam?' he asked. I said I was and thanked him. He walked off while I continued up the hill knowing that I was still faced with the problems which had sent me down to the water's edge. I'd have to teach myself to control such urges.

This crisis was replaced by another. One evening I rode my bike home from the Settlement. It was about ten o'clock. This trip home was always difficult at night. There were no lights in the streets except for the tiny slits emitted from car headlights. The tram lines, and particularly their slippery passing loops, constantly threatened to throw me from my bicycle. I knew every turn in the lines between Everton and the city but safe riding was still difficult, although not as difficult as when buildings were burning after a raid and the air was full of smoke.

I arrived home even more exhausted than usual, and called

Alan. There was no reply. Just then the phone rang. It was a Liverpool hospital: Alan had been admitted there after being hit by a tram. I got back on my bike and headed for the hospital. In the emergency section, I saw a man whose face was so bloodied and bruised that at first I did not recognise it. What may have been a wave of embarrassment passed over this battered face. 'I must have had a little too much to drink,' he said, in his self-deprecating way.

I can't remember what I said but I left the hospital with a desperate feeling that the various segments of my personality were about to fly apart. I rode home and rang my friend, Maisie, who was married to a stockbroker. In more relaxed times we had occasionally created cover stories for one another when there was the rare opportunity of something interesting to do. Now I just wanted to tell her what was happening to me. Then a taxi arrived at the door. It was Alan and he had discharged himself from the hospital. Almost immediately, someone else arrived to take him back. Henry Cohen, the professor of medicine at the university, who like Alan was one of the 'bright young professors' appointed in the late twenties, wanted to keep Alan in hospital 'to dry him out'. I was pleased that I'd have some time to sort myself out: but also alarmed by Henry Cohen's comment. It meant that others knew about Alan's drinking.

These events left me feeling that the two sides of my brain had become disconnected; in short, that I was going mad. I felt and 'saw' the connection between the two hemispheres coming apart. I had never felt anything like that before. I learned later that schizophrenics can have such hallucinations about their body parts; also that, under extreme anxiety, patients report the frightening experience of body distortion. This is called de-personalisation and is sometimes accompanied by de-realisation — feelings that the surroundings were also being distorted. Normal people sometimes experience the same sensations from extreme fatigue and lack of sleep.

I had neither the time nor inclination to establish which of these might be behind my vivid hallucinations. A car was pulling up outside. It was Mary Mott. Maisie had rung her and she had come to take me to Hope Lodge. I'd lost my grip on reality. I was wearing my best dressing-gown, not my normal clothes, as I left with Mary. On arriving at Hope Lodge, I went to bed. I still had a clear visual image of what I thought was happening in my head.

I slept for the best part of a day in the spare room and then spent some time studying the complex pattern of cracks above my head. Was this further evidence that I no longer existed in a stable environment? Then Mary came into the room and everything fell back into place. The ceiling had been fractured during a recent bombing raid. Whatever its cause, the madness was over. I thought at the time that Mary's love had cured me. This may seem very New Age: right and left hemispheres, and all that. But it's what I experienced. Incidentally, this was many years before the different functions of the right and left cerebral hemispheres became a major topic in popular psychology.

Things Come to an End

I was soon forced to leave the Settlement. It was in good shape and had adequate funds. I had to help resettle — separately — my mother and Dink who, after forty years of hostility and arguments about the relative merits of the Bavarians and the French, were finally separated by a German bomb which destroyed the front of their house. The beautiful glass and china and their finely crafted cabinets were mainly in smithereens on the pavement outside. I happened to be in London and my brother and I arrived to find my father standing on guard over the wreckage, which he claimed he could put together again. We helped him rescue what we could. Dink stayed on in the back of the house while my mother, whose bedroom was in the front, at long last could get away. She wanted to take any furniture which remained intact. That seemed a bit mean but I arranged for her to stay in a hotel while I searched for somewhere more permanent.

While searching in London in July 1943, I suffered severe withdrawal symptoms for Mary. My need for her affection returned. I wrote to 'My Dearest Mary' almost daily — except when I ran out of envelopes and had to ask her to send back some old ones. In the letters I always refered to myself as 'Your young friend'. I sound very young and in need of continual praise and reassurance, as is shown in these extracts.

It was nice of you to say I write good letters. They just flow out (as in my talking but with the advantage of NO repetition) ...

Please send me another of your letters. They make me feel so good.

Having read your letter I've quite got over my nervous prostration — though I do not look forward to seeing Mummie even for an hour.

I fervently hope I shall never have to end my days in a hotel like this. There are six or seven old things who look so depressing. They have such hopeless expressions on their faces, and I'm not surprised as the breakfast is pretty horrible ...

I can't believe that today is only Friday. Your young friend has excelled herself this time. Found a very nice room for Mummie, arranged for the furniture to be moved on Monday and Alan arrives on Tuesday.

Further letters to Mary relate how Alan and I borrowed stretchers and camped in my mother's future home — a single room — while we decorated and equipped it. I was back at my old trade and still good at it. We went out for all our meals, returning to some old haunts. Alan dined with Mary's husband Francis at the Athenaeum Club, the home of the intellectual elite among the London clubs. It was still to his liking. When he returned to our 'camp site' he remarked: 'I should say, it is a little oasis of education and culture in a centre of smoke, ugliness and money-grubbing.' This was a play on the first report of the aims of the Settlement. Alan rarely missed an opportunity for word play. We dined at the Studio Club, where some members now wore service uniforms. Alan went out and bought me flowers but nothing was quite the same as it had been fourteen years before. Things rarely are. Alan tried hard, and was very attentive, and I knew I would still do it all over again, but the original gaiety had gone.

I noted the change in me in another missive to Mary. I had just had my first visitor to my mother's room, Hugh Meredith, Alan's friend and best man at our wedding, whose wife had died the previous year:

> He expressed pleasure that I really had long hair, whereupon I immediately produced my false plait. Due hilarity followed. He seemed to be going out of his way to be complimentary to your young friend. But I think ten years with Alan has improved me. I certainly feel more able to deal with Hugh now than when I was a young bride.

I added, later in the letter, that 'nothing happened between us.'

My mother did not stay in her new room for long. The following year she was diagnosed as having cancer. I told Alan and his response was immediate. 'You must bring her back here,' he said without any prompt from me. She moved into our bedroom and we slept upstairs. She was terribly demanding over the next few months before she died.

I came to London to make arrangements for her funeral. I stood on Euston Station with tears streaming down my face, less because of the loss of my mother than that some coal dust had blown into my eyes. I was wiping them when an attractive, well-dressed man approached. He wanted to know if he could help, adding that he was Russian and knew a little about eyes. He carefully wiped mine, then asked me to lunch. I accepted. I was having dinner that evening with Bill and Marjorie Holford at their London house, so I took a risk and brought the Russian along. I expected them to be shocked: instead they encouraged me in my turpitude. They even suggested I should sleep there but I preferred to be alone in my bad behaviour.

Part of the pleasure was the secrecy; knowing I was doing wrong, and knowing the high cost of being found out. That night I 'went to bed' with my acquaintance, which is how people in those days used to put it. He was keen to parade himself in front of me, but I made a point of not looking. I must have had my first and only

Marjorie Brooks' (Holford) portrait of Cécile, 1940.

orgasm. I was overwhelmed by its intensity and I had no idea that for some this was almost an everyday sensation. So I never expected a repeat performance. At that time — at thirty-four — I still really knew nothing about sex — except that men seemed to like it. It was a surprise to find there was something in it for women too. I was still as bewildered by the sexual world as Alice had been with Wonderland. Whenever I came to London my friend was always at the station to meet me. Then one morning I woke to find that my mother's diamond brooch and my grandmother's gold bracelet had been stolen. That cured me.

As for Dink … When one of the workmen's cottages which my grandfather had left to his grandchildren and where my father had for years collected the rent became available, he left Finchley Road and went to live in Hornsey with his tenants. He took with him the remnants of the house: some cutlery, a few glasses, and a white and gilt plate which had hung in the hallway. He had to learn to look after himself. I remember that he put pieces of cheese on the kitchen floor so that the mice would not climb onto the table to feed. Dink could not bear to think of trapping them.

He continued to travel by train to the country, where he would walk all day. He always took his lunch with him and a bottle of home-made lemonade. One day he suffered a stroke while walking in a street far from home. The police took the unlabelled bottle from his pocket for testing while the ambulance took him to a nearby hospital. When I heard the news I took the first train to London and went straight to see him. He couldn't speak but managed a wink. He died soon after. I was amused when I was questioned by the police about the bottle and its contents which they thought might be poison or drugs.

I went back to Dink's workman's cottage and decided to keep it on for when Alan and I made trips to London. Some of my wealthy friends in Liverpool heard about our pied-à-terre and inquired whether we would let it to them occasionally. I dampened their enthusiasm by saying it was not in a very good location nor was it furnished very well.

When the war ended I was working as an army welfare officer with the West Lancs Territorials. It was my task to make recommendations on issues like compassionate leave, often sought by service personnel wanting to control the damage the war was doing to their relationships. Those four months were sad and squalid — but I learned a lot.

Life Four
Going Upstream

A Grimy, Run-down Carrier of Coal

I can't remember the day World War Two ended. Possibly, that memory has been overwritten by later memories of two personal and peaceful events. In one I am at the tiller of a seventy-two foot canal boat; in the other, with no secondary school experience, I become a tertiary student. Both events changed my life, or, perhaps more accurately, lives.

Peace was at hand when I casually picked up a copy of the *London Illustrated News*. It featured an article by Tom Rolt packed with beguiling descriptions of what it was like to be travelling steadily in a narrow-boat, seventy-two feet long with a slender seven-foot beam and a shallow draught of two feet nine inches, through the network of canals crisscrossing Britain. The article took me under Georgian bridges and over Georgian aqueducts, up and down hills by way of Victorian locks, into canal pubs, and past warehouses of simple industrial architecture styled in soft red bricks, and cottages with thatched roofs. These were scattered along a network of 6,500 kilometres of canals, hand-dug some two centuries earlier. I was seduced by these images.

Rolt concluded with a plea to save both the British inland waterways which were becoming mud-filled and overgrown, and the prosaic narrow-boats which had trouble in economically shifting coal, cotton, fruit juice, pottery and cheese against competition from first the railways and then trucks.

Alan and I wrote immediately to the newly constituted Inland Waterways Association and sent our subscription to become member number twelve. On an impulse, we ended the letter by asking whether there were any narrow-boats on the market. A letter came back from the chairman of the association, Robert Fordyce Aickman, suggesting we should engage in a little 'pertinacious inquiry in backwaters'. Eventually our inquiries located the *Phosphorus* at Rickmansworth, north of London on the Grand Union Canal system. She was on the market for three hundred and fifty pounds and we bought her unseen as we were worried that someone might see her and snap her up before we did. My impulse to purchase was very strong.

Eventually we drove to Rickmansworth and to Frogmore Wharf where the *Phosphorus* lay neglected. When we saw her we realised that no one else would have been foolish enough to purchase her. She looked a grimy, run-down, retired carrier of coal; which she was. What were we going to do with this coal-ingrained hulk, immobile and three hundred and twenty kilometres from our home? As a diversion we did a bit of gongoozling (canal language for prolonged and uninvited staring) at a narrow-boat rising in a nearby lock. It was brightly painted with castles, roses and other traditional motifs. There were touches of the gipsy wagon about it which excited me, given a family claim to gipsy ancestry. The boat man, dressed in the traditional garb of red tie, singlet, coat but no shirt, sent water gushing through the paddles in the lock gate which control the flow. The heavily loaded boat rose, before chugging off at the higher level. We thought the whole process looked terrifying, though the boatman handled it coolly. It seemed beyond us, but we left Rickmansworth determined to get the *Phosphorus* moving again.

Alan knew the proprietor of John Parke and Sons, Barge

Builders and Repairers, Graving Dock Owners, so we organised for the *Phosphorus* to be towed back to the company's dock on the canal at Bootle, just outside Liverpool. It was a long trip through the canal network even when undertaken by an expert: three hundred kilometres as the crow flies can become six hundred, because canals follow the most level and most easily dug route rather than the shortest. When the *Phosphorus* arrived at Bootle we went to welcome her and to chat with John Parke about converting her into a houseboat. We brought along a set of plans devised by Tom Rolt for his boat but we soon revealed a considerable degree of ignorance about canal boats. We didn't know that narrow-boats usually worked in pairs, with an engine boat towing a butty boat, which did not have an engine; or a horse towing a boat from the towpath.

No doubt the boat builders were amused to see their prejudices about the paucity of practical information possessed by an academic — and particularly a philosopher — so amply reinforced. We had bought the wrong type of boat and now we would have to buy an engine for a craft which was ill-shaped to receive one. But I don't like to think of the *Phosphorus* as a mistake. We came to love her very much. And, just incidentally, the *Hesperus*, the engine boat of the pair, had been purchased by Lord Lucan, who always wanted to 'cover as much new ground as possible,' which meant the *Hesperus* remained unconverted and something of a wreck.

Marine equipment was difficult to obtain in postwar Britain. We had to go to Wolverhampton, a centre for heavy machinery not too far away, to purchase a fifteen-horsepower two-stroke diesel; slow but reliable. We also wrote to a friend in Cornwall to get a double-burner kerosene stove. Meanwhile, the shipwrights were putting up struts and beams to carry the roof, and gradually the boat, which had been open to receive cargoes of coal, became a long dark tunnel. All of this was happening at the cost of three shillings and sixpence per hour for labour. I requested windows which would open outwards to catch the

114

breeze. The shipwrights laughed as they told us that windows like that would be smashed the first time we entered a lock without shutting them. The fit was that tight. They gave us sliding windows, and a number of tips about life on the waterways. Meanwhile we painted, no small task with a seventy-two-foot hull.

Eventually, the conversion was completed. Butty boat *Phosphorus* had become houseboat *Phosphorus*. We borrowed a professional steersman from the shipyards as 'driving instructor' for our first few weekend forays. Alan's brother Stewart, an engineer, was on holidays and came along too. Our instructor started the motor and took our floating home into the centre of the canal for the first trip. He sought out 'somewhere quiet' so that I could take over, while we circumnavigated Aintree, site of the Grand National Steeplechase. Then the great moment arrived and I took the tiller. It was the most wonderful feeling I'd ever had. I could feel how a good pull to the left on the tiller became a slow drift to the right by the bow. Sometimes I felt powerful and in control; other times impotent — but always excited.

The second weekend we went to Wigan Pier, along canals cut through the residue from coal mines dug one hundred years before. We tied up behind a pair of cumbersome broad-boats, each with a fourteen-foot beam, and each carrying one hundred and fifty tons of coal. The *Phosphorus* was about to enter her first lock under our control but with a little help from our professional boatman. It was

Cécile, at the tiller, and Alan.

115

exhilarating when our narrow-boat went into the broad lock, the gates slammed shut, and water poured through the bottom sluices until we too could open the gates and chug out at the higher level. There was further excitement as, nestled in a large tank of water on a swing bridge, we passed over the black waters of the Manchester Ship Canal. The *Phosphorus* then eased through a deep grassy cutting, on the way to penetrating our first tunnel.

This was to be a weekend of many new experiences and, seeing that our steersman was going home that evening, we were hurrying to get through the tunnel before he left. Hurrying, that is, to the extent that a narrow-boat ever hurries. When we arrived at the oval entrance to the tunnel, however, a pair of narrow-boats painted with roses and castles was tied up, obviously awaiting permission to enter. A tattered red flag fluttered over the entrance. I walked along the towpath to find out when we could move. Halfway up a grassy bank was a thatched cottage where an old man was working in his garden. I told him we were new to boats — as if that were necessary — and asked when we could pass through the tunnel. He thought we wouldn't be allowed through on a Sunday. Then he told me of times when the path below us had been crowded with horses towing narrow-boats. The flag was changed frequently then, with boats arriving at either end of the tunnel at the same time. I had to ask what the flag at the tunnel entrance indicated, and was told that it meant we could not proceed into the tunnel and could only enter when the red flag was removed and flying at the other end. I was learning.

I went over the hill, through which the tunnel passed, to the flagman's house and met a resolute old man. He said he'd take the red flag away at six next morning. Not before. He was obviously not the sort of person to change his mind, so I walked back to the boat. The woman from the butty boat was heading for me, looking not at all pleased. I felt like an intruder. While there were far fewer of them than there once had been, the canal boat people were a close-knit community who desired little contact with 'folk off the land'. I expected her to say that pleasure boaters like us had no right to be on their waterway. I would not have had any trouble with this, but all she wanted was to ask what the tunnel man had said about starting times. I told her and, so she wouldn't think we might jump the queue,

Interior of the Phosphorus.

added that we never got up early. She turned to leave, then paused: 'And you better get bikes off roof. It'll be a tight squeeze for you in the tunnel even without them.'

We had brought our bikes so we could shop in the villages, tour the countryside, and phone friends from public phone boxes to tell them where to find us on the occasions when we wished to be found. The man from the cottage joined us. He too doubted whether we'd get through, and, with the slightest hint of a smile, referred to the *Phosphorus* as Buckingham Palace, because of its relative grandeur. There was only a small space in an unconverted narrow-boat in which the crew — and often the family — had to cook, eat, sleep, and steer.

The red flag was down by the time we'd woken, and the work boats had gone through the tunnel. We untied our bicycles and took them from the roof. Stewart had just rejoined us and was at the tiller, and my job was to watch from the bow. I was of little use, however, because there was no way I could have made myself heard above the engine which was thumping away in the confined space of the tunnel. Slowly, the *Phosphorus* disappeared into the darkness. We had the headlamp on but its shaky beam

Cécile, in the foreground, with friends aboard the Phosphorus.

illuminated only the damp roof of the tunnel immediately above us. Through the blackness I could just make out the light at the other end. I didn't know that, some twenty metres back, Stewart was having problems with the engine. Mud stirred up from the bottom had blocked the inlet duct for cooling water and we were in danger of being trapped — and suffocated. But he said nothing, mindful of the inexperience of his crew. The tiny light, about the size of a mouse hole, gradually expanded over the next twenty minutes, until we burst back into the gentle English light, which for a few seconds was almost blinding. Still I had no trouble seeing the tunnel man enthusiastically waving his flag as we passed. He seemed almost as pleased as we were to have us through the tunnel and out of his area of responsibility.

We cleared the cooling duct then moved on between meadows and past steep wooded banks. Occasionally, through breaks in the trees, we could look down on a green valley. I became lost in the anticipation of endless summers spent passing slowly through this dreamy English countryside. Then I noticed that the small bow waves, which earlier had almost hypnotised me as I lay with my head hanging over the bow, were no longer rippling towards the bank. We had stopped, stuck in thick squelchy mud. Alan, Stewart and I each took a barge pole and pushed as one. The *Phosphorus* didn't move. We made some jokes about not touching people with barge poles then I went to make some coffee. We were in no hurry to move. We had enough fuel, food and water to see out the summer.

While discussing the prospects — or even the desirability — of rescue, we heard the distinctive sound of a marine diesel engine. Some time later a pair of work boats appeared. I was not confident that we amateurs were welcome on the waterways and unsure whether the approaching boat people would want to help us. Then we heard them throttle down and, as the man in the engine boat came level, he shouted to me, 'Wanna snatch?' It sounded a trifle rude but I said I did and was thrown a well-used rope which I tied to the front stud. The engine boat backed off, then accelerated. This resulted in only a shudder running through the *Phosphorus*, but the second tug sent us sliding into the deeper water midstream. We passed our rescuers a couple of the packets-of-five Woodbine cigarettes, which we kept as tips for just such services.

We were still gliding along when I remembered a short list of useful hints for amateurs like us, published by the Inland Waterways Association. The first hint was to keep to the middle except on bends when you should be on the outside. That was where the deepest water would be. I could see a sharp bend coming up so I scrambled to the rear of the boat to pass on the tip to Stewart, who was steering. I then went forward with a short pole which combined a spike and a hook. The strategy was to use the spike end to push the bow away from the bank and the hook end to plunge into brambles so that the boat could be pulled closer. I felt the *Phosphorus* was slipping too far from the outside bank so I hooked into a clump of blackberries and pulled with all my rather limited might. It takes a lot to divert a seventy-two foot wooden boat even when it is travelling at only six or seven kilometres an hour. Instead of redirecting the *Phosphorus*, I managed to haul myself out of the boat and onto the bank, fortunately at the one spot where there were no blackberry bushes. The boat sailed on for some distance before Alan noticed I was missing and stopped.

Little by little I established some contact with the canal communities. We would tie up at one of the many piers, or in occasional inland ports, and I'd cycle to the village shopping areas. Sometimes Alan came with me. Sometimes he would go with Stewart to the pub where they'd drink in the saloon bar while their aquatic superiors were in the front bar.

Stewart liked to be with Alan. He depended on Alan to run his life, and to protect him from its harsher aspects. He was like a puppy waiting for instructions and approval from its owner. In most aspects of personality Stewart was quite unlike Alan. He was unsure of himself and tended to come out with inappropriate comments. He lacked Alan's talent for self-deprecation and his cool mastery of so many topics. But there was something about him, physically, which made him a pale shadow of Alan. He was tall and there was a similarity in his walk. It was enough to provide me with intense personal anguish over the next thirty-five years. At that time, however, he was just an occasional irritation, like when I tried to keep alcohol off the *Phosphorus*. Whenever we were about to take our dry ship into the canals a latecomer would appear on the bank carrying a considerable cargo: Stewart with a bag of Scotch.

Riding to the shops, we'd pass small factories, mills spinning cotton brought up from the sea ports by canal boat, and watch girls tending the spools. We might visit a dairy and buy a pint of milk — provided we promised to leave the bottle at the next lock. Once, a woman sold us half a dozen eggs. We had become accustomed to an egg a month during wartime rationing, and decided to splurge and put all six in the one omelette. Then on to the fish shop where the stuffed head of a carthorse was mounted on the wall. I examined the severed head. The fishmonger noted my interest and came over. 'My old favourite,' he said. 'Used to tow round my delivery van. Now I have a motor.' I'd ride back to the *Phosphorus* loaded with local produce — and folklore.

Occasionally we'd have trouble with the diesel engine, and I'd write to John Parke seeking advice. The replies were the essence of tact:

Dear Mrs Dorward

Thank you very much for your letter. I have been anxious about your progress and am sorry you have had a little trouble so early but I feel that until you get to know the engine and your craft there will be a certain amount of trouble which will not occur later on. Please allow me to make some observations.

Which he did with considerable deference.

Despite our inexperience these were happy times. Even Alan's drinking seemed less important. Sometimes he would be unable to cross the eight-foot elm gangplank to get aboard safely. Once I had to pull the *Phosphorus* under a nearby bridge so he could be manoeuvred down onto the deck.

Life with him could be wearing and occasionally I thought about what it might be like without him. But I left only once, for a week. We had been walking in Hyde Park after attending the second wedding of Humphrey, one of Alan's friends from their student days. He had just married a woman much younger than his first wife, who had died. To my surprise I began crying and could not stop. I sobbed out that it was time for Alan, like Humphrey, to marry a younger woman; also that I was absolutely worn out. 'Let me go back to the boat alone. I must be alone — and you must leave me,' I blurted out.

Alan walked me to the bus which took me to the station. From there I caught the train to Peterborough, a railway junction a hundred and twenty kilometres from London, where *Phosphorus* was waiting on a quiet section of the canal. Alan went to Scotland to stay with Stewart. I gradually came to terms with myself and phoned him. He had been almost as upset as I had. He said he would come back by train. I went to meet him in the Morris, which we garaged nearby. But I didn't really want to see him: I wouldn't pay the penny required for a platform ticket. I waited outside.

Alan came out and hugged me and we went back to the boat where he calmed me down, probably by promising to give up whisky. I hoped this gesture might be the prelude to something special. But our sleeping arrangements remained unchanged, piles of rubber mattresses, in the fore and aft respectively, of a seventy-two foot boat. About a year later I heard that Humphrey's young wife had committed suicide, and was grateful I had managed to stay alive.

On my cycling trips among the canal and farming communities, I began to notice the many beautiful children, some working with their parents on the boats. I was continually being reminded that I wanted a child. It had been easier to avoid such thoughts in Liverpool with my extensive round of social events and social causes. But when I was alone at dawn at the tiller of the *Phosphorus*, with Alan sleeping heavily almost at my feet, it was difficult to keep from my consciousness the thought that I was in my late thirties and would never have a child.

In one village I passed a little girl with a stunningly beautiful face standing in the doorway of the butcher's shop. My desire flared. I was not aware that I had started to cry but tears were pouring down my face. I looked across the path at the picturesque cemetery and conjured up an eccentric rationalisation. Experience with the characters from my favourite authors, the Brontë sisters and Jane Austen, was instructive. I knew they wouldn't cry in the main street of a village, without apparent reason. I hurried through the cemetery gates, and walked among the headstones until I was able to control myself. I wanted the locals to think I'd suffered a recent and tragic loss but there was no indication that they even noticed.

When I arrived back at the *Phosphorus*, a weathered old boatman was admiring her. 'She's an old Ricky boat, she is,' he told me. 'I knew 'er soon as I seen 'er.' He had been on the *Phosphorus* when she was carting coal and wanted to know where we were taking her. When I told him, he looked concerned: 'Oh, the New Cut. Have you got the right lock key? I can get you one. And a 'orn? I can get you one of them too.'

I asked him why I needed a horn. He explained that when you

go through a bridge hole you can't see any boats which might be coming the other way, and they can't see you. 'You've got to give them a blow,' he said. I told him I'd like that. The boatman came along to help us through a right angle bend. Before he left, I asked how one safely passed a boat coming the other way without getting stuck on the canal bank. 'Just steer straight at the other boat,' he explained enigmatically. I wanted to ask what happened if the other steersman was working to similar instructions. But, in a flash, the boatman was gone and we were alone to tackle our most severe test yet. This was a flight of fifteen locks, starting just outside Audlem, in Cheshire, and stretching up the hillside.

The hillside was deserted when we pushed the *Phosphorus* into the first lock, shut the gates, and let the water flush in. On cue, the *Phosphorus* rose to the next level. We had hoped to see this untrammelled passage repeated through all fifteen locks. But already there were danger signs. When we were in the second lock I saw tiny figures running down the towpath to prepare the next lock. We were going to have to pass descending boats in the pounds, the enclosed areas of water which linked the locks.

By the time we had cleared another two or three locks, the whole staircase of locks was teeming with people, and their boats were descending on us. We hurried the *Phosphorus* out of the lock and stood meekly in the rain, holding wet ropes which secured either end of her against the towpath, waiting for a descending craft to get by. But this boat was horse-drawn and couldn't get past us; its tow ropes were tangling with our superstructure. The boat people shouted at one another, then at us. We were not very popular. One boatman took pity on us and waved us past him and on to the next lock. But we were just too slow, too tired, too wet, and not clever enough to bring off the manoeuvre.

Eventually, the lock-keeper also took pity on us. He helped us through the remaining locks and tied up the *Phosphorus* under the vast canopy of two oak trees beside his cottage. We had been almost four hours coming up the hill, and were soaked and exhausted. We fell inside the boat, emptied the water from our shoes, and took off our wet clothes. Soon we were sitting wrapped in blankets with our feet in a bowl of hot water. We ate local bread adorned with country bacon and eggs, eased down with whisky-spiced tea. I went to bed early while Alan trudged back down the hill in the rain to a pub 'for a drink or two.'

It was about this time we introduced George to life on the water. George was our grey cat. When we brought him aboard for his first journey, he sniffed the boat from bow to stern, and checked that it had a convenient lavatory and a promising galley, before he climbed on the roof and peered over the side. He was confident, with neither life jacket nor instructions in swimming. Once he knew he received regular food and had a cat box available he was happy to come with us. We were travelling on the Shropshire Canal. Apart from the locks at Audlem, the Shropshire Canal was noted for its long unbroken stretches of water. The canal builders cut deep into the hills and built up embankments across the valleys rather than installing locks in the undulating countryside. Sometimes we looked upwards at an arch of trees which completely enveloped us; other times we looked down on a winding country road which would suddenly disappear into a tunnel, constructed so that vehicles could pass under the canal. At such points there might be a battered sign on the canal towpath, indicating the road below led to a pub with a name like the Navigator Inn. The navigators dug the canal and carried away the spoil. Their name was shortened to 'navvy'.

The grass along the Shropshire Canal always looked greener on the side opposite the towpath so we slid the *Phosphorus* onto the muddy bank and pushed our long elm plank onto the grassy verge. We had lunch there, but did not linger as we had a young Australian student from the University of Liverpool with us, who needed to board the London train at a town some distance downstream. We had tea while we travelled but again pulled in to eat dinner which had been cooking during the afternoon as we chugged along. Food was always more delicious on the water, in this case country roast beef with steamed vegetables followed by fresh raspberries. We were then able to drop the student off at a nearby station.

The sun was setting, the birds were twittering, and ... a horrific thought struck me. Where was George? He hadn't been seen for hours, since lunchtime in fact. I did a quick search of his favourite hiding places on the boat then sadly conceded that we had left him behind. Four hours since lunch and travelling at six or seven kilometres an hour meant that George must be about twenty-five kilometres back. We couldn't turn the boat around, the canal was much too narrow. So I would have to wait, frantic, until the morning, then ride back on my bike.

By six next morning I was riding at top speed along the towpath, heading for our lunch spot of the previous day. The canal banks were already lined with men sitting on stools, hoping to hook a fish for breakfast. All wore caps which they raised as I passed: 'Good morning, ma'am.' My replies were not enthusiastic. I was too worried about George. He hated strangers and I thought all these fishermen would help to drive him away from the canal. Most of the canal bank looked like our lunch site and I didn't know where to start the search. I stopped at a small pub and asked permission to put up a poster. I did this without much optimism.

LOST
One pound reward for grey cat
Boat Phosphorus

The landlord was reassuring and dismissed my worry that, even now, George was heading back to Liverpool. 'George will wait for you. Cats always do. You'll see,' he said with apparent authority. He told me there was an effective news network among the boats and any reports of a sighting would be relayed to us. And so it happened. A boatman stopped us midstream to report

Cécile's 72ft Occupational Therapy project.

that a little girl had found a grey cat near our luncheon spot. We still couldn't turn the *Phosphorus* around, so we hired a car and went to find the little girl in question. She took us to a cottage on the canal bank and pointed underneath at the hen house. And there was George. We were all delighted: the child with her one pound note; Alan and I with recovering George; and obviously George with being back with us. He purred on my bed all that night.

The excitement and the bliss of touring in the *Phosphorus* in the late forties had almost led me to ditch the course of study I'd embarked on earlier. Chugging through the Midlands with a number of friends or just with Alan, past picturesque countryside and memorable docks and buildings, seemed an attractive life. But I knew that soon I would be needing a paid occupation. Alan would be retiring when I was forty-three at best; he was not well, and philosophy would always languish at Liverpool. His career became less secure after a sombre visit from the vice chancellor seeking his early retirement. I felt good about gaining a profession, particularly as my experience during the war had convinced me I was much more capable than I'd previously thought.

The 72ft Occupational Therapy Project

It was almost preordained that I should choose occupational therapy as my future career. It was 1946 and for ten years I'd been friendly with Constance Owen who urged me to do more — or perhaps some — study. We were both members of the Personal Service Committee. Conn had become interested in occupational therapy in the twenties when a friend of hers suffered a mental illness and was admitted to hospital. Conn gave up her university studies to become a teacher, and eventually won a scholarship to the United States, the only place where occupational therapy training was then available. She returned to Britain with a PhD and became principal of the first school of occupational therapy. One afternoon a week she provided occupational support for psychiatric patients, and asked me if I would like to be her honorary assistant. It was the first time I had come in contact with such patients, although I had often considered that I was on the brink of lunacy myself.

I enjoyed helping make toys and I got on well with the patients. After the war Conn decided to start her own occupational therapy college in a collection of deserted Victorian houses outside Liverpool. There seemed to be no opportunity for

Constance Owen (Conn).

me to participate in this venture as I had no background of formal education. Having been a professor's wife for about fifteen years I couldn't bring myself to become a secondary student. One day Conn made me an offer I couldn't refuse: I could study with her for six months without any tuition fees, then sit for the preliminary exams in anatomy, physiology, psychology and first aid. If I passed I could enrol formally at her Liverpool School of Occupational Therapy. This seemed to be a considerable hurdle as I was thirty-five and had never sat for a written exam apart from Miss Haycock's grammar tests.

The preliminary exams turned out to be fairly basic, and I passed without much trouble. However, the first year of the formal course was difficult for students like me who had not previously encountered science subjects or the general methods of science. Most evenings Alan and I ran through the day's lectures together. Alan was great on scientific method, as you'd expect of a student of Russell and Moore. But it was different with anatomy. We'd sit at the table and study the architecture of each other's arms, tentatively tracking muscles, bones and tendons. All this anatomical detail was a revelation for the professor of philosophy. He said he'd thought his arms were 'just made of meat', and he was not altogether joking. Sometimes this study took place on the boat, where Alan was building up a significant library. We could moor the *Phosphorus* then come back to Liverpool by car or train or taxi for lectures.

Training with Conn involved clinical as well as theoretical work. As part of the clinical training, I went out to institutions with qualified occupational therapists. We worked in local mental hospitals, TB hospitals, and children's hospitals. One day Conn came to me with another exciting offer. She had arranged for occupational therapy to be introduced into the old Liverpool Workhouse, which was now a home for old people where the residents were separated strictly by gender. Conn wanted me to be there for her 'opening up' day, when the women who lived upstairs would be led down to mix with the men who were on the ground floor. They would all be given occupations to perform rather than being kept in bed. Conn knew I'd been horrified when I worked as a volunteer at this Dickensian centre before the war. She wanted me to see the changes she'd recommended come into being. We brought the women down one by one. It took a long time: some hadn't been down the stairs in years; some had scarcely been out of bed for years. 'Eh, look at him. A man,' one of the women said to me. Others made more colourful comments.

The aim of occupational therapy at that time was to provide something for patients to do once they were well enough to do it. We were trained to assess what they were capable of doing. I had to learn, then teach, a whole range of crafts. I was good at them, but not always sure that some of the patients were well enough to learn them. The devotion of most occupational therapists to craft, and particularly cane work, was becoming a standing joke. Even the satirical magazine *Punch* featured cartoons with hospitals overflowing with cane baskets.

Learning crafts also provided some tough physical tests for me. We had to use a variety of tools including cross-cut saws in what was called occupational carpentry. The trend for

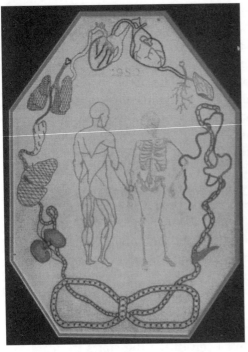

occupational therapy to become counselling was still many years away.

However, it was another craft, embroidery, which caused a moment of crisis when I was about to graduate as an occupational therapist. I had to submit a sample of my work to 'an embroiderer'. I meant it to incorporate both my craft and anatomy work: internal organs linked with blood vessels and swathes of intestine, in a style which drew something from art nouveau. The embroiderer said it wasn't embroidery and refused to even consider it, until Conn came to the rescue and told her to think again.

When I had been awarded the Diploma of the English Association of Occupational Therapy, Conn asked if I would like to stay at the college as a tutor in (very basic) anatomy. Many students were finding their university lectures in anatomy rather difficult. They didn't know much about bone structure or anatomical terminology. My job was to provide them with the essence of the lectures. I came to love this task, although on the first occasion when I had to address a group of about seven or eight students I was terrified. I can't do this, I thought. They won't listen. Why hadn't I just remained the 'wife of a professor'? Meanwhile, there was a continuing din as my students grated their chairs on the floor.

I knew I had to go on, so I took a deep breath and looked them over. I started with: 'Are you too near the gas stove and getting too hot? If you are, then move your chairs away now, so you won't be scraping them on the floor later.' That was the making of me. The students stopped shuffling and paid attention. I knew I could do it, and was soon known around the college both as 'Mrs D' and as something of an eccentric lecturer. I enhanced this reputation when I stopped students taking notes or copying diagrams during my classes. I told them they had books containing facts and diagrams. What I was trying to do was to help them understand those books, not be a substitute for reading them. Today's tertiary teachers will recognise that this is a continuing dilemma.

One day I brought Conn, my friend, mentor and now employer, back to the *Phosphorus*. She knew of my bursts of sadness that Alan's drinking brought on, and of my disappointment at my childlessness. Possibly, when she had made her initial offer immediately after the war, she had thought I would leave Alan and therefore needed a career. Conn now seemed to understand how my hopes for revitalising my life with Alan were focused on the *Phosphorus*. She ran her eyes over all seventy-two feet of her then said: 'That's the biggest occupational therapy project with which you'll ever be involved.' She might have said 'biggest and most successful'. For Alan was transformed once he stepped on board the *Phosphorus*, although he did have some bad evenings: there were many pubs along the waterways. He worked the locks with panache. While I'd hesitate and wonder whether we'd get through he'd say, 'Let's give it a go.' He also became skilled as a steersman. Just occasionally he almost looked healthy, although that didn't last long. I think he rather enjoyed poor health. Just the same he did have a fibrillating heart and a weak chest. Which meant that I did any heavy work on the boat. The story developed that I was rather bossy and liked to run the show. But I had to be like that.

This was when I lost Mary Mott. She died in 1953 before she was

Mary Mott.

seventy. She'd had such an impact on the shaping of my life it was hard to imagine she had gone. One night on the boat I dreamed that her spirit visited me. As soon as I was aware of her presence, I said: 'How good of you to come.' I was grateful she had taken the trouble to come, but I was also very upset. Mary did not appear bodily but as an intense presence without shape or form. The following night she returned, again in a dream. This time I was not overcome with gratitude, but took it more naturally. I was walking along a pavement. I could clearly see the paving stones and the kerb, and that Mary was with me. Again, not in bodily form, but moving with me. I knew she could not stay, and I said so. I also said the effort of parting had to be made. I wanted to be the one to make the effort. I was extremely distressed, but did not wish to show it while Mary was there. So I told her that at the next corner I would turn back. Which I did.

I thought about Mary often after that night but never dreamed of her again. Life went on.

During the weekends our friends still crowded aboard the *Phosphorus*. Those who couldn't get inside sat on the roof as we passed increasing numbers of other converted coal-carriers. The houseboat fashion was taking hold. Alan was the gracious, confident host as he took our friends, their children, and the children's pets touring. I imagine he was more like the young man who was appointed to the Liverpool chair in 1928 rather than the ageing philosopher who would never meet the expectations of his peers.

Those expectations had been high. Alan had gone to the University of Liverpool with the backing of the leading philosophers in the land. G E Moore, Professor of Logic at Cambridge and editor of the leading philosophical journal, *Mind*, wrote to the selection committee:

> He seems to me to be exceptionally acute and exceptionally clear-headed: he is a very conscientious thinker and of a thoroughly scholarly habit of mind.

G F Stout, Professor of Logic and Psychology at St Andrews, wrote:

> Dorward I know intimately as he was my assistant. I can speak strongly in his favour from every point of view, both as a philosopher and man.

There were others. Professor A S Pringle Patterson, from Edinburgh, noted:

> He writes with distinction, and combines acuteness in criticism with maturity and sanity of judgement. I do not think, therefore, the fact that he has not as yet produced a full-sized treatise is a serious count against him.

Sadly Pringle Patterson's expectation about Alan's treatise remained unfulfilled after more than twenty years. In those days British academics were able to devote twenty or even thirty years to producing their single, significant work, which might take many more years to be acknowledged, let alone fully understood. But Alan was never going to write anything which presented new ideas to the academic world. His one contribution was a booklet on Bertrand Russell which he wrote in 1950 for the British Council. It was clear and competent, and pointedly it looked at Russell's advocacy of impulse as a basis of behaviour, but said nothing really new.

Colleagues in Liverpool wondered how the man who had matched arguments in intellectual bouts with Russell, Moore and Wittgenstein had become ineffectual, at least when it came to setting down his ideas in learned journals and books.

These were still the days of the God Professor but colleagues found Alan accessible, decent and kind. He showed he was still a very good philosopher at the weekly seminar but he was unable to put his ideas down in print. Was that because of his drinking? Did he drink because he wasn't writing? Or not write because of his drinking? Was the problem the shift from Cambridge, the philosopher's heaven, to provincial Belfast and later commercial Liverpool where only a few were interested in his ideas? Or was he just another example of how difficult it is to overcome alcohol addiction?

There were times when Alan seriously tried to stop drinking but his resolve would only last for a week or so. There was ample opportunity for drinking in the postwar years. Only a handful of students in this utilitarian city took philosophy. His department remained small and there were often no honours students. Meanwhile some of his students were winning distinction and becoming professors elsewhere. Alan dismissed sadly the intellectual claims of some desperately-seeking clerics doing postgraduate degrees: 'They just want to have Dr in front of their names on the sign outside their churches.'

Amid all this disappointment, the *Phosphorus* stood out as a symbol of Alan's success, all seventy-two feet of her stemming from the wonderful single plank of elm which constituted her keel. I'm told that some saw me as another success symbol but I don't believe that. There was no doubt that the *Phosphorus* was a social success. The visitors' book contains many famous names

— three Nobel prize-winners in physics, the anthropologist Margaret Mead, and a philosopher of food, Kenneth Lo, who revealed the secrets of Chinese cooking to many in the west. At weekends the *Phosphorus* was the place to be. But there were also 'ordinary' names: like the first entries, W J and Mary Sheckleston from the boat *Spectre*. They told us stories of the boom days of canal boats and, as they left, Mrs Sheckleston signed for both of them. Obviously her husband could not write.

Sometimes the *Phosphorus* was difficult to get to or even find. My barrister friend Leadley wrote: 'I can see no hope of getting to see you while you are at Market Drayton but if you will indicate where you will be next weekend I will investigate the possibility of coming over.' On trips when we wanted privacy we sometimes travelled without maps so that when asked we could say truthfully we did not know where we were heading. Occasionally, we would stop and ride off on our bikes to discover the name of the nearest village. When we asked village people where we were they would look at us in a way which said they thought we were very strange. We'd then add that we came from a boat, as if that explained everything.

Sometimes we'd ride separately away from the *Phosphorus*. At Worcester I came across Alan's distinctive Edwardian bicycle propped outside the cathedral of Our Lord and the Blessed Virgin Mary, which is near the River Severn. We

exchanged greetings with a mock formality. 'Fancy meeting you here,' he said. 'And fancy meeting YOU like this,' I said. Then he said 'Would you like me to show you the cathedral?' 'Of course. It would be marvellous.' Perhaps the villagers did have a point about us.

Meanwhile, I was building up a reputation for my teaching of anatomy, and sometimes went to London to tutor occupational therapy students before exams. I loved staying on the *Phosphorus* when she happened to be in London. She could be tied up outside the Zoological Gardens which backed on to the Regent Canal. Harrison Matthews, the scientific director of the zoo and a friend from pre-*Phosphorus* days, gave us a key which allowed us to open a small gate near where we moored and traverse the site at night. I watched my beloved giraffes, lions, monkeys and even some kangaroos in my personal nature park.

Crossing the Wash

Alan retired as Professor of Philosphy in 1954, and had his portrait painted. He looks rather disappointed. By then the *Phosphorus* had become central to our lives, and on his retirement day we cast off at Chester, twenty-five kilometres south of Liverpool. We kept one floor at twenty-eight Percy Street so we could return whenever we wished and rented the rest to provide some income. Alan never came back to Liverpool.

I felt Alan would benefit from visiting his intellectual home, Cambridge, where he had been a rising star mixing with the superstars. Many of his friends were still there, and the children of our Liverpool friends were there as students. The problem was that we had reached the stage where we didn't want to go anywhere without the *Phosphorus*, and the linking canals running approximately east-west weren't deep enough to allow us to cross from the Grand Union Canal to the Great Ouse River which led towards Cambridge. There was only one thing we could do — change canal systems by crossing the Wash.

This was easier said than done. The Wash is a tricky North Sea bay abutting the Norfolk and Lincolnshire coasts. Two channels lead out through the sandbanks to deep water. Our task was to cross, for some distance side-on to the waves, from one channel to the other, a total distance of about twenty-five kilometres.

The Wash had secured its place in history when King John lost his jewels and baggage there on an incoming tide in 1216. We had no wish to join them and had been carefully planning the crossing for a year, starting with a letter seeking advice from Lord Lucan who had crossed the Wash earlier in the *Hesperus*, which still closely resembled a coal carrier, with a tent up front for shelter. It was an event of some significance.

In August 1955 the *Manchester Guardian* published my story of our crossing, under the heading:

CRUISE OF THE PHOSPHORUS
A Canal Boat in the Sea

It was more than just a cruise. It was a major adventure, or perhaps a series of adventures as we took to sea in a flat-bottomed boat. We started at Peterborough by taking on our seawater crew. One was handy at washing-up and shopping, the other was a retired merchant seaman who now owned a boat like ours. As part of our planning, we had purchased a massive anchor in case things went wrong, and two long, second-hand ropes to accommodate the massive rise and fall in the tidal waters at Wisbech where we waited for ideal conditions. At Wisbech grain and timber ships moored alongside us, and we looked like a punt by comparison. We waited seven days for perfect weather and spent some of that time at a famous inn named The Dog in a Doublet. We also secured anything on the boat that was not nailed down. We hoped it would not be a rough passage but knew it could be and did not want anything rolling about.

The pilot we had organised earlier took us out on the ebb tide, timing our trip so that we would turn, just at the change of tide, into the King's Lynn channel for the run back to the shore. For ninety minutes we headed out. There was some wind and moderate waves but our flat-bottomed boat rode the waves comfortably. The decisive moment came when we had to turn towards King's Lynn's Deep for the journey back. We were broadside to the waves and the *Phosphorus* began to roll. We had no doubts now that we were at sea. We rushed unsteadily from one end of the boat to the other checking whether the water was coming over our decks and threatening to swamp us. But no, old *Phosphorus* was behaving well and righting herself easily from one rolling wave to the next.

This drama lasted an exciting ten minutes, just long enough to give us a real taste of the sea, and of a little danger. We were just congratulating ourselves on our skill when the *Phosphorus* hit a sandbank. Our boating friend climbed onto the roof and tried to push us off with a twenty foot pole. However, very quickly both *Phosphorus* and the pole were stuck in the tonnes of sand which were rushing in on the tide. Gradually we pushed the *Phosphorus* into deeper water and reached the main channel along which the incoming tide would carry us back to shore. Next, a fishing boat made up on us and I could smell fresh shrimps being cooked. I waved a basin in one hand and a five-shilling piece in the other. To our delight the shrimp boat came alongside to do business. It was the best five shillings' worth of shrimps we'd ever see.

Our pilot asked the fishermen to organise a riverman to meet us at the jetty to take us up on the tide to the Denver Sluice, the first lock on the Great Ouse. The pilot left us and the riverman took over. In two hours we were through the lock and back in non-tidal waters for the first time in a week. It was several days before we simmered down to normal river life. Some time later we tied up in Cambridge beside Magdalen Bridge. Then the Moores came on board, G E in his lecturing slippers and both smoking small clay pipes. Alan, at least, was home.

We had a gracious life at Cambridge with many of the children of old friends coming to see us on the boat. I sought new things to do on the river and bought a tiny punt with a motor. I zoomed around on moonlit nights, travelling along the Backs of colleges which looked like three-hundred-year-old film sets. Twice a week I took the train to London to see students at the occupational therapy school regarding their problems with exam preparation.

When we seemed to be well settled and even talking about buying a riverside cottage, I took a job at the Cambridge Mental Hospital. I started in early 1956 at this 940-bed institution with its extensive gardens and high fence. There was a separate building for younger patients who were becoming independent: part of the hospital's shift from being a lock-up institution to one where patients had more contact with the outside world. At the entrance to the hospital were two large wooden gateposts and each morning I paused there and 'left myself hanging on the posts'. It was a precise ritual which generated for me a clear image, the aim of which was to forget the personal Me and my problems so the other Me would have all my energies available for my patients. It seemed to work.

Then staff started leaving the Occupational Therapy Department and by September 1956 I was running it. In November I formally became Acting Head Occupational Therapist. I was at the centre of things and had six qualified occupational therapists, an occupational carpenter, a gymnastic instructor, and three male and eight female nurses working with me to keep patients occupied. I realised the wonderful scope of occupational therapy to help people as I developed new projects for a group of very withdrawn patients. They started by tearing up paper and cutting cloth, and ended with papier-mâché toys and stuffed cushions. They also became better adjusted patients.

One day I was furious: one of my patients who was almost ready to go out to work had been put back under lock and key without any communication with me. When one of the young doctors asked how I was, I burst out with the story. This outburst resulted in my being consulted, and my patient being reinstated in the hostel. Soon she was outside and working.

I had a woman in once a week to keep the *Phosphorus*

shipshape. Alan seemed happy, particularly when he was with G E Moore, but his health was a worry. My diary has frequent but cryptic entries — Alan sick; Alan better; A sick again; A improved; A sees doctor ... We didn't talk about his illness although he did mention he had 'prostate problems'. There seemed no reason for immediate alarm and, at the mental hospital and aboard the *Phosphorus,* I made preparations for Christmas 1956.

Ten days before Christmas I took a quick trip to Liverpool to bring back some nice things, including a pair of brass Georgian candlesticks, to improve our quality of living on board. When I returned the next day Alan was in hospital — and dying. He had been very sick once before, and thought he was dying. On that occasion he read with selected friends the description of the death of Socrates from Plato's *Phaedo.* It seemed an entirely appropriate way for a philosopher to go. He recovered quickly after the reading.

This time it was serious. Prostate problems meant cancer. There were no theatrical touches. He just asked me to promise 'not to give Stewart up' then died. It was 16 December 1956.

I was devastated and did not want to go back to the *Phosphorus.* Alan's clothes were there, and many of his books, and I suppose his whisky. The Chadwicks took me to the Master's Lodge at Gonville and Caius College. (James Chadwick was by then the Master.) Next day, I wrote in my diary: 'Alan died last night.' Just that. I never mentioned him again in the diary. That was the only way I knew how to handle my loss. I had depended on Alan: through him my character had been formed and was still forming. He had given me, perhaps not always intentionally, what he termed the inestimable ability to be satisfied with my own company. My only problem had been the drink which had constantly loomed to threaten my peace of mind and deny me my conjugal rights.

I remember only fragmentary details of the funeral which left from the Master's Lodge at Gonville and Caius. I resurrected the

Retirement portrait of Alan Dorward.

black duffel coat which had kept me warm on the *Phosphorus* to wear at the funeral. Aileen Chadwick would not let me wear it: she lent me a black coat and skirt. Despite Alan's ambivalence about religion, there was a clergyman officiating at the funeral. He said he would just say a few words but said many more than that. I thought Alan would raise the coffin lid and say, 'That is quite enough.' The thought made me smile. There were darker thoughts, like the one which said I'd never had any responsibility for the running of my life — only the lives of others. How could I manage? Stewart also had his problems. The source of his advice and information about the world had gone. He went out and bought a set of the *Encyclopaedia Britannica.*

I quickly went back to work at the mental hospital. We were constructing a nativity scene and it had to be finished in less than a week. The patients had made all the characters from papier-mâché then dressed them. The occupational carpenter had helped with the stable. All was revealed on Christmas Eve — Jesus, Mary and Joseph, the Wise Men from the East, the guiding star, and sundry animals. One of the patients looked at Mary, shining in blue satin, and asked in a loud voice: 'Is that the Queen Mother?' I almost laughed to think that I'd been so sure they'd know what the display was about.

Life Five
Hanging on the Gatepost

Australian Landfall

I couldn't remain long at Cambridge after Alan's death. Memories of him were everywhere. I could go back each evening to the Master's Lodge at Gonville and Caius College, as the guest of the Chadwicks, but I couldn't forget that the *Phosphorus* was still tied up behind King's College, filled with Alan's books and clothes. The tactic of leaving the personal me hanging on the gateposts allowed me to work briefly at the hospital, and the patients seemed to keep on improving, but I couldn't continue.

I sold the *Phosphorus* to some American physicists and returned to Liverpool. But that worked no miracles. I was forty-six and alone. I had never been alone before, and thus never forced to take responsibility for myself. The pleasure I had learned to generate from my own company was proving elusive now that Alan was no longer available as my unobtrusive guide. All I had left was my continuing membership on some of the Liverpool committees. I had originally joined them in the role of the professor's wife: now, if I remained, I would be playing the professor's widow. I didn't want to go backwards like that; I had to break away, and those committees provided a means of doing so. Lady Hobhouse of the Blue Funnel Line family was an important member of a number of them. I had written to her from Cambridge asking if any of their ships went to Fiji, as one of Alan's friends had invited me to spend six months there as part of a working holiday. When I arrived in Liverpool a letter was waiting from the Blue Funnel passenger manager:

> Sir John Hobhouse passed to us your letter of 24th May addressed to Lady Hobhouse concerning a passage to Fiji and he asked me to communicate with you on your return to Liverpool and give you as much help as possible.

The letter offered me a trip to Sydney at one pound a day on the new Blue Funnel freighter, the *Hector*, which carried thirty first-class passengers. Blue Funnel would organise for me to get from Sydney to Fiji. The timing could not have been better and I accepted at once. This would be the first leg of an around the world working holiday extending over two years.

The *Hector* was leaving from Liverpool, which for some reason meant I could take any amount of baggage. I included a substantial collection of artefacts from my ten years on the *Phosphorus* — canal art, pictures, metal cans and plates embellished with traditional roses and crowns, lock handles, and maps. Some I took as gifts, others to remind me of my recent past as I started on a new life. My trip to Fiji was regarded by my English friends as a great adventure, so far away and rather exotic. The same friends also told me how lucky I was to be travelling on a freighter and how much I'd enjoy stopping at places like Port Said. I would agree with a smile, thinking: lucky perhaps, but God, you don't know how much I'll be missing Alan.

The trip was fascinating, and Cairo, while not exactly enjoyable in the way my friends predicted, was educational. I was standing at the rail watching the traders come aboard to sell their wares when I was surprised to feel a hand moving under my dress. It took me a moment to realise I was being assaulted by one of the traders. I moved away, somewhat wiser.

I made my first Australian landfall when the *Hector* called at Albany. I'll never forget Albany's long wooden jetty, and a tiny locomotive coming out to deliver and collect cargo. There seemed to be few other signs of life in the small rural town which had been the first point of white settlement in Western Australia. Goodness, is this all there is to Australia, I thought, remembering the long floating platforms, the miles of docks, and the vast buildings which constituted the Port of Liverpool. I walked into town and was relieved to find that it had electric lighting. The shop windows were filled with wildflowers for a spring festival. I saw my first local flame trees, a small eucalyptus with bright red flowers. My thoughts about Australia had changed for the better between my arrival and my departure three hours later. But I'd yet to see anything resembling a city.

Adelaide was undoubtedly a city; and more so Melbourne, where I stayed with Olive Rayne, my friend from the Liverpool Occupational Therapy School who was the head of the school at Royal Melbourne Hospital. My letter about Melbourne in October 1957 to my friend Beryl in Liverpool was not flattering: 'We came up the river and it was disgustingly cold — far worse than I could have imagined. The place reminded me of Liverpool on a particularly horrible winter's day. It is really awful to think I have come all this way to be frozen. I felt like going straight back on the *Hector*.' My next letter to Beryl presented a happier picture: 'Forty days after leaving Liverpool the *Hector* sailed into Sydney Harbour. You can't imagine how beautiful it is and how warm.' I was stunned by the grandeur of the harbour and the beautiful beaches along the coastline.

My first culture shock came quickly when I called on the friend of a friend to whom I had been given a letter of introduction. I stood at the gateway to a large house in Cremorne, and asked for directions from a gardener who was weeding a bed of roses. The gardener led me to the front door of the house, pulled some keys from the pocket of his khaki work-shirt and took me inside. He was my friend's husband. My English view of the established order of society, where gardeners dug with a certain deference and the householders paid them to do so, had just taken a heavy knock. At about the same time, while staying briefly with an acquaintance, I was told to earn my keep: I was handed a straw broom and told to sweep my room. Needless to say I didn't, and an apology was offered. I decided to find a place of my own.

The next shock came when I went for my first swim in the surf. I found myself being knocked over, then under, time after time. I berated myself for being clumsy and not getting a proper footing as the waves broke over me. I'd brace myself for the next wave: and go tumbling down again. Finally I understood that the strength of the waves was the problem. I watched the locals handle them, learned quickly and was soon an enthusiastic bodysurfer.

In Sydney I learned the extent to which the Liverpool Occupational Therapy School was the centre of a worldwide network. The director of the Sydney school was a friend from the Liverpool school and had been a frequent traveller on the *Phosphorus*. I had no trouble getting a job. Occupational therapists were in short supply in Sydney, which had recently suffered a major — and probably its last — polio epidemic. I worked at an institution at Manly called Far West Children. Many of the children had been paralysed by polio, and came from country New South Wales for specialist treatment and rehabilitation.

One of my first patients at the Far West was a little girl about six, with braces on both legs. She couldn't stand alone and was accustomed to being swung by the arms between adults, her feet only occasionally touching the ground. I was convinced that she should be able to stand — with a little help. But there was no equipment available to provide such help. So I manufactured a puppet head on a stick for the child to play with and also to use

Jackie.

as a third point of balance. I wanted to get her accustomed to balancing with her arms down rather than up. I started by holding the child between my knees, then I gradually relaxed my grip until she was standing alone. 'Jackie stands with stick for one second,' says my diary. The first time Jackie stood was one of the most memorable images I have taken from my time as a therapist. When the girl realised she was standing alone, she screamed in fright and I had to re-grip her with my knees. Gradually she became more confident. My diary records when she stood alone for 110 seconds. Soon she could move around with a set of wheels: not a walking frame, but an old pram with the wheels tightened so that they wouldn't spin too rapidly and send her sprawling.

We took the children out of their beds, where many had been spending most of their time, and up to the roof to play games. The play sessions were restricted, as many of the children were in extensive plaster casts or strapped on to frames designed to prevent an imbalance in the muscle systems as muscles recovered strength at different rates.

There was very little formal equipment available. We constructed a Heath Robinson style maypole using an old bicycle wheel attached to the top of a post. Old toys hung from the wheel on lengths of string. Then we placed the children around the pole and they had great fun hitting the toys towards their friends and warlike toys at their enemies of the moment. Soon we had a very tangled collection of strings which required a pair of scissors and new cord to set right.

The three months working holiday in Sydney passed too quickly. It was now January and my letter to Beryl noted the heat:

> The temperature rose to 107 degrees today. It's marvellous. Just like being under a hair drier — but all over. I went out in pants and a cotton dress only — and my hat, which I wear most days. But the women here always wear stockings.

I sailed for New Zealand to stay on a sheep farm outside Wellington with the sister of one of my occupational therapy friends and her husband. I recorded in my diary: 'The house is large and airy but has no servants. There are no farm servants either. The 1200 sheep seem to look after themselves ...' I visited the thermal regions of the north island and wrote:

> I saw what I would take to be part of the bowels of the earth, simmering away gently, and stinking to high heaven. All over the place, from out of the most ordinary grassy hillock, or from under some flowering gorse bush such as one might see on Hampstead Heath, jets of steam issued from unseen cracks. Had Alan been here I'm sure he and I would have proposed that secretly a network of fine electric wires had been laid underneath to have us all on.

Alan was still very close; our mutual, quirky view of the world lived on.

Fiji was my next stop. I had left the impression with my friends in Liverpool that I had been invited to Suva to stay with a family. Actually, I was staying with Humphrey, Alan's

An 'Alan-like' calm in Fiji.

Cambridge friend who had become a major colonial official. While in the service of Empire, he had acquired a 'bad reputation' as a womaniser. No one would have believed me if I'd said that I would be staying at Humphrey's house as just a good friend. But that was true when I arrived and true when I left. However, just in case neighbours should get the wrong impression, I stopped wearing my elegant dressing-gown outside the house and wore Alan's instead. It made me look very respectable.

Humphrey's house was built from wood and its long verandah reminded me of the *Phosphorus*. The house was beside a lagoon lined with palms bearing coconuts. I could watch, whenever I cared to raise my eyes, the surf breaking over the lagoon's outer edge. A cooling breeze blew from it through the windows and doors. The atmosphere was so calm, so Alan-like, that I was not surprised to feel somewhat overwhelmed. In situations like this Humphrey reminded me of Alan, although their personalities were poles apart. Alan used to tell me, with a certain vicarious pride, that Humphrey had been a heroic nocturnal climber of the towers and statues of Cambridge colleges. He had taken the gilt crown from the statue of Henry VIII at Trinity College which Henry had founded. After graduating he returned the crown by parcel post. Another of their friends, Aldous Huxley, was also staying in the house in Fiji.

Enough of Lotus Eating

I had three months of idleness in Suva. I toured the island; went to receptions, dinners and afternoon teas; swam in the surf just in front of the house, or just lazed in bed. I began to feel I'd had enough of lotus eating. Or perhaps there were not enough lotuses in Suva to satisfy me. During this time I heard fantastic stories about my host. They sounded like extracts from a lurid novel in which I was a minor character. Humphrey obviously had been involved in long term liaisons with the local women and these were often detailed in the stories. I featured only occasionally — but vividly. Such stories could only have been based on imagination. Certainly I wasn't his type, and he was far too old for me — and even more decrepit than poor old Alan.

It seemed time to move on. I remembered Miss Graham, a wonderful woman I'd met on the passage to Suva. She had been returning from New Zealand for her fiftieth year of service in Fiji with the Methodist Missions. When I told her I was planning to stay at the Commissioner's house she too told me eagerly about Humphrey's dubious reputation. She also described the difficulties she had in getting domestic help for the mission's school and associated hostels at Lautoka, some one hundred kilometres north of Suva.

I decided to take the plunge and take on the job of matron of the hostel attached to the Methodist girls' school — despite the fact that a missionary regimen would be a stern one for me: no drinking, no sleeping in, and regular Sunday worship. I was allowed to smoke; everyone seemed to smoke in Fiji. My reaction was mixed as I told Beryl:

> They sing the most awful hymns night and morning — and teach them to the girls. They also say a long breakfast rigmarole and have a conversation with God which is a bit much. I try not to listen. But they work like slaves for hardly any money and I'm glad to help them out a bit.

During my first days at Lautoka I was taken to a firewalking ceremony held at dawn on a hillside just outside town. I had seen the languid life of colonial administrators, and a little of the busy life of the Methodist missionaries. The firewalking ceremony was something else again. It started with drumming and chanting and incense burning. A temporary structure thatched with palm leaves enclosed a pit six metres long which was filled with glowing stones taken straight from the fire. I moved forward to take a closer look but the heat and the pungent smell of heated kava drove me back. Down in the misty valley six men swathed in rather dirty white clothes were intoning prayers before they followed a group of drummers up the hill. The crowd — Fijians, Indians and Europeans — jostled one another to get a good view. Water was sprinkled on the stones and hissed into the crowd as steam. When the firewalkers slowly crossed the pit then sank to their haunches before a shabby temporary altar, it was almost an anticlimax.

I returned to the gentility of the mission which previously had been an old colonial hotel. My quarters were on the verandah outside the dormitory. My task was to supervise seventy Indian schoolgirls who were the grandchildren and great grandchildren of the Indian labourers who had been imported to work in the cane fields. I started the day by ringing the six o'clock wake-up bell, then checked that the girls got up, made their beds, and swept the floors before school. Once a week I drove to the market to purchase food, with an Indian woman who

Schoolgirls at Lautoka where Cécile was matron of the school hostel.

did the cooking. The kitchen had no chimney and the wood fire in the middle of the room filled it with smoke. I was not allowed to stay there for long because the cook felt it was too smoky for me. Out of the kitchen came a straightforward menu of curries with rice or flat bread, twice a day every day.

Occasionally I did what matrons in institutions everywhere did — checked to see the girls' hair was free of nits. It wasn't. I soon discovered to my horror that I too had them, and treated myself with a generous application of the preparation I used on the girls.

But it was not these routine duties which left the most lasting impression of my stay there. One of the first things I did on arriving at the mission was to inspect the earthen trenches which constituted the hostel's lavatories. I found the outlets clogged; apparently they hadn't worked properly for more than a year. I arranged for them to be re-dug immediately, and learned later that this operation had made a lasting impact. The primitive lavatories would be my memorial: from that day the girls visited what they called 'Mrs D's toilets'.

While I was in Fiji there was an epidemic of poliomyelitis. The Colonial War Memorial Hospital asked the British Red Cross to appoint me for two sessions a week to help rehabilitate eight polio patients, all of them boys under ten. I went into action using my small Austin Countryman as my mobile office and store. As usual, I had no rehabilitation equipment so I tapped into the Liverpool occupational therapy network to get some. I started with the Sydney school. They sent some coloured building blocks and interlocking shapes. These gave me an idea.

Fiji was a land of heavy smokers, even by the standards of the late fifties. Almost every house had its pile of empty Capstan and Gold Flake tins. The thought came to me that, if we could attach the lids to the bottoms permanently, the tins could all be fitted together and we'd have the makings for castles galore. I ran through my plan with someone who just happened to be handy with a soldering iron. He volunteered to help me and the castles project was under way. The children scraped the labels from the tins — lovely destructive work. Soon castles were rising into the air, and the next thing we had to do was provide weapons with which the kids could knock them down. Much of my time was spent crawling under beds to recover tins, or ducking to avoid those being thrown at me.

I also worked with a group of young men, again polio victims, who were in wheelchairs. I found that planks placed across the tops of their bedside cupboards formed a bench at which they could work. Soon they were producing paintings and craft objects and I started on plans to establish small businesses where these could be sold. But my year-long stay in Fiji was coming to an end, and so I didn't have time to implement the plans. I was booked on the liner *Orsova* which would soon take me to Los Angeles.

I didn't especially enjoy the trip, although I became friendly with a number of people, and attended a lot of drinks parties in a cabin near mine. I imagine I was invited to allay any objections to the noise, which went on till three or four in the morning and ended up with visits to other cabins. I had three gents trying to visit me, but I did not fancy any of them and kept them decidedly out!

I had intended spending only a few days in California. However, someone ran into the rear of my friends' car, my feet went through the windscreen, and I spent two months recovering from a pair of injured ankles.

I received a modest compensation payment, which went towards a trip by mule down the Grand Canyon, the spectacular mile-deep gorge sculpted by the sediment carried by the Colorado River. I had been wanting to do this ever since reading about the canyon in a children's paper at the Hampstead library some forty years earlier, about the same time

Cécile and guide at the Grand Canyon.

I was being stopped by my mother from reading *Jane Eyre*. There had been no prospect of my making the trip before I received the compensation payment — I was always travelling on the tightest of budgets.

I reached the southern rim of the canyon by the Santa Fe express, then continued by bus. A young cowboy type of fellow took me to a corral surrounded by spruce and yellow pine trees and selected a mule for me. Its name was Salem, not exactly an auspicious name for the beast which would take me down the Angel Trail. Salem was a very wide mule and I had to stretch my legs painfully apart to stay secure. As the decline became steeper, the path began to zigzag. It also moved closer to the edge. I hoped Salem would know when to turn, or we'd both drop off into the chasm. I tried to reassure myself that he was an old mule who'd been on the track before. Why should he choose to ignore a turn and drop over the edge just because I was on him? I would give him no instructions, and avoided looking down into the abyss, as I had no head for heights.

Eventually, when we stopped for lunch, I made two disturbing discoveries. One was that when I got out of the saddle I could scarcely stand up. My knees were bent; I was all bent. I thought briefly that I would be unable to continue. The second was that I was my guide's only customer. I had assumed others would have joined us back along the track while my gaze was fixed straight ahead. I asked the guide where the others were. 'It's early in the season. There aren't any others,' he explained.

The temperature rose as we resumed the descent after lunch. The overriding colour of the canyon was a deep red, but we also moved through soft pastel shades which reflected the different strata of sedimentary rock over which Salem was plodding. Finally, we were among the cactus at the bottom. However, the most exciting section of the journey was still ahead: a narrow suspension bridge crossing the Colorado River. This was a bridge of considerable movement: it went up and down as well as swaying from side to side. Had I been required to cross it at the start of the trip I would simply have died of fright. But I'd survived many moments that morning where I could have died of fright, so I shut my eyes and trusted Salem would not fail me.

Finally, I was sitting in a restaurant at the bottom of the canyon, nursing my painful joints and eating delicious roast chicken. The cook came and slid in beside me, very close. He made some clumsy advances which I rejected rather imperiously: 'Considering I've just come down the wall of the Grand Canyon on a mule and can hardly bear to sit on my own behind to eat, what you are proposing is absolutely ridiculous.' That cooled his enthusiasm.

Next I went to Canada to see my brother Raymond. He and his wife Frances had settled in Calgary, Alberta, where he worked as an engineer. Raymond had also invited Stewart to stay while I was there, and we drove to Calgary airport to meet him. Raymond asked if I was looking forward to seeing Stewart again. I hid my anxiety. He looked enough like Alan for the reunion to be painful. Also, he was now as dependent on me as we both had been on Alan. My understated response was: 'I'd be happier if Alan were arriving.'

Raymond pushed a double bed into the only spare room in the house. He assumed for reasons I could not comprehend that Stewart and I would want to sleep together. I didn't care one way or the other — so we did. It left me feeling sad but seemed to make Stewart happy. For three weeks we took in the spectacular scenery of Canada in mid-winter, then Stewart flew back to the Hebrides, while I started an occupational therapy job in Kingston, Ontario.

Three months later I moved on to New York and Washington, mainly for the art galleries. I had the unusual experience of visiting the Washington Art Gallery during a fierce snowstorm, and I had the whole building to myself, with all those wonderful European works of art.

Life seemed different when I returned to Liverpool after my two years of travelling. I was now more self-reliant, and the pain of missing Alan had eased. My friends noticed the change, and that I was obviously restless. They asked where I would go if I couldn't settle back in Liverpool, which seemed likely. I told them Australia, because I liked the relaxed atmosphere there. Then one day I was reading the British occupational therapists' journal and there was an advertisement seeking someone with teaching experience in anatomy and crafts to join the Royal Perth Hospital School of Occupational Therapy, which had opened that year, 1961. Gordon and Flora Stephenson, my friends from Liverpool University days, had gone to Perth in the early fifties.

Gordon was a planning consultant to the state government.

I decided to apply. By the time I did, Olive Rayne, my old occupational therapy teacher and now the foundation director of the school, was getting desperate. She was the only full-time staff member and needed help urgently. I was the only applicant. I offered to come for six months, and to pay my own fare for the voyage by sea. I wanted to be free to leave if I was unable to survive the full-time teaching. The school agreed to the six-month contract, but said to come by air. I agreed but kept my house in Liverpool in case I didn't like Perth. I rang Bill (by then Lord) Holford in London to tell him of my plans. He sounded enthusiastic. 'Perth's a nice place. I've just built a bridge there,' he said. That was the Narrows, the elegant concrete structure which crosses the Swan River near the city. It was the result of one of Gordon Stephenson's early planning recommendations.

Adventures in the Bush

I arrived in Perth in summer and was welcomed at the rather small and basic airport by Olive Rayne. We headed for the occupational therapy school which was housed in what had been the Kensington Hotel, an 1880s pub in working class East Perth, known to staff and students as the Old Kenso. The licence had been surrendered and the lounge, ladies' lounge and bars now housed the school. The word BAR in brown glass remained on one of the windows.

Some hospital staff lived in the upstairs rooms and I joined them. Our showers were at the end of the corridor, and had formerly been used by hotel guests. I waited my turn for a shower in what I liked to call my peignoir, which was a pale pink cross between a dressing-gown and an overall. It was very elegant and much commented upon by my colleagues, who queried the name. I told them that the French word *'peigne'* meant a comb. In the days of servants, young ladies used to have their long hair tended after they had dressed and the peignoir protected their dresses.

I could easily walk into central Perth from the Kenso. The city was as I imagined London to have been when my parents were young, but much smaller, of course. It had a population of 400,000, not much traffic and the suburbs had yet to start spreading. The large mineral development projects in the north of the state were just starting to be discussed. Perth people reminded me of the Liverpudlians who worried that Londoners might be looking down on them, which they often did. Perth residents thought they were being scorned by Melbourne and Sydney and easily became defensive. They often talked about how badly Western Australia was treated by the 'Eastern Staters'.

The pride of Perth was its beaches, its river and its central traffic artery, St George's Terrace, which was then a fine boulevard of Victorian and Edwardian office buildings, some with a special goldrush flourish. The height of buildings and the variety of their pediments meant that the footpaths seemed to be continually sunlit. A lasting impression from these first days was that of hearing my own footsteps as I moved around Boans, the large department store which claimed to stock everything from a needle to an anchor. I'd never been in shops in London or Liverpool which didn't have sound-deadening carpet on their floors.

There were other firsts for me, and some very eurocentric impressions. I felt the city had no history; it had no really old buildings, no Roman ruins, and only one art gallery, and that was small and seemed to show mostly conservative British and some Australian landscape paintings. There was no sign of anything modern.

My Sydney experience with the gardener-owner was given a special twist on my first day at work in Perth. There seemed to be no class distinction; everyone was equal or at least acted as if that were the case. But not quite. As I was about to enter a hospital ward, a young man in a white coat stepped aside then pushed open the door for me. A woman about my age watched what seemed to me the most normal of social exchanges. But she was obviously displeased, and waited until the man had gone before cornering me and demanding: '*Who* do you think *you* are, letting that doctor open the door for you?'

No one had ever spoken to me like that before. I realised that in the hospital, where doctors were concerned, there were social boundaries almost as rigid as those I had just left. I made a particular point of keeping in the background when doctors were around lest one of them should talk to me and attract the wrath of some of the nursing staff. I was spoken to severely on other occasions, and wondered whether I had come to a land of barbarians. I had considerable doubts about staying, but I wouldn't return to Britain. I wouldn't allow myself to retrace my steps. It sounds funny now but at the time it was devastating for me. I still believed I had a particular place in the scheme of things. So, early one morning, I found myself standing on Cottesloe beach with the idea of ending it all.

The water was so clear I could see the sand whiting swimming past in the shallows. There couldn't be the excuse of dirty water which saved me from drowning myself at Liverpool. I dived in, swam past the pylon and headed for Rottnest. My plan was to drown along the way. A kilometre offshore I reassessed my situation. Perhaps I should give Australia another chance. I turned and swam back to shore — with difficulty. The offshore easterly breeze which had made swimming out rather easy ensured my return trip would not be without effort.

Not long after this I found myself in a bed at my hospital. I'd always had a severe back problem which seemed to have been made worse by my swim in rough water. I was placed in extension to ease the pain. I was also given aspirin despite my warning that it could set off the skin eruptions and general discomfort associated with my old bugbear urticaria. I seemed to have been cured of it before I left Liverpool but the aspirin brought it back.

I recovered before term started and was given my first batch of students, with the instruction to 'do with them what you will.' I treated my girls like members of a family; no, like my family. This meant classes could be dramatic; sometimes almost operatic.

I grasped students' arms to make a point, I shouted, and I gesticulated. They laughed back at me — in a nice sort of way. The damping down of my natural behaviour to fit the English social milieu, a response to Alan's counsel, had lifted. But occasionally remnants of the class system would break loose: like when a student told me with pride that her father owned a shop. That seems no cause for pride, thought the old me. Then I remembered that I was starting a new life and that things were different here.

I showed students how to adjust the weaving looms to maximise the exercise that would help patients recover from their particular injuries and, at the same time, give them the pleasure of creating something. I also taught my students screen printing, then in its infancy in Perth. Sadly, we were teaching the British curriculum and I'm sure now that these were not skills the students would ever use when working in local hospitals. I didn't know this at the time, however.

I joined the Spinners and Weavers Guild, expecting that I would learn something to enrich my teaching. I found the guild comprised only about twenty members and, apart from Mrs Beckett who had worked as a dressmaker to Alexandra the Queen Mother during the reign of George V and had sewed silk for parachutes in World War One, and a couple of the men who were skilled with large looms, I found that I was teaching the others, not learning from them. The ladies (except me) wore hats to meetings. I also discovered that the country which rode on the sheep's back knew surprisingly little about wool. I was asked whether some wool from a grey sheep was 'fine steel wool'.

In the thriving agricultural centre of Wagin, guild members encountered a woman who did know about wool. She arrived at our display with a fine fleece from a black ewe. Could we weave it into a blanket? Her seven-year-old son would be going to boarding school soon and a comfort blanket from his favourite sheep would make him feel more at home. There were some strange people around here. And some strange customs.

I appeared in the local newspapers, complaining that the thick wool we needed so that patients could weave carpets could not be found in Western Australia. We had to import it from Scotland.

Much of my teaching was done in a small cottage at the back of the Kenso. There weren't enough chairs at the school so we sat on the floor. I began to feel that my students were not just my family but my children.

I decided I should teach them to use their eyes and look carefully at pictures — as my parents and their artist friends had done for me. Here I didn't have the advantage of a series of art galleries packed with exciting paintings from which I had drawn my own inspiration, but we made frequent visits to the old Art Gallery of Western Australia. My students often found these visits amusing. I always seemed to be getting into arguments with people who would announce, when standing in front of only a mildly non-representational canvas: 'A monkey at our zoo could do better than that.' I'd get mad and confront them. I'd tell them that they were just glancing at the painting rather than looking at it carefully. I told them how this might be done. I had lots of arguments, and won an occasional convert. I also made my students evaluate each other's designs or pictures, so they could get used to looking critically at art rather than just glancing at it. I enjoyed opening their eyes.

My methods of teaching also seemed to be different from other methods used around the hospital. I had a considerable emotional investment in them and when my methods were criticised for being 'different', I submitted my resignation and bought a small restaurant in the foothills. My resignation was rejected. One of my friends remarked that this was fortunate: a restaurant was not the ideal business for someone with so little expertise or interest in food preparation. My students seemed pleased that I was staying. They had started to call me 'Mrs D' and described me as 'that eccentric teacher'. If they saw me at the beach or shopping they came up to greet me: 'Hello, Mrs D,'

'Good to see you, Mrs D.' My students in England would have slipped away, with both parties feeling slightly embarrassed.

I was unaccustomed to all this instruction, plus the accompanying administrative and assessment duties. I also had to take my students to the Anatomy Department at the University of Western Australia where I'd sit and fume as the lecturers provided for my students a rather condescending story about the architecture of the human body. Teach them something difficult, I'd feel like shouting. But I maintained silence. I still knew my place. All this activity had me working Monday to Friday, 8.30 am to 5.30 pm. Those are typist's hours, I'd tell myself loftily. In Britain I gave only two or three lectures a week, or a few anatomy tutorials, or filled in while a staff member was away ill or on holidays. I thought the continual work would kill me if I didn't develop an effective escape strategy.

Most Friday evenings I set off for the bush to ease the pressures of the previous five days. I'd have an early dinner and then drive, sometimes south but usually towards the warmer north, where there were also fewer roadside fences, making it easier to find a camping space. I took with me a small barbecue grill on which to cook my chops; also my lilo, and my shovel. I treasured that shovel. I felt that it hadn't been much of a weekend if I hadn't dug my car from deep in the sand at least once.

I started with short trips to Yanchep, an isolated coastal fishing centre and national park fifty kilometres north of Perth. In my diary were entries like: 'Yanchep. Swim, rest in sun, crayfish salad lunch. Got bogged.' And (a couple of days later), 'Crayfish again. Bogged again.'

Everything about Yanchep was wonderful. It was wonderful sleeping under the trees, with a net to protect me from the mozzies. I'd lie down and gaze up through the branches at the millions of stars. If the moon was full and immediately overhead I'd see a second layer of 'stars'. Hundreds of glowing lights appeared among the swaying branches. I'd never seen anything like it before. Maybe it had something to do with the shiny leaves of the eucalyptus trees; or maybe it was just part of the magic of the park. Next morning it felt marvellous to crank up the back of the lilo and have breakfast sitting up in bed in the open. If I were camped near Yanchep beach I'd have a swim before

Breakfast in bed.

breakfast. There was a clear green pool close to the beach, protected by a circle of reefs over which the waves broke, and deep enough to provide shelter for several cray-boats — hence the diary entries about crayfish lunches.

After breakfast I'd study the ground for footprints or droppings to see if any native animals had passed by while I slept. My hope was to wake up with a kangaroo beside my bed. Not surprisingly, this never happened. I'd admire the wildflowers and the grey-green trees and shrubs. I enthused about almost everything in the Australian bush.

I always followed a set plan when seeking a camping spot at night in more remote areas: turn left onto a track, then turn left again at the next track and stop as soon as there was some sheltered space. The routine was designed to prevent me from getting lost when driving out next morning. It was not always successful, as a diary entry indicates: 'Got lost for the first hour.' Occasionally my strategy would put me in interesting situations. One night I found what seemed like a nice camping site, had my gin and tonic and chops for dinner and went to sleep. I woke with the headlights of a truck only three metres away. There was a lot of noise where previously only cicadas scraping their wings on their bodies could be heard. The driver explained that I had camped across the entrance to his farmhouse. Fortunately we all

Cécile setting off on the Nullarbor Father Christmas run.

thought it was very funny: an elaborate version of parking on someone's driveway in the suburbs.

By Christmas I was ready to cross the Nullarbor with two friends. The road was unsealed and full of large potholes which did considerable damage to automobile springs. Wrecked cars were scattered along the route. Here I discovered the ultimate example of the relaxed Australian way of life. We arrived at a roadside motel, when everyone was asleep. The doors were unlocked and we found ourselves a room and put ourselves to bed. No one was awake next morning either so we put some money in an envelope and left. At the next stop we came across a pilot with a small plane which was being used to deliver Christmas presents to children on widely scattered sheep stations. I went along for the ride.

I had friends with me on this occasion but being alone, somewhere in the middle of nowhere, never worried me. I was never frightened, although I might be now. I was once travelling alone through Payne's Find, a small abandoned gold mining town on the edge of the north-eastern wheatbelt in Western Australia, four hundred and twenty-five kilometres from Perth. An emu ran across my path. I swerved but hit it and, in panic, put my foot down on the accelerator rather than the brake. My out-of-control station wagon missed the big trees at the side of the road, knocked over some little ones, and buried its bonnet in a sandhill. The front wheels were wrecked and the wagon clearly couldn't be driven. I summoned up the courage to walk back and see how the emu was. I found it at the side of the road, decapitated and disembowelled. Poor emu.

I returned to my car and spread out my gear under a tree. I was quite content. I had all the food and drink I needed for the next few days. I thought that something would turn up, but hopefully not too soon. The first car which passed was heading north. I did not move. There was no point in stopping the occupants, since they wouldn't be going near a phone. But the driver obviously saw the dismembered emu, the crashed car at the side of the road, and me sitting happily under a small tree. He must have decided that I had suffered concussion in the accident, or perhaps I was crazy, or both.

'It's perfectly all right, thank you,' I said as the driver approached and offered help. 'I'd rather like to spend a few days here. I don't need to be back to work for three days.' The driver said he'd alert Payne's Find as to my location, but one of his companions said this was impossible, because the phone 'went off at ten' in the morning. This sounded strange, but I discovered later that many country telephone exchanges were often operated only intermittently by the local women.

The next car to pass along this lonely road also stopped. They'd heard of my accident while in Payne's Find. They said they would 'tell 'em in Dalwallinu — they'll do something.' Dalwallinu was the next town on the way back to Perth. I cautioned against haste. 'I'm not in a hurry. Don't make anyone do anything in a rush.' Not likely, I thought, but shortly — well, two hours later — a third car stopped. The driver had also got the message at Payne's Find. He approached me, waving a tow truck operator's card.

'I believe you want a tow truck,' the young man said. He told me he was ferrying a car to Perth and would alert the tow truck company whose card he carried. I told him not to let the company hurry with its rescue bid as I was very happy where I was. He gave me that bemused look, which hinted that he too thought I must be concussed or mad. He assured me help would come, but he wasn't sure when that might be. Certainly he would not be in Perth before nightfall. I had a drink and dinner, and went to bed after a satisfactory day beside the road. I was hoping to be allowed at least one more such day.

About one o'clock in the morning a tow truck pulled up almost beside my lilo and a young couple climbed out. I got up in my nightie and was told by the young woman: 'Hey, would you believe this. He just came around to my place and asked if I wanted to go up the road two hundred and fifty miles. I didn't believe him. I've still got my bedroom slippers on.' The young man hoisted up my car while I thanked him, but I thought that I didn't want to go back to Perth just yet and that it would be a help if people didn't insist on helping me.

Just Like a Man

As I organise my thoughts about the next set of events I have in front of me three sheets of thin paper on which is recorded a far greater adventure on the road than that at Payne's Find. I was on my way to Shark Bay when I bogged my car near Eneabba, in sand plain country three hundred and ten kilometres north of Perth. I had followed my usual procedure for finding a stopover. Ten hours later I was parked by the roadside and writing an account of the astonishing events I had just experienced. The account begins with: 'If I don't write this down I'll never believe it happened.'

I had taken my second left turn and the sun had just set when I drove into a patch of deep red sand which had drifted across the patchy gravel road. There was no possibility that I could dig myself out of this one, so I activated my usual procedures for such an emergency: I poured myself a gin and tonic. Then I started to walk through scrubby country towards where I thought I had seen a light shining in the distance. It was pleasantly cool and quite exciting as I had no idea where I might be going. Then the light disappeared. I spotted two kangaroos, with their ears twitching, against the faint glow of the sky. Poor things, I thought; if I were a man I'd probably shoot you. I walked on. Three lights appeared where there had been only one before, then disappeared. Eventually I came to an extensive brightly lit clearing. In the centre was a very large tent with a number of smaller tents here and there around the perimeter under the scattered trees.

I saw a young man as I moved into the large circle of light but he didn't seem interested in my arrival until I said, 'Hi'. He paused but still showed only a modicum of interest. I told him I was stuck in the sand back along the track. 'Better see the Boss,' he said without enthusiasm, and took me into the large tent. Four young men followed. I said I was thirsty. Cans of cold Swan beer arrived from the large refrigerator. I was asked if I'd eaten. Yes, but ages ago. Next, a plate of food — half a chicken, roast potatoes, sweet potatoes, peas — was placed in front of me. I said I couldn't possibly eat all that. 'Eat what you can, then,' came the reply from somewhere behind me. I ate the chicken breast then gnawed at the leg. It was delicious.

The Boss, another strongly built young man of about my height, appeared wearing khaki shorts and boots. He said: 'I'll shift you, if you want to be shifted tonight.' I told him I didn't really care as long as someone knew where I was. I'd walk back to my station wagon, sleep, and wait to be rescued in the morning.

'Rubbish. We'll go now,' said the Boss. He led me to a tremendous truck with six wheels, four-wheel drive, four hundred or was it four thousand gallons of fuel, and a long steel hawser for towing. He pushed on both sides of my behind to get me into the passenger seat, but in a way which suggested that the manoeuvre was more for pleasure than function. We went back to the sand patch and the Boss soon pulled my station wagon onto the firm surface of a gravel pit. I thanked him, and then came a surprise. 'Lock everything and come back and have some more beer. The others are going to Perth. You can stay the night.' Then he added: 'But you don't have to sleep with me.' He must have expected agreement, as he was pushing me up into the driver's seat before he'd completed his proposition. I decided to risk it anyway. On the way back to the camp, I steered while he operated the gears. The Boss was letting me play with his powerful toy.

We drank more beer and the Boss described to me how seismic shots worked, and what they were telling his exploration company about the oil and gas reserves beneath the surface. Then he shifted the conversation from the professional to the personal. He'd been in the Australian desert for eight months and was sex-starved. Before that he'd been working in Pasadena, but he didn't like American women. He was, however, attracted to older women — or so he said. I picked up on the theme of sexual deprivation. I told him I'd rather be a man than a woman, because I could easily find a young woman if I were a man. But, as a woman, I couldn't easily secure a man. The only way I could achieve a satisfactory life as a woman was to forget about men. 'Nonsense. What you need is a good waking up,' he replied. Or words to that effect. He left no doubt that he was well-equipped for just that task.

I denied that what he said was true. What I can't deny is that it was a great pleasure for me later that night to hold a man in my hand: it must be the same for a man to fondle a woman. The tent was half open and the cool breeze played over us. The stars were brilliant. Much later the Boss went out to have a shower, while I gloated over the delights of my nomadic interlude. I'd never met a man like him. I suppose he also achieved a certain satisfaction that an older woman should arrive out of the blue and be prepared to make love with him. I dare say he had never met someone like me, either.

The Boss came back from his shower, then went away again without saying a word. Did I hear the truck drive away? I couldn't be sure. But I wasn't going to hang around. I collected my belongings from around the tent and walked back towards my car. I was near the sand patch where this all started when I saw lights approaching. It could have been the big truck. I flattened myself on the red earth as the truck thundered by, showering me with dirt. I can't think why I felt I had to hide. Was I afraid the Boss had run out on me and I didn't want to know? Was I afraid of being persuaded to go back to his tent? Or, of not being asked back? Anyway, I went to bed in my car and slept.

Next morning I walked back to the drilling camp to ask my companion of the night before to show me the rig and the readings he obtained with it. He'd promised to do that the previous evening. But the truck was nowhere to be seen. Had it been hidden to disguise the fact that he was still around? I decided not to pursue this to a possibly brutal conclusion. I might spoil everything. Instead, I walked back to my car, turned the key, and headed north for Shark Bay. I was literally hugging myself for bringing off such an unlikely adventure, at my age and with no regrets. I'm acting like a man I thought, a man who takes what he wants then leaves. But I was also the same woman who, perhaps because of my experience with my cousin, could never make the first move.

At about this time I was becoming known to a wider audience; or rather my distinctive deep voice was. I began appearing on Catherine King's ABC 'Women's Session'. Between 1944 and 1966, Catherine King's program of interviews, readings, news and discussion had a big following among women across this vast state of Western Australia. I first read over the airwaves a piece I had written called 'The Moth', on the difficulties of granting freedom to a large moth. During one of my early visits to Yanchep, when I was staying in an old tram which had been converted into holiday accommodation, a large moth resisted all my attempts to get it to fly out of the tram windows. I did not fancy having it flying into my face during the night so I slept outside, leaving the tram window open. Next morning the moth had gone. A talk based on my trip into the Grand Canyon was also well received, although I felt it inappropriate to include my response to the amorous cook.

To hear the program during one of my trips, I went in to the post office at Denham, the centre of the enchanting collection of placid bays, sandy beaches, and rich bird and fish life which is Shark Bay, and asked if I could listen to their wireless. The switchboard operator said, 'That's her,' as my voice drifted through the building. Others also made this association. People came up to me in the street, at the beach, or in shops: anywhere I opened my mouth. 'We heard you on "The Women's Session",' they'd say. Occasionally, they still do.

I soon realised I would be staying at the Occupational Therapy School longer than my contracted six months. I wasn't ready to leave my students, my bush and my beaches. Six months at the Kenso became twelve months, and my mileage in the bush increased massively. My travels extended through the Murchison goldfields: Mount Magnet, Big Bell and Cue. Three trips through the Kimberleys to Darwin followed.

I'd been at the Kenso for fifteen months when I was invited to share, 'on probation', a house in Broome Street in Cottesloe, with a young social worker named Lillian. After some weeks I was deemed acceptable, and became a permanent resident. Most evenings Lillian and I walked down a back lane to the ocean for a swim in the modest waves which built up on a reef close to shore. Along the way we would pass a tiny cottage at the end of a long back garden. I often told Lillian how I'd like to own that cottage.

An old jarrah weatherboard house in the next street, Deane Street, also caught my eye. It had a rusting corrugated iron roof and, more importantly, views down the street of the Indian Ocean. I knew that house was just what I wanted. One

Twenty-seven Deane Street.

173

day in 1963 I knocked at the front door. A little old lady answered and we introduced ourselves. She was Mrs Emily Jackson. In conversation with each other we would remain Mrs Jackson and Mrs Dorward. I asked Mrs Jackson whether her house might be for sale.

The timing was perfect. Her unmarried sister had just died and the house had to be sold to meet the terms of the will. Mrs Jackson said she would be putting it in the hands of a real estate agent the following week. She told me she hoped whoever bought the house would allow her to stay on. She had lived there for forty years, and wanted to end her time there.

Mrs Jackson showed me how the house could be divided into two flats, with the back verandah becoming a second kitchen. That space was filled with packing cases which still contained the furniture she, as a recent widow, and her unmarried sister had brought there forty years earlier. Mrs Jackson suggested she could take the smaller of the flats. This seemed a satisfactory arrangement for both of us and I bought the house. It was purchased with the legacy from my Bavarian grandfather. I had sold the two workers' cottages in London after the war, but had always kept the money separate as a memorial to him. I felt that my grandfather would have liked to have me living among the pine trees which grew in the garden. I felt good about that.

I hadn't inspected the flowing back garden before putting down the deposit on number twenty-seven Deane Street in April 1963. Mrs Jackson hadn't seemed keen for me to do so. When I finally did, I was surprised to find I had bought not just the house but the cottage I'd previously admired from the back lane as well. I went inside to discover that I had also purchased a second tenant, Miss Anne Louise Hamersley, the eccentric member of a celebrated Western Australian family. Her aunt Margaret had married John (later Lord) Forrest in a match where Margaret was thought to have 'married down'.

Miss Hamersley was sitting at a large pine table when I entered. 'I am not a teetotaller,' she said, at once and unprompted, apparently anticipating a question frequently asked of tenants by landlords.

'What's your tipple?' I asked.

'Sherry,' she replied.

I told Miss Hamersley I looked forward to joining her in a celebration shortly. I also decided the cottage should be called Hamersley Lodge. I quickly came to admire Miss Hamersley for her many eccentricities, even though some of the family seemed to shun her for the same quirks. Her clothes were scarcely the latest fashion or even particularly clean. Her blouses didn't fit all that well and one day I noticed she was displaying her belly button. I told her that I was having some friends to lunch in the garden. She was invited — if she put a dress on. She said she had put on weight and her clothes didn't fit. I recommended that she should at least put on a petticoat.

Despite, or perhaps because of, her eccentricities, Miss Hamersley retained some powerful supporters. One day a man, well-dressed and affable, called at the house and asked for her. I thought she must be sick and that this was her doctor calling. However, on her way out Miss Hamersley introduced me to her caller. He was Ross (later Sir Ross) Hutchinson, the state minister for health and Liberal member for Cottesloe, and he was taking her to the opening of State Parliament, to be followed by afternoon tea. Miss Hamersley, for her part, collected membership subscriptions for the Liberal Party. Often they were rather reluctant recruits: Miss Hamersley was not the sort of person to readily acknowledge a knock-back. She had been president of the Cottesloe Primary School Parents and Friends and collected continually for them too; and for a range of other community causes.

Miss Hamersley had help — an elderly woman who came in each week to do her washing. This meant boiling her clothes and bedding in a bricked-in wood-fired copper, backing onto the outdoor dunny situated halfway down the back yard. Miss Hamersley, my cottage tenant at five shillings a week, and Mrs

Jackson, my house tenant at ten shillings a week, shared this facility. I used to see them having their morning chat halfway down the garden. Each had their individual rolls of toilet paper hanging from two wire hooks on the back of the dunny door. I had never seen anything like this in England. When I arranged for a hot water system to be installed in my flat, as well as an inside toilet and a space for a washing machine, Mrs Jackson kept her chip heater.

Number twenty-seven was on a large block of land. There were three or four places where I had set up beds so I could sleep outside whenever the impulse took me. The gipsy in me disliked the idea of sleeping in the same place each night. I installed a shower in the garden, hidden by bushes, for showering after visits to the beach. It was chilling to discover that while I had been engaging in this outdoor living, Eric Edgar Cooke had been roaming the Perth suburbs, particularly Cottesloe. During the hunt for this random killer, Perth residents locked themselves indoors and afterwards never returned to their old summer ways. I can't remember changing mine.

My builder gradually divided the house into two flats. I moved a heavy wardrobe across the corridor as a temporary divider while he finished the work. When I returned home one evening the wardrobe had moved so far into my living area that it blocked the entrance to my sitting room. I tried to push it back, but my octogenarian house tenant on the other side was striving quietly to maintain her increased living space. I gave up pushing and we began negotiating through the wardrobe. Mrs Jackson pleaded she would not have enough room until her relatives carted their furniture away. She won the day but agreed to allow me enough room so I could edge into my sitting room.

One Sunday morning Mrs Jackson and I were sitting on the garden steps. I asked if she was pleased with the pathway I'd constructed, which led to the new front door of her flat. I expected a thank you. Instead, she turned on me: 'Look at this path! The surface is so rough I could just as likely break my leg here. I won't use it.' I was very angry, and was about to launch my counter attack, something like, 'You have no right to speak to *me* like that ...' Then I realised she had every right to complain, and told her I was glad to be in Australia where everyone was equal. I knew also that in

A theatrical moment with author Tom Hungerford.

Australia I still had to 'learn my place'.

English friends calling at Deane Street often remarked that number twenty-seven was like my house in Liverpool. It was not at all like our eighteenth century Georgian house. But I knew what they meant. I had brought over some of the items of furniture from Percy Street. The arrangement of the fireplace was also similar, although this was almost by chance. One of my first Perth friends, the writer Tom Hungerford, gave me an over-mantle similar to that around our old fireplace.

The big difference from Percy Street was in my choice of symbols. Hanging beside the fireplace was a small oil titled *String Bags,* by the Sydney artist and set painter Desmond Digby. As with many of his paintings, *String Bags* depicts the sort of woman I was determined never to become: frozen faced, conventionally well dressed and gripping three string bags bulging with household items. I'd hung the painting where I would see it constantly. I'd seen a number of friends of about my age become tied to secure humdrum lives centred on their homes.

Many of my new friends were artists I'd met at the Western Australian Art Gallery, including Guy and Helen Grey Smith. I also met Kate O'Connor at the Skinner Gallery. I noticed this elderly, stylish woman who reminded me of the painters from

String Bags, *a painting by*
Desmond Digby.

Paris who used to visit my aunts in the twenties. The resemblance was not surprising. Kate O'Connor had spent forty-five years painting in Paris before she returned to Perth. I wanted to meet her. I asked a woman standing near me if she would introduce me to Muriel Dawkins, who I knew was Kate O'Connor's niece. I met Muriel and she and I became very close friends. I soon met her husband, Alec Dawkins, who was a pioneering orthopaedic surgeon. I saw him frequently after that in the wards at Royal Perth, but I kept out of his way. To be acknowledged by a doctor — particularly an eminent one — was hazardous for a mere occupational therapist.

My old friends Gordon and Flora Stephenson would occasionally take me to the Swan Valley, twenty-five kilometres from Perth and then the state's major wine-making centre. From the fifties Gordon and Flora had dined and lunched at the Houghton Winery with legendary winemaker Jack Mann and his wife Angela. Or the Manns would come to the Stephenson residence. I'd eat and drink with them, and listen to Jack lament he was no longer thirty. He would have liked to start again, growing champagne grapes and making 'the world's best champagne' in the cooler climate of Mount Barker, three hundred and fifty kilometres south-east of Perth. I'd leave when Jack and Gordon talked about cricket and threatened to go to a game.

I met up with another and younger group of friends in Perth, following an unusual meeting over a table of food at the art gallery. According to Leoné Ferrier the meeting went like this:

A tall elegant woman wearing sandals came up to us and said, in a very deep voice: 'You all look very interesting. Who are you?'

I said that I was Leoné Ferrier. 'Ooh, Leoné Ferrier … the painting with the black sky. I remember your painting. What a painting …' I'd just won the Under 25 Perth Prize with that painting and I was pleased with the praise. The woman invited us to a barbecue at noon on the following Sunday at twenty-seven Deane Street. She added: 'But I must warn you that I have a rest at three o'clock so you'll have to be gone by then.'

We all met and went to Cécile's place. Sure enough, she was expecting us. There was lots of food — but nothing was prepared. Absolutely nothing at all. So the guys went down and started the barbecue. I stayed and got the food ready. I realised later that she didn't know what to do with unprepared food …

I suppose this sounds a bit like me — but I could cook food in a steamer. I'd done that for many years on the *Phosphorus*.

Number twenty-seven became the centre of a diffuse family, largely of young artists. Miss Hamersley fitted easily into this unconventional group. So did Alan's brother Stewart, who had followed me to Perth and lived only a few doors away. I'd always felt sorry for Stewart. He was handsome and thought of himself as a ladies' man but he always seemed to put both his feet in a very

Open house — Cécile, left, and a group of young artists at twenty-seven Deane Street.

large mouth and destroyed many a romantic endeavour in the process.

Things never quite worked out for Stewart. The 1914–18 War interrupted his engineering studies at the University of Edinburgh. His skill took him to the front line in France, dealing with lines of communication. On his return from the war, he was forced to start his studies all over again, rather than picking up where he'd left off. He set up his own mill to make tweed but the Depression caused it to fail and Stewart suffered a severe psychological breakdown.

Alan, who had a good knowledge of the psychological techniques of the time, managed to get him over it but, in Perth as in Britain, Stewart continued to have trouble organising his life. He looked to me for help. When living nearby, and later in Mrs Jackson's flat next door, Stewart drove me mad. He'd turn up at my door as soon as I arrived home from work, just like a friendly puppy, and frequently asked me to marry him. I firmly refused these offers.

If Stewart had problems with self-management Miss Hamersley had no trouble managing him. She had him drive her to the Mosman Park Hotel whenever her sherry supply needed refurbishment. She could control me too. I would drive her to Fremantle, where she had committee meetings, some with the mayor of Fremantle, Sir Frederick Samson. She never told me what the committees were about but, since Sir Fred insisted on a cup of tea as the preferred drink for his meetings, he may have set up some tension with a sherry tippler.

When I bought the house at twenty-seven Deane Street, the cottage, and their respective tenants, I also bought fourteen cats. Now I am a cat lover, but not a fourteen-cat lover. One of the cats, Black Lady, was mine. Miss Hamersley owned a grey half Persian, and tried to feed the others, which gathered outside the lodge at feeding time. It was hopeless, particularly as, from time to time, they had kittens. Miss Hamersley and I decided we had to do something so I rang the RSPCA for help.

It took three painful months to reduce the number to two, Black Lady and Miss Hamersley's grey.

Miss Hamersley started to become ill at about this time and, on a number of occasions, needed treatment at Fremantle Hospital. I always went to see her, and was often tempted to slip her a small bottle of sherry, but I didn't dare do it. My fear of draconian nursing sisters remained. When she died Miss Hamersley's sisters came to remove, and most probably discard, her belongings. They invited me to go with them to the funeral at which members of the Red Cross Service Unit, in uniform, led the cortege. I renamed her cottage Heavenly Lodge but that didn't have the appeal of the original so it soon became Hamersley Lodge again. I converted Hamersley Lodge into a bedroom-studio for me. I brought down a huge spinning wheel which I'd collected at a mission station in the Kimberleys and a substantial loom. My friends laughed as I hung my favourite paintings and got out some silver for what I called my studio and they called 'the garage'.

I still saw a lot of Lillian. We continued to go swimming together, and toured the river in my small aluminium runabout which partly replaced the *Phosphorus* in my affection for aquatic craft. The runabout took us to scenic spots around the Swan where we ate breakfast, or up the more distant Canning for lunch. I began to regard Lillian as I imagine one would a daughter. At the same time I could see a veil of uncertainty being drawn across her face whenever we were together. I knew she was troubled, but about what I had no

Cécile and Lillian seated, with Leoné punting, on the Canning River.

idea. All became apparent one evening at the Deane Street beach. We were the only swimmers left, and had just finished drying ourselves. Lillian turned towards me, then rose on her toes and kissed me on the lips with some intensity, pushing her tongue into my mouth. I was outraged. I forgot my training and slapped her face. 'How dare you!' I said. She began to weep. We became close again in an instant. She told me how she had become increasingly uncertain about her sexuality and asked me for help.

I was not in a strong position to help anyone. I knew almost nothing about sexual relationships between women, though I'm sure my intense relationships with older women in London then Liverpool must have attracted occasional, if unfounded innuendo. But I listened when Lillian told me that unwittingly she had developed strong feelings towards other women, and they seemed to be ready to reciprocate. She had wanted to talk about these feelings, but found that she couldn't. Finally, she sought help from W A (Bill) McRae, a local sporting icon, educated at Harvard, and a Jungian analyst. He had recently spent time with C G Jung at the institute in Zurich, and he listed Sybil Thorndike among his clients. Lillian said she liked him but couldn't talk to him. He was a man. She asked me to come along to her sessions and provide some support. I was willing, providing Bill McRae agreed to it, which he did.

We sat in large green chairs in the consulting room, which looked out onto an orange orchard in the Perth foothills. The couch remained unoccupied. I sat in silence. Soon Lillian was talking, guardedly, about her hostility towards her mother and all the problems that posed; and how she felt she was enclosed by brick walls which prevented her from talking to anyone about her feelings. The metaphor was extended: she felt like a squirrel in a cage. But she held back on her most personal feelings. She was still unable to communicate easily with men. Meanwhile I started to feel I was Lillian's mother. I went to see Dr McRae at his city rooms in the Oddfellows building and told him of my apparent change of identity. He said this was necessary for

Lillian's recovery. She should be able to unload her worst feelings for her mother on to me. I suspect we both felt we were playing a game — but it seemed to be working. Lillian became more confident with each session.

I had my own therapeutic games, one of which I called Tigers. Lillian and I played it during lunch breaks or in the evening. We padded like tigers through the bush at King's Park. We confronted, then growled, then sprang at each other. We scratched at each other. We sent each other tiger post cards and tiger soft toys. The aim was to make Lillian into a real tiger; not someone to be pushed aside by her mother or any of her associates. It sounds like rather strange behaviour but it seemed to help.

Cécile and her Dormobile, her home away from home.

Life Six
Just Dordling Along

A European Winter

The occupational therapy students at Royal Perth Hospital launched me into another new life when I was fifty-eight. Typically they followed a set sequence on graduating: work for a year then travel to Europe. They would return and tell wonderful stories of their adventures, usually on low budgets, and their visits to the art galleries of the world where they used my techniques for viewing pictures. Good heavens, I thought, these girls have travelled around Italy and Greece and I've never even been to Rome — despite the fact of my Italian heritage and that for fifty years I'd lived so close. All those years on the *Phosphorus*, exploring the English inland waterways, had blocked any other destinations from my mind.

By the time I became eligible for long service leave in 1969 my students had shown me clearly what I should do. I retired and made plans to devote myself to a life on the road, calling on friends and art galleries along the way, and looking for clues which might be mailed back to the developing artistic talents at number twenty-seven. It was a life which lasted until I was eighty-four.

I investigated the best way to combine driving and camping,

and ended up purchasing a Bedford Dormobile, a campervan with an extending roof and a name which seemed just right for me. It would await my arrival in London. I read about touring in Europe and began planning, between dinners at the Oyster Beds, breakfasts on the Swan River, and working on the construction of a weekend shelter among the trees on a block in the Perth foothills, which I owned with Lillian and some other friends.

Some months after my retirement I set off by way of Canada to see my brother, then to New York where I boarded a night plane to London. As I approached Heathrow, I thanked God I hadn't told any of my friends or relations that I was coming. I was to be met by the man with the campervan. The representative of the Bedford Vauxhall company was there and he began by asking: 'Are you alone?' The tone of the question seemed to imply that it was a crime for a woman nudging sixty to be travelling alone. 'Well, yes I am, and I'd be glad if you drove for a while,' I replied. This seemed to satisfy him. We collected my luggage, and headed for the car park where a sparkling new white Bedford Dormobile awaited me.

So, this was it! My mobile home with a bed, a couch, a folding table, a gas cooker, a fridge, a toilet bucket, but not too much more. The van would keep going — Vauxhall and Bedford had a reputation for reliability —and I knew I could drive it, but I wasn't so sure I could live in it. It was much smaller than I had imagined when I ordered it in Perth. I was even less confident I would survive living alone on the road. I had not slept well the previous couple of days in New York, anticipating possible disaster. Would I end up frozen to death after a breakdown on a mountain road? Or crash? Or be attacked at a lonely camping spot?

The Dormobile man took me over Westminster Bridge and we soon found a side street. He showed me how everything worked, then asked if I could turn the camper around. He left after I'd assured him that I could. My next task was one which came to dominate my life for the next twenty-six years — to establish myself in an economical camp site with good facilities. In London this was a more difficult proposition than just making two left turns into the bush and unpacking my gear under a clump of trees. I parked in a camping space called the Crystal Palace Harbour in the early afternoon, and went to some nearby shops to purchase coffee, butter and milk, a pot and pan, and some pot scrubbers. But I had been away for seven years, and had forgotten the English institution of early closing on Wednesday afternoons. Not a single shop or cafe near the camp site was open. I sat in the van, tired, hungry and dejected. I'd never be able to live in so small a space. I'd made a silly mistake. I'd better sell the van now and go back to Australia.

But then I spoke to some campers in the next bay. As soon as they replied I recognised they were Aussies. I could have cried. I was feeling so homesick for Cottesloe, and Australia generally. They came from Adelaide and were travelling with their daughter. They invited me to eat with them. I produced some duty-free whisky and the celebrations began. These continued at a local pub where I had my first half-pint of (warm) English bitter. The couple told me they too had been initially upset when their van seemed cramped, and everything was stiff and difficult to manipulate. But things quickly became easier for them to work, and travelling solo meant that I would have a lot more room than they had. I slept moderately well that night. Whenever I woke and began to worry about starting my adventure, a sip of brandy from a flask placed by my bed kept up my courage.

Next morning, I was feeling much happier. I caught a bus to Trafalgar Square and went to the National Gallery where all my old favourites were hanging in their usual places. I lingered in front of Lippo Lippi's *Worship of the Golden Calf*, the calf leaping across beautiful blue sky over a multitude of worshippers. A lunch of cold roast beef (Scottish) and salad, and a glass of *vin rosé* at the gallery restaurant completed my revival. I collected a car sticker announcing PERTH WA at

Australia House, and went home to attach it to my van.

I had contacted an old friend who was staying at the University of North Wales at Bangor, and arranged to visit her en route to my old home in Liverpool. Next day I was travelling in a fog along a winding road. I found a telephone box and rang my friend to say I would have dinner before arriving at Bangor. Then I poured myself a small gin and bitter lemon before switching my attention to my pillar-box red socks. They had been worrying me all day: quite wrong with brown shoes and pale green trousers. I changed them and immediately felt better. I felt better still after eating a pork pie and some celery, and something called faggots, which I had bought at Stratford-on-Avon earlier in the day.

I was beginning to like eating 'at home' which meant in car parks with views. I drew back the curtain and looked out of the window. There was a babbling brook; Brahms was on the radio, and life in my travelling home was pretty good. I would have liked to spend the night there but I had to go on to Bangor.

My friend invited me to sleep in her spare bedroom but I declined. I wanted to continue practising sleeping in the van. That night I slept in my sleeping bag on a roomy double bed made by flattening all four seats.

Three days passed pleasantly, and then I headed for Liverpool. As I drew closer I became anxious about how I would react to twenty-eight Percy Street after an eight-year absence. The anxiety peaked as I came through the King George V Tunnel and parked my van outside our old home. This time I took the self-interested me into the house to deal with the ghosts waiting for me. That was difficult but not as bad as I'd expected.

I set about cleaning up the attic, where Alan's library and remnants of our twenty-five years together and his forty-five years in academe were gathering dust. A dealer from Oxford picked through the first editions and other old books and bought those he wanted — which was most of them. It was like disposing of part of Alan's life. Then the furniture: I decided to ship Alan's large desk to Deane Street and, strangely, the oak corner cabinet in which he'd kept his whisky.

The letters generated some sad moments, but also many happy ones as I read through and sorted them over the next few weeks. I collected together letters which I thought would interest Trinity College, Cambridge: Alan's letters as a student to Humphrey, my host in Fiji; Bertrand Russell's references when Alan was seeking academic jobs; exchanges with friends such as Moore, Haldane and Chadwick. I bundled them up and stacked then in the back of the old Morris roadster, ready to be posted. I went back inside for just three minutes to check that I had everything. On my return the large box containing the letters had been stolen. I never saw them again. I imagine the thief decided they were of no value and ditched them. I was desolate: my carelessness had effectively obliterated a large part of Alan's life. It would be thirty years before I would admit to anyone what had happened. It was all too painful.

Meanwhile, I lived in my van outside number twenty-eight for five weeks, with only rare retreats inside to sleep. I lunched in the van with Conn, my friend who had started me on the road to occupational therapy and an independent life. Other friends such as Maisie who had frequently been entertained in our formal dining room came to eat and talk in the van. They seemed to understand why I did not want to socialise in the house, although the tenants at number twenty-eight and the neighbours probably thought it all rather strange. I needed a place where I could develop my new life without being overwhelmed by my past; where I just needed to turn the key to be free.

That happened one morning when I suddenly decided to drive south and east to Cambridge, prior to the start of my European tour. One diary entry says simply, 'Cemetery'. I spent two evenings in the cemetery at Cambridge, parked close to the austere granite slab which marked Alan's grave. My diary records, rather clinically: 'I am peacefully installed in the cemetery. All exaggerated horrors have now gone. I feel free of unnecessary emotion and ready to travel.'

Two weeks later I was heading across the channel to spend Christmas 1969 at Vence near Nice in southern France. I only just managed to catch the ferry after getting lost in the back streets of Southampton. I had never crossed the channel before in daylight so I had never seen the Isle of Wight or the Needles. The sun was out and I stood on deck to get a good view. I was wearing the old black duffel coat I'd found gathering dust in the Percy Street attic. With that, my chestnut wig which I wore when I wanted to present myself as young and outrageous, and my stretch trousers, I must have looked quite the thing. Sadly, however, I was the only passenger on deck so my outfit went unappreciated.

The swell built up so I went down to the bar for a brandy and soda to sip slowly as I lay flat on a long stool. Then another brandy ... I woke as we moored in Cherbourg harbour. In no time I was at the wheel of my van and driving in La Belle France which had seen some changes since the workers' strikes and the students' near-revolution drove Charles de Gaulle from the presidency the previous year. None of these changes impinged on me: I was interested in travelling through the countryside.

I wore a big grin as I drove away. I was so happy to be quite on my own and absolutely independent. I could go wherever I pleased — like a gipsy. I drove in freezing weather through Cherbourg, Valognes, then stopped at Coutance. It was starting to rain so I thought I'd stay overnight. *'Je veux rester dans la voiture,'* I told a garage attendant, without planning to use the word *voiture*. I was pleased about that as it was a more appropriate word for the Dormobile than *l'automobile*. I bought some petrol and spent the evening on the driveway, after using the shower. For the first time I put sheets on the bed and the sleeping bag on top, rather than just sleeping in the bag. It was much more comfortable — and much warmer.

Next morning I had egg and bacon for breakfast before stopping at the Mont-Saint-Michel, the legendary rock on the border of Brittany and Normandy. The stark conical outcrop played a central role in Anglo-French conflicts in the Middle Ages, and held recalcitrant monks captive during the French Revolution, before being declared a national monument by Napoleon III. I walked up the steep street, past shops of every kind, until I reached the church and monastic buildings above. I'll never forget the wonder of it all. Moving in the late afternoon I drove fifteen kilometres and stopped near a wharf, where I sheltered by an old cargo shed. I decided this was the place to spend the night — especially as I could still see the rock.

Normally, I need a drink around five-thirty in the evening to keep me going, but that evening I didn't want one. It might have disturbed the feelings the rock had inspired in me.

Next morning revealed a number of old fishermen on the dock, studying their boats which had been left high and dry when the tide went out. They cast slightly amused glances at the woman in her van banging away at her typewriter recording highlights of the previous day. I would have liked to stay another night. The sense of isolation appealed to me. However, having revealed that I was alone on the wharf, I thought it prudent to move on.

It was bitterly cold as I crossed the Alps heading for the warmer south. The roads were terrible. They made the driving I'd done in Australia on loose sand or gravel tracks seem like a picnic. Trucks skidded and came to rest at alarming angles; cars turned over in ditches, while I crawled along at a snail's pace. I was learning a lot about driving, also about how happy I could be living in a van, whatever the weather. But I thought it would be wise to get off the road. I went up a side road and was looking for a place to camp when I met a farmer who invited me to shelter overnight in his house. I said I wanted to stay in the van so he swung open the large barn door and I drove inside to share the space with sheep, chickens and a cow. Next day the large barn doors were swung open and I drove out to find that the weather had improved.

I had arranged to visit a London friend who had rung me

while I was still in England to report the strange delusional behaviour of her husband, and to ask me to come and help. Her husband was convinced that people were trying to poison him. When I arrived he'd had workers erect security wire at the top of the fence, and new gates, and beams to keep the poisoners out. I parked inside the new gates then had to listen to repeated stories about the wily poisoners and why they wanted to kill him. He believed his wife had joined his persecutors. We had a number of sad lunches with excellent food, but where the meal was intermittently checked for poison.

Each night I went back to my van to sleep, and to ponder on a comment once made to me by my friend Agnes Stapledon: that, on the road, I would become more of a psychotherapist than an occupational therapist. And so it happened. In this case it was clear that the poisoners had been conjured up by my friend to make it impossible for him to leave the house and face the outside world. If forced to delve far enough into himself, he would probably realise he never wanted to face a world which had delivered him such severe physical and emotional trauma in childhood, in marriage, and in the war. Without help he would remain with absolutely no insight into the origins of his psychological state.

I began leading him back to his earlier life. It was soon apparent, however, that the risk of precipitating complete personality disintegration was too great. I had no right to take that risk, particularly without some back-up support for him. I felt I couldn't stay around and do nothing, but it took me almost a week to bring myself to leave. The security of the place was appealing, even with madness rampant.

In Vence I visited the daughter of one of Alan's colleagues from the University of Liverpool, and went to see some paintings by Matisse which were held there. I stayed for two weeks. Some of that time I spent in bed in the back of the van with a severe outbreak of urticaria and a cold. My friend brought hot water-bottles, and delicious soup and home-made fruit flans. When I felt better I did some spring cleaning and resumed changing the configuration of the van from a bedroom to a sitting room with a table, and back to a bedroom again, at twelve-hourly intervals. For four days I didn't even start the Dormobile.

I was happy living like this over Christmas and the New Year. We had a French Christmas dinner on Christmas Eve, with one of the five courses being frogs' legs. I'd felt a special bond with frogs while on the *Phosphorus*: their croaking kept me company in the evenings while Alan slept. Perhaps it would be better if I imagined they were chicken not frogs. But I dismissed this as false sentiment and ate with gusto — and a good garlic sauce.

I felt too secure here, but knew I should be back on the road; that this sort of security could endanger the boldness required by an ageing woman traveller. I had to escape. The point about buying the van was not just to allow me to travel about, but also to be able to drive away whenever I felt trapped. The anxieties about solo travel were those of my friends, not my own, I told myself; so one day I just drove away, destination Marseilles.

An hour after my release I was driving in the snow-capped mountains when I was provided with the opportunity to do something I'd wanted to do for a long time — wash some clothing in a *lavoir*, the villagers' communal facility. A mountain stream was directed through a pipe into two large stone troughs, which had sloping stone slabs on which to scrub the clothes. I took a couple of towels and a pair of stockings, and delighted in soaping them on the slabs and sloshing them about in the running water. I started in the top trough but soon realised that the soapy water would run into the second and larger trough. Rinsing would take ages. So I washed in the second trough and rinsed in the first. I felt very clever, and wondered whether the women of the village had also thought of that.

I travelled slowly around the south coast of France. One stupendous view followed another. Blue bay followed promontory, then another bay and another promontory. An occasional blue fishing boat netted squid in the intensely blue water. The Côte d'Azur indeed. Gazing inland, the view featured the snow-capped Alpes Maritimes. It was very cold and the roads were often slippery, but whenever I stopped people approached, wanting to talk to me about my travels. Vans like mine were rare in the early seventies and one driven by a woman must have been unique. The locals inspected it, and my Frigidaire and dining table — or bed, depending on the hour.

Once at dusk I pulled into a car park near Cannes. I saw in outline a man gazing over the deep blue water. Behind him was a large conveyance: a driver and his truck, I thought. I moved closer. The man was a camper and his 'truck' a campervan, but at least twice the size of mine. Camping technology had eclipsed my Dormobile already. Momentarily, I thought about getting a bigger van; then I remembered the narrow village roads through which I just managed to squeeze my small van. Also, I loved my Dormobile. Already it had so many associations for me with memorable events and wonderful places.

The Côte d'Azur was noticeably populated compared with what I'd experienced in Australia outside the cities. I noted the use of terracing, and how well the houses merged with the countryside. Was there a hint here for how I might deal with the Kalamunda block? I spoke with many residents but almost no tourists. The season for pleasure boats and sunbaked bodies was still some months away. I was pleased about that. It meant I could just walk around and explore. If there had been crowds of people I might have needed a partner so that I could promenade. I travelled through Cannes and Toulon and, after a great deal of asking for directions, arrived at a friend's place in Marseilles. There was a large courtyard in which I could park my van. The weather was terrible: grey skies and rain, just like Liverpool.

For three days my van stayed in the courtyard while I spent my time painting my friend's rooms — a return to my Women Decorators days.

When I did get out on the road again it was obvious that something was wrong with the van. I had no idea about what went on under a car's bonnet. No idea at all. That was not a problem on this occasion, however. When I stopped just outside Arles, the van attracted a number of helpers. They decided it wasn't serious — just a small fracture in the carburettor. Someone did a temporary repair job so I could get back to town to arrange for a part to be sent from the Vauxhall factory in Britain. Then someone else volunteered to do another repair so that I could drive around while waiting for the part to arrive.

How I enjoyed myself during this enforced stay in such an area of early Roman influence! Arles was a centre which backed Caesar when he rebelled against Pompey in the civil war of 50BC. It allowed great scope for my fantasies based on the life of a woman in Roman times. It was also where Van Gogh painted *Sunflowers* — more encouragement for fantasy. Meanwhile I slept in my van, occasionally at an all-night garage when I felt the need for security. Here my sleep was interrupted by a dog which looked and sounded as if it belonged in *The Hound of the Baskervilles*. The owner was almost as noisy when he ordered the dog to be quiet.

I slept well, ate well and did a lot of walking while the van was being fixed. Then I headed for Aix-en-Provence, where my friend at Marseilles had organised for me to provide English conversation for students at the local university. I did that happily for two or three weeks. Then I left the last of the old friends I'd see on this journey and set out for Italy where perhaps I'd find new ones. The real excitement was about to begin.

While driving along the coast I began to think again of the warnings I'd had about the lack of secluded spots for free camping in Italy. I certainly couldn't see any. There was a set of railway tracks and a road between me and the beach which meant I could not turn off where I would have liked. So I left the main road and took a mountain road. Up and up and up. In no time I was in six or seven centimetres of snow. I passed a man and his donkey, then a man and his mule. I resisted the temptation to photograph them. I didn't want to intrude; also, it was very cold outside the van.

I was amazed to see that the sides of most of the mountain were terraced, right through the snowline. Near the top was a village, where I was strongly advised by the garage man to return to sea level. I could easily freeze to death, he said. I agreed it was too cold, but I was glad to have had the experience of driving in the mountains during a February snowfall.

The man at the garage told me of a quiet spot in which to camp just outside Genoa. I went straight past it the first time and couldn't turn back for several kilometres. I almost decided to miss Genoa and camp outside the next town, but I persisted and turned around. It was a happy decision.

Life with the Circus

The garage man's 'quiet spot' overlooking the ocean, on the edge of an enormous car park in Genoa, turned out to be less quiet than I'd been informed. I'd had dinner and was about to go to bed when a man arrived and told me I couldn't stay overnight but, if I took the van to the city square, I could sleep there. I followed his advice.

A couple of hours later I was woken by an extraordinary cacophony of noises, many of them animal. Circo Americano, from the United States of America and celebrating Columbus' birth in Genoa and his later voyages, had come to town, and the Big Top was being secured. I had to move aside a little as the Dormobile was about to be encased in canvas.

Soon I was camped between the dining station for the 'circus boys' and the waves of the Mediterranean, which I could hear breaking on the rocks just below. I had a front stalls view from which to watch the rest of the circus arrive and the tents go up. Nineteen elephants clumped up from the railway station and were installed in their red-striped tent: I was soon talking with one of their keepers. I also made friends with three stilt walkers, and Mr Roy who dived from a considerable height into a portable water tank which he carried on the back of his truck along with his diving tower. Meanwhile the tent pegs were hammered in, three men and three sledgehammers to a peg. Bang, bang, bang ... the timing was perfect. It needed to be. For me the operation was a circus act in itself.

Next a wire security fence was run around the tents, circus people and animals, and me. I had, without planning it, become part of the Circo Americano. My new stilt walker friends brought me photographs of their performances at their previous show in Rome. The sky diver and his wife invited me to their caravan, and I was amazed at the elegance of their parlour which rivalled an English drawing room. My Dormobile, which only twelve hours earlier had been sitting alone in the square, was now surrounded by sleeping-trucks, kitchen-trucks, animal-trucks, and just plain trucks. It attracted no particular attention. All of this was starting to seem like a dream. I kept quiet throughout the first day; I didn't want to draw attention to myself. I watched everything in between making trips on foot to a nearby supermarket. The stilt walkers and the sky diver and his wife all said they'd vouch for me if I were stopped at the gate. But that was never necessary.

On the morning before opening night brightly patterned costumes were hanging out to air on lines strung between the caravans. It was a beautiful day and my washing was out too. The horses were being polished up and brushed down by the boys, and a layer of sawdust was spread over the flattened earth on which they would prance. I was one of a crowd of 6000 at the opening; the theme was of the discovery of America by Christopher Columbus. During the interval I slipped around the back of the Big Top to visit my van. I wanted to use my toilet and pour myself a drink. One of the circus men stopped me but, on looking closer, smiled and walked away. I went shopping the next morning and the same man let me out and back in again. I had become part of the circus community. After all, I too lived in a van and was constantly on the move.

As I lay on my bed next morning, the van's rear door open, watching the sea breaking on the rocks, I thought about moving on. It would be so easy to embrace this interesting, protected lifestyle. I had a secured camp site with a great view; I was surrounded by new friends and could watch all sorts of interesting things happening at any time, day or night. I need never make plans as to how I might entertain myself: the circus turned on continual entertainment. (Although I did slip out to see Maria Callas in the title role of *Medea* at the Genoa Opera House.)

I knew I had to leave now — or I wouldn't be able to go at all. I went to the Big Top for a last look and was again riveted by the horse training in one ring and the young man juggling on a slack rope in another. The clown Barney and the sky diver Mr Roy came and sat on either side of me. I told them I would leave at midday; that if I stayed any longer I'd never be able to drag myself away. The clown seemed sad as a clown is supposed to be. So was Mr Roy.

As I prepared the van for departure, I realised I was having the same feelings I'd had when I left Vence after Christmas, even though the circumstances were so different. As I drove through the grounds feeling unhappy, the *artistes* waved goodbye. They had become my friends and I felt I belonged there with them. However, as I passed through the gates, sadness immediately turned to elation: I had cast off the crippling restraints that a desire for security imposed on me.

That evening I passed through La Spezia, a sizeable town and port on the way to Pisa. It was getting dark and I thought I'd better pull in at the next camp site. But before I could do so, I noticed a promontory cutting right into this beautiful bay. I drove down with the sea on both sides of me and parked near the ruins of an old castle. I decided to stop for dinner; then stayed the night. I had intended leaving early next morning but everything was so beautiful I was still there at lunch time. I sat with the doors open and luxuriated in the warm sunshine pouring over me. What hotel could match this? It was so warm that I could experiment with a new method of keeping clean by draping warm damp towels over my body. It seemed to work well, and I filed this information away for times when there were no showers available.

Pisa was to be the start of a long and interesting stretch of Italian stopovers that included Rome, Naples, Vesuvio, Reggio Calabria. I parked outside the St Matthew National Museum, rich in medieval treasures. The medieval period always affects me, and an hour in this museum left me really churned up. I walked over to my van and flattened the seats to form a chaise longue. I reclined in the warm sunlight, had lunch and some dry white chianti, and watched the world of tourists, locals, children, dogs and students pass by. I wondered yet again, in my European way, how my students in Perth could perform so creatively in an environment that had none of this richness.

I conjured up a plan to park overnight as close as possible to the National Museum, so that I could sleep in its aura. I noticed a small parking area for the museum principals and decided to come back when all was quiet, park, and see what happened. Just the thought that I would be able to do this filled me with the belief that the world was a beautiful place, and that I could do pretty much as I liked in it.

To test this hypothesis I went to Marina Pisa and bought some prawns and whitebait. Would they set off an outburst of urticaria? Suppose I woke up with my eyes closed by the allergic reaction and no one to guide me? Never mind: risk it. I fried the seafood in olive oil — and it was delicious. There were no subsequent skin eruptions. I began to wonder whether my wretched urticaria might have been the result of my internal tensions, not diet.

My belief that I could do as I liked proved to be misplaced. A guard evicted me and my van from the car park at two in the morning. Later in the morning I returned for a last look at the museum. My viewing was distracted by an attendant who followed me everywhere. He attempted to corner me and reach under my dress. I told him forcibly I was not interested, in English and with an occasional Italian word and lots of gestures. That seemed to cool his enthusiasm. This amorous attitude by Italian men towards me, when I was just a few days short of fifty-nine, was extraordinary. It was not even as if I were wearing my chestnut wig which made me look ten to fifteen years younger and made some men in cars honk in some excitement. Men are easily fooled I mused as I drove towards Rome, now only two hours away.

My emotional response to Italy had already been particularly powerful, even though I couldn't speak more than a few words of the language. I knew my reaction to Rome would be something else again. Stories of my students' visits there had been the original stimulus for these travels. In preparation for my entry, I pinned on my Menelaus cameo, carved by my grandfather Luigi Isler of Rome. I was ready to be astounded.

I found a camp site with lots of trees outside Rome and drove into the centre of the city most days. My van was parked outside the Colosseum as I prepared and ate a dinner of veal and pasta to celebrate my fifty-ninth birthday. While washing up afterwards, I looked out through my window at the tiers of illuminated arches. It was not difficult to imagine the Colosseum packed with people. I heard the roar of the populace as the lions enjoyed the Christians. I parked outside the Borghese Gallery, which Cardinal Scipione Borghese built in the early seventeenth century to display his collection of sculptures, so that I could rest between emotionally exhausting visits there. I also parked the van outside the main concert hall, La Academia di Cecilia, where I experienced the highest point of my musical life: the towering organ recital of Bach. And, of course, the institute's name enhanced this very special effect on me.

Near the institute a language school advertised an intensive course in Italian: three hours a day for a fortnight. I decided it was appalling that with my background I could use only a few words of Italian. So I enrolled for what would prove to be a frustrating assignment.

My van was again in the thick of things when I went to the premiere of *Carmen* at which evening dress was compulsory. I'd intended leaving the van in the camp site and travelling into the city by bus. I discovered, however, that the last bus left the station at midnight while *Carmen* finished fifteen minutes later. I couldn't afford a twenty-minute taxi ride so I came into Rome early. I found a parking spot within five minutes of the theatre and close to my language school. I did some business around Rome and spent three hours at the school. I was getting a slightly firmer grip on the language but was never going to master it. I often felt slow and stupid. But at least I was making the effort.

About six o'clock it began to rain. That made my five-minute walk in evening dress a problem. So I strolled over to ask the commissionaire at the Teatro dell'Opera if I could park in the theatre courtyard. It seemed most unlikely that he'd agree as that was a space reserved for the opera's principals. Certainly, said the commissionaire, who even pointed to a space. The next problem was how to get to it through the impenetrable maze of one-way streets. On my walk back I carefully noted the *UNO SENSO* signs so that, in the chaos of six o'clock traffic, I could drive straight to the theatre in a few minutes. The commissionaire, in top hat and gold braid, recognised me immediately. I smiled as he waved me into the position he had reserved only a few metres from the theatre entrance.

I celebrated in the van with a gin and orange followed by a meal of pasta. Outside, I could hear the performers arriving as I prepared myself for an elegant entry. By some miracle I did my hair very well, given the limited space of the van. I put on my long dress, then a small tiara. I was ready to step through the rear doors of the van to face the crowd of Roman matrons and their escorts. I looked in one of the long mirrors as I entered the foyer of the theatre and was pleased with what I saw. In my diary I wrote: 'I must say I felt perfectly equal and in some cases more so. The men were a fairly ordinary lot, only a few with long hair and one or two with plum coloured jackets.' During the intervals I slipped out to the van where the drinks were cheaper.

The next day was Friday 13 March, and I wanted to see the Sistine Chapel. I couldn't decide whether to go into Rome by bus or risk driving again. I'd had such a charmed run with the gods at the opera that perhaps I shouldn't tempt them. Then I thought, how ridiculous to allow myself to be frightened when I'd already done so much driving in terrible traffic. So I drove to the Vatican. I had never travelled into the city centre so quickly. But by the time I'd walked to the chapel entrance there were thousands crowded inside, with guides hectoring their national groups in Italian, English, French, German and Japanese. I hate crowds. Consequently I didn't look up. With all that chatter I knew I wouldn't be able to take in the glory of the ceiling, which represented four years of work by Michaelangelo. I just sat on a bench at the side of the chapel, eyes on the floor, and pondered how I could see the paintings without all those noisy people spoiling my experience. I retreated to my van parked outside St Peter's for a rest, lunch and some restorative beverages.

The van offered the solution to this, as to so many problems. I would sleep outside the Sistine Chapel and be first in the queue the following morning. Around midnight, I parked outside the entry gate and went to bed. I rose early, had my breakfast of coffee and egg and bacon, then headed for the gates at eight o'clock. I wasn't first but third in the queue. None of us in the queue spoke but we all had the same aim. When the gates opened at ten we raced past the attendants and straight to the chapel.

The other two hundred people behind us in the queue didn't come straight to the chapel, but were waylaid at other exhibits and I had forty minutes of uninterrupted exhilaration. This was the highlight of a lifetime spent viewing art. I could die now, I thought, after such an experience. And all this was being done on so little money. It was proving cheaper for me to live in the van outside the great museums of Rome than at twenty-seven Deane Street, Cottesloe. I didn't have to entertain anyone but myself, and more often than not I was invited to eat in other people's vans. It was, however, important to find free camp sites wherever they were available. They could save a lot of money.

When I left Rome for Naples and Pompeii, I was tired and emotionally exhausted. I stopped overnight at a garage, where my legs were closely studied by the proprietor. Next morning I saw Naples, but didn't like the traffic. I wanted to go on to Pompeii as quickly as possible but the traffic was chaotic and the traffic signs apparently non-existent. There were interminable jams and, during one of these, a woman in an adjacent car passed across two lemons and an orange. I could see they'd be handy later with my gin and tonics. I thanked her.

I had a little scrape with another car in one of these jams. I got out, locked my door and prepared for battle. I won, to the approbation of my audience of drivers who had left their cars and of passers-by. All were gesticulating wildly. I'd like to say I won because of my newly acquired skills with the language but my lessons in Rome had not been a great success. I won because I out-gesticulated the Italians!

One of my roadside supporters, a man with a motorcycle, stayed to ask me where I was going. I told him — then he noticed my cameo. He said he worked at a cameo factory which was on the way to Pompeii; he'd direct me through the traffic. When I arrived at the factory the workers were enthusiastic about Luigi Isler's Menelaus. Onyx ... the only one of its kind ... nothing like that now ... worth more than five hundred pounds. The workers' comments were flattering, but I knew all that. I bought some earrings, then headed for Pompeii.

When I arrived I was told by a man I could take a bus to view the crater. Leave the car, he said, no cost for parking. I took no notice and drove on. The atmosphere made me feel more and more uncomfortable. I felt I was surrounded by sharks just waiting to strike. So I went on to Vesuvio where my map told me

I'd find a camping area. What the map didn't say was that the site was closed in winter.

I drove through what seemed like an endless slum before coming to a narrow cobbled road, defined on either side by stone walls. The road went on and on, up and up. At last I came to a restaurant. I asked where the camping area was. I was told I'd passed it; that it was not open anyhow. Just drive up to the crater and stop there, someone said. No thanks, I didn't want to be there alone. I decided to eat at the restaurant and sleep in the parking area, even though the chef offered me a bed in his chalet further down the hill. I politely refused. What no one told me was that the restaurant staff and the man on the gate leading to the crater road all went home at 10 pm. That left just me, alone on a narrow road, feeling threatened.

I'd never been really nervous before and I wasn't then. I went to sleep despite being disturbed by thunder and lightning, which I don't like. Then a car arrived and began flashing its headlights on and off at my van. Men gathered around. They beat on the windows, and called out 'Lady! Lady!' I lay motionless in my bed. Even my breathing seemed to have almost stopped. I felt like an oyster whose protective shell was about to be split open, revealing a shivering defenceless body. The intruders gave up after fifteen minutes and I thought they'd gone. Then headlights began flashing again. More cars arrived and there were more voices talking close to my van. There was a renewed assault on my shell, this time with a screwdriver. This went on for about an hour. My breathing was becoming less and less perceptible. Just when I was sure the van would spring open at the seams another vehicle arrived. There were now more voices near my van, American and Australian voices. I peeped out and saw a van like mine. I knew I was safe now but it took me an hour or two to calm down. Then my fear was replaced by anger. I was particularly annoyed at myself: I had broken one of my rules by parking in a position from which there was no easy escape route.

The next day at a small seaside town near Naples I began

talking at a garage to a cultivated man with a car carrying Roma plates. I told him of my chilling experience the previous night. He just laughed. I asked him if it was safe for me to go to Sicily alone. Certainly, he said. But he would say that. Things were easier for older men, there must be thousands of them driving alone. See a lone woman on a long trip, and that is quite something. I thought that perhaps next time I'd disguise myself as a man.

Finally, I compromised with my travel plans to go right to the Italian toe. I continued south to Reggio Calabria. The Italian coast was stunning. I'd thought the Côte D'Azur was beautiful but by comparison it was sophisticated tourist country. In Italy I saw farms worked by bullocks, and donkeys with panniers along the road. Eventually, through my binoculars, I could see the flow of lava at the crater edge of Mount Etna and the lights of Messina across the water. Out of my back window a full silver moon was rising. I resisted the temptation to take the ferry across to Sicily. One of my mottos has always been to leave unexplored a little of what life has to offer.

I returned to Rome, where I picked up a young well-dressed woman who was hitching on the autoroute. She took me all around Rome looking for I knew not what. Finally I noticed her sisterly interest in the street girls standing around small fires on the pavements. I was being taken on a tour of the beats, while she decided on a spot which might be most lucrative. I dropped her off after an hour of this with the equivalent of five shillings to have coffee while she waited for a client.

After a day in Rome I headed off through Assisi, through the walled town of Perugia, and then to Florence where I felt as though I too were floating on the clouds of glory depicted in so many paintings. I took frequent trips into the Uffizi, the former administrative offices of the Medici. All those Botticellis ... all those sculptures. I had to go though the freezing cold back to the van to recover my strength, before returning again and again.

Then I went to Venice, briefly, as an insurance policy in case I never got back there; then Verona, Como and into Switzerland. The roads around the Pass were slippery and tricky but I reached Zurich safely. I kept moving, through Holland, where I spent time with my cousin Marie and watched large vessels traversing the major canals, and then to Germany.

I was losing my enthusiasm for writing detailed commentaries in my diary. However, I did record a new security tactic I tried there. Whenever I arrived at a lonely camp site or stopped beside the road, I swiftly drew the blinds and played loud pop music, rather than Brahms. I wanted possible marauders to think young people were in the van. I'm not sure whether I fooled anyone, but the strategy kept me happy.

A Real Tiger

Eventually, in May, I was viewing the cliffs of Dover again. What a welcome I received from the old English sunshine — through a haze. I left the ferry in my van, determined to camp as close to the ocean as possible. And I did. I found a tiny road which led around the edge of the chalk cliffs, ending in a cleared space beside a rifle range. No one was about and the sea and the countryside were all mine. A few cars approached but saw my encampment and went away. Later, on the way to London, I discovered the site of an old railway track. The rails had been taken up and pheasants walked along one bank beside the line of sleepers which disappeared around a corner. Primroses bloomed on the other bank; and a fawn appeared on the line grazing on the lower branches. I felt I should be thanking someone for all my wonderful camping spots. But I don't know who to thank. Mary, Leadley, my barrister friend from Liverpool, Alan ... I'd like to think that!

In London there was news waiting from Cottesloe, which I still called home. One of the many letters came from Lillian. It began with, 'This is a want-to-get-this-off-my-chest letter.' She described over eight vivid pages her improvement, but also her difficulty in standing up to a strong woman who seemed to have sexual intent. She wanted a supportive reply from me. She wrote:

> So you see what I mean about you being my freedom, my release from prison, my feeling that I belong in the real world of people who feel, instead of the usual world of people who have to suppress everything and live behind brick walls, or in their cages like squirrels.
>
> You released me from that world by allowing me to tell you my feelings, especially those that most cut me off, the lesbian feelings.

Obviously the release was not complete. At times she couldn't pick up the phone for fear it was the woman seeking a social engagement. She felt she had no ready answers to give. She recalled her training in King's Park to be a tiger and admitted her transmogrification was incomplete:

> Real TIGERS like you have got ready answers just as they have ready claws; but baby tigers like me don't have ready answers so they have to keep at a distance.

I was already thinking I'd have to bring Lillian along on a trip so we could talk face-to-face in the van.

The travel bug had bitten and I couldn't stay in one place for long. Throughout 1972 I worked on a plan to drive back to Australia. I had inquired about visas for Afghanistan and other countries along the overland route when civil war in Pakistan ended that project, largely, it must be said, because of the warnings and general fussing of my friends. I discovered Crete and also returned to some of my favourite places. I had another look at Rome. The Eternal City excited me all over again — but this time I brought some extra knowledge with me. I knew to sleep outside the Vatican gates to avoid the queues, and how to get the best parking places at the opera house.

The Spanish Steps, the much-storied place of assignation for young lovers, provided me with an interlude in my van which was not without irony. It started when I asked a passing senior police officer where there was a plot at the top of the steps for me to park my van overnight and he told me. I always invited any pleasant looking person into my van to see how I lived — and, as the police official was more than just pleasant, I showed him in, with the van in its evening configuration. He was so unlike other Italian men I'd encountered: his advances came from his eyes, not his hands. I thought he was so well mannered it would be rather nice to do as he seemed to be suggesting — as the young people went noisily by the van. I knew that his name was Victor but little else. My diary states: 'V stayed a while.'

He would leave me messages on my windscreen suggesting further meetings. They were always in the afternoon. Perhaps he had a wife and family waiting for him to return home in the evenings. I never asked. All I knew was that he dressed well and was a gentle and interesting lover.

I was particularly surprised one day when he claimed to be very tired and indicated that I should 'do the work'. This position was surprisingly pleasant. My diary notes that he 'showered me with presents' and that my self-esteem grew. I was over sixty and enjoying myself.

Then I decided that I was losing control of the situation and I didn't know how to escape it politely. One day I climbed into the driver's seat, turned the key, and drove from the Spanish Steps and never returned. The interlude was over. As I noted before, I could behave like a man: love (but not *real* love) and leave.

Outside Rome I picked up a young couple. They had been hitching for years, off and on, and were now both twenty-two years old. They told me they'd been to India before; also Pakistan, Afghanistan and Nepal. I felt a surge of interest in returning to Australia by the so-called overland route, through the Khyber Pass. My passengers were obviously experienced hitchers. They travelled light; just bedding and some spare underwear.

But they carried what seemed to me to be far heavier psychological burdens. She was from Sheffield and had a very strong accent which I did my utmost to disregard. He was a physics student from Corpus Christi at Cambridge and also had a strong provincial accent. I asked him how he got on at Cambridge. He said: 'Not well, socially.' I could easily believe it. I was surprised how little he seemed to know in areas outside physics.

Despite my prejudice about provincial accents, I invited them to spend the night in my 'upstairs' beds, which opened up when I raised the roof. In return they offered to buy me a meal at a trattoria near the camp site, but it closed before we could get there. So I opened some tins. Next morning we were off, they for Venice and me for Bologna.

I spent the night south of Bologna, beside what looked like a deserted barn. When I got up next morning about twenty workmen bearing shovels and rakes were assembling around the van, apparently waiting for their orders. I had camped outside, or perhaps inside, some sort of municipal centre. I greeted the men as I emerged through the rear door, and they waved and smiled. I drove north and, when I was a suitable distance from the assembly, I stopped and emptied my 'slops' (or night soil as it is politely called). While I was doing this two of the older men from the centre cycled by. There were roars of laughter and nods of understanding from them — and back from me.

Bologna tantalised my senses with its elegant colonnades and towers; its paved streets. From there I drove to Siena. The petrol gauge was on zero so I went to the first garage I saw. No one was there, of course. It was lunch time. So I ate my lunch in the shade of the petrol pumps, thinking they'd come back at two o'clock. But I had not taken into account siesta. I went to sleep and was woken just before three o'clock by a man asking if I wanted petrol. I couldn't help laughing as I'd been waiting (comfortably) for nearly two hours.

I eventually returned to Britain but, as the weather became bleaker, I took off again for my first look at Greece. I recall coming into Athens and to the Parthenon where I made an immediate and favourable judgement about the hundreds of tourists visiting there. They were dressed in brightly coloured clothes that contrasted with the background of flinty grey rock and added something alive and modern. I couldn't help recalling the ghastly crowds of chattering tourists I'd encountered in the Sistine Chapel. I had been afraid of finding much the same here — but fortunately I was wrong. People were sitting about on the stones, quietly contemplating. They didn't impinge on the scene with crass remarks about their surroundings.

I met Stewart, who flew in from Australia to travel with me for the next two weeks. The highlight was a trip to Delphi and the Sanctuary of Apollo. The scenery became increasingly wild and spectacular as we approached Mt Parnassus, where the camp site was situated some distance down the mountainside. I parked on the edge of a sheer drop which overlooked a valley and an inlet of the Bay of Corinth. Stewart slept in a hotel opposite. When I woke the sun had just come over the eastern hills and was touching the peaks of the mountains opposite. The waters of the bay were still in shadow. I soaked in the view through the open rear door of the Dormobile while I was having breakfast in bed. If anyone chose to look in at me, rather than gaze at the view, they were welcome.

This wonderful and changing scenery overwhelmed any irritation which might have been evoked by Stewart's determination to help me with my travels; also Stewart's attempts to provide me with advice about money which was a topic which did not interest me. But at least, on this occasion, he failed to ask me to marry him.

Occasionally I shut out this talk so that I could entertain mischievous thoughts about the Delphic Oracle, given Stewart's need for direction in his own life. I thought of him posing questions to the oracle, 'a woman over fifty years of age and dressed as a maiden, and enveloped in intoxicating mephitic vapours' ... me, in fact.

We divided our first day in Delphi into three parts — the lower temples followed by a rest and a campari and soda. Then the larger temples and theatre, all in bright sunshine. This was followed by lunch in the van, and another rest until the museum opened at three.

The weather was still fine as we crossed two spectacular mountain ranges the next morning and came down to Thermopylae on the main Athens highway. We were looking for a hotel where Stewart could stay but couldn't find one. I was exhausted — and desperate. I even stopped at a lit-up driveway believing it to be a hotel and was answered unintelligibly; so much so that I wouldn't be surprised to find that we'd chanced on the local mental hospital. I hated the thought of spending the night with Stewart in my van. At last, only sixteen kilometres from Athens, we found a hotel.

I was pleased when Stewart left for Singapore and I could return to solo travel. I made my way to Epidaurus, one of Greece's most treasured ancient sites. As I arrived I was warmly greeted by a bearded young man who said he knew me; that we had met briefly at Toledo. It was nice to be remembered, and made so welcome. Then, as I walked up towards the well-preserved third century theatre, a marvellous apparition passed me coming down. It carried a long Greek sheep crook, wore a stocking hat, and had a long beard. I couldn't help exclaiming aloud. He might have been a shepherd from biblical times. I loved recreating times past: here it was done for me.

Driving in the direction of the island of Spetses I saw a young woman walking beside the muddy road. The weather was bad so I offered her a lift. She indicated with gestures that her village was off the main road. I indicated I didn't mind that at all. When we arrived the whole population of about one hundred turned out to meet us. They all had the same name as all were related. I was taken into three or four houses and shown pictures and letters from relatives in Australia. They gave me coffee and loukoumia, which was like Turkish Delight although the Greeks wouldn't call it that. After a few minutes in the final house a young girl wearing trousers and a bush jacket entered and spoke to me in English. She was born in the village but had been living in Montreal. She told me that when the Germans occupied Greece in World War Two, they did not find this village, it was so far off the beaten track and so well hidden.

I left with many thanks and handshakes. As I drove away, cloud descended and soon I was in a fog which lasted halfway to the coast. I emerged into clear but cold and grey weather and drove into a small port where I saw SPETSES written in chalk on a board beside one of the boats. I concluded, wrongly as it turned out, that this was the ferry I was seeking to take me to the island. I went into a cafe. An old man, who said he spoke English, asked if I was alone. Most men seemed to ask that. He told me he too was, but did not tell me anything understandable about the ferry. Next day when I'd found the ferry it had started to rain so I did not make the crossing.

A dark young man was standing near the ferry jetty with his wife and child. He was looking extremely frustrated. He told me he was in a hurry to go to a job interview and had been unable to get a taxi. I offered to take him wherever he wanted to go, little realising his destination was Athens some one hundred kilometres away. There were language difficulties on both sides. At this point the bracket holding my spare tyre under the van broke. The tyre dropped to the road and soon a lorry driver stopped to help me secure it. We had to slide on our backs underneath the vehicle to get the tyre back in place. My passenger refused to help: his city suit would get dirty, he said. Then I saw that the fuel was low and for some time I expected to run out. I was glad to see a cluster of houses. Perhaps there was also a garage. But no. Eventually and inevitably we stopped dead. I explained to a kind young man on a motorbike and gave him fifty drachmas to fetch some petrol (much as I once gave a one pound note to a taxi driver in Waterloo Road when I ran out there). He returned after fifteen minutes with the fuel. We started off again and filled the tank at the Isthmus of Corinth, then continued to Athens at full speed, urged on by my passengers.

I became a regular visitor to Greece. The warm winters reminded me of Cottesloe. I loved the scenery and the way the colours changed as each hour passed; the old women on their donkeys, whom I studied through my binoculars; and the young men with fine flashing dark eyes who made me thankful — or perhaps sad — I was not forty years younger.

On my sixty-first birthday I drove from Athens to Corinth to Patras to Pirgos to Olympia, where I toasted myself with champagne. A Greek man came up to me and said in English: 'Greece is a good place for you.' I couldn't disagree. Travelling with me were two French Canadian hitchhikers. I took them to the ruins at Olympia where I could provide some instruction on the history of the place. The sun was gentle and shining through a mist as we explored among the glistening stones and greenery, past the remains of the colonnade and out to the stadium.

Then I drove towards Vassas where I told my hitchers we'd see the temple dedicated to Apollo of Epicurus, Greece's most isolated temple. But I had no idea how bad the surface of the road up the twelve-hundred-metres hill would be. I was driving in an apparently endless cloud, with thunder and lightning and hail, and my petrol gauge almost on zero. I stopped and decided to turn around. But, at that moment a bus arrived. We stopped it and climbed aboard, and asked where the temple was.

A column appeared from the mist immediately above us. It was the Temple of Apollo. We left the bus and, still in pelting rain, climbed up to the temple. We were very high but could see nothing of the surrounding country: only the adjacent building stones and Doric and Ionic half-columns and walls so carefully constructed two and a half thousand years earlier. We ended up soaked but happy.

After returning to the van, I found some petrol at a village and a restaurant which served delectable lemon chicken. We headed south over muddy tracks to the caves at Piros, then across to Githion, and from there to Molai and Monomvassia where I parked on the edge of a cliff facing out to sea. Crumbling mountain roads took us through marvellous scenery to Sparti, Tripolis, Argos, Nafplion … through another twenty towns and villages before I arrived back at the Acropolis car park on dusk.

Two heads quickly appeared at my window to ask me to a party up the hill. They said to look out for a red car. In due course I drove up Observation Hill and stopped near a red van. The occupants knew nothing about a party. I waited but no one came. Perhaps I was in the wrong place; or had misunderstood what was said; or perhaps someone was having me on. It didn't matter. I went to sleep where I'd parked, and woke to the Piraeus in one direction and the Acropolis in the other, and the rest of Athens nestled in between.

I decided I should learn the language of this wonderful country. I went back to Athens and asked a woman of about my age behind the counter at the YWCA about lessons. No, all classes were full, she said. But I could perhaps learn from a young teacher who was free in the afternoons. She asked for my address, and I began burbling on about the van and the interesting nights I'd spent with hippies parked unofficially near the Acropolis …

'I am so glad you are having such a good time with them,' she said icily. I could see she had shut down on me. I told her I'd come back when I'd decided what to do, then made my getaway.

Meanwhile back in Cottesloe, some fifteen thousand kilometres away, the devoted Stewart bought a detailed map of Greece so that he could plot my progress from my incoming letters.

On 30 March 1972 I found myself on the ferry again travelling back from Aegina to Piraeus. It was the fortieth anniversary of my wedding day in the Haverstock Hill Town Hall. I was thinking of Alan as I tried to determine the position of the Persian fleet in the battle with the Greeks in the fifth century BC. He had always been keen to show me what he called the 'very place' described by Herodotus in the first Western history. The attraction of touring Britain in the *Phosphorus* prevented that. But he taught me so well that I could view the scene then reconstruct the battle unaided.

I must have visited Greece ten times. On arrival there, after my first visit, I'd head straight for Olympia. I was visiting old friends. Zeus, Aphrodite, Ares, Apollo, Hestia ... They were almost members of my family. Dink had told us about them so often in my childhood, while my mother was always talking about the Muses. This familiarity made a walk among the classical sculptures in the Olympia museum something very special. Most special to me was a 470 BC ceramic statue of the beautiful youth Ganymede being abducted by Zeus to become his cupbearer and presumably lover. It was a small statue, about forty centimetres high, with Ganymede gently holding a hen in his left hand while Zeus clutched him about the chest.

That hen served as a teaching device when Leoné, my young artist friend, was travelling with me. I took her to Olympia and sent her to view the statue while I rested at the camp site. When she returned I asked if she'd seen the hen. She hadn't, so I became very stern: 'And you — an artist — you miss that. You didn't see it because you didn't look properly.' It was my old theme from the occupational therapy school. I sent her back with instructions that this time she should 'look properly'; which she did.

In my visits to Olympia I sometimes took on the role of guide for a wider group, telling visitors about my family of gods and muses, as well as the significance of certain ancient sites. I'd hear: 'What's so special about that mess of stones forming an arch?' and the words would suck me into the group. 'I'll have you know your mess of stones is the entry arch to the Olympic stadium.' Meanwhile, on the edge of the crowd, Leoné could be seen smirking.

Dordling Not Dawdling

I was by now convinced that I could be ridiculously happy living in my van for the next twenty years. I still had a small part of twenty-eight Percy Street available as a base, plus my house in Cottesloe as a refuge from European winters and an open house for local artists. My happiness was enhanced by the excitement of driving through Greece and I began to refer to the Dormobile in my diary as 'my caravan'. A gipsy caravan, perhaps? I liked to think so, given my father's claim of a gipsy inheritance through his Hungarian mother. I coined a word to describe my mode of living — dordling. Not dawdling. I might often have wandered around at my leisure but, when the mood took me, I could cover ground at speed.

Back in England, my love affair with the inland waterways was re-established. Friends who had been our guests on the *Phosphorus* now owned their own narrow-boat, the *Beatty*. They invited me to cruise with them down the often tree-covered Regent's Canal from Little Venice to the Thames. I hadn't travelled on that section of the canal system before and looked for it first from the land. I knew it slipped through East London and passed behind St Pancras Station, but on earlier attempts I hadn't been able to get to where I thought it should have been. Maps weren't much use because access to the area was so difficult from the street.

One morning I woke in the van, parked beside a kerb near St Pancras Hospital. As usual at such 'camp sites', I woke to the sounds of revving car engines, and slamming car doors. I peered through the blinds and there were cars everywhere. I had chosen this site for my inner-city camp because it was close to the hospital. This was September and I was to have my second cholera injection; all part of my plan to avoid the approaching winter.

I washed my face and teeth then strolled across the road, bearing my slop pail and a kettle of water for rinsing it out. I emptied the contents of the pail down a street drain. If anyone saw me, they would not be curious. It was anything-goes in that part of London in the early seventies. Then I had my usual breakfast, propped up in bed. I read for a while before walking to the hospital. Service was rapid that day, and I found myself standing on a street behind St Pancras railway station with three hours to kill. I had a sudden impulse to look for the lock cottage on this section of Regent's Canal.

The street I was walking along was enclosed by corrugated iron all along one side and a high brick fence on the other. I asked a woman for directions to the canal. She told me it was close: that first I should go down the road to the Coroner's Court. I continued on to a little park which had been a cemetery. There in one corner was the Coroner's Court, with a hearse waiting outside for a corpse to be released for burial. It all looked like a film set. Now I felt I knew where the canal should be. I checked with a passer-by. 'Yes,' he said, 'just go under the three bridges and up the stairs and there it is.'

I followed his instructions, but there were in fact ten sets of railway tracks with accompanying trains, passengers, signals, and a large fence between me and where I knew the canal must be. I saw a railway man standing by the tracks, and thought he would show some interest in a strange woman standing on the edge of a track used by express trains. But he didn't. I had to call out to attract his attention. Reluctantly he told me to go down some stairs and under a bridge, then turn left, turn right, and … and there it was, the lock cottage.

The name PLANK was painted on the fence in solid agricultural lettering. What a great name for a lock cottage, I thought. The woman living there told me that Mr Plank had been the keeper of the lock for more than forty years. Only last year she and her husband had taken him to the Canal Museum at Stoke Bruerne. It was the lock keeper's first trip up his canal, and he'd loved it. He died soon after. The cottage had a garden with tomatoes, potatoes, fruit trees, dahlias, snapdragons, and very green lawn that ran down to the black water which led eastward towards the Thames. I saw a cleared space behind the house, which I added to my mental list of prospective long-term parking spots for my Dormobile. Across and upward from this quiet place I saw St Pancras and Kings Cross stations, four gasometers, and the GPO Tower. The centre of London was roaring, only a few minutes walk from the lock cottage — if you knew the way.

Next day I went back to Rickmansworth and left the van in the boatyard where the *Phosphorus* had been built in 1926, and where Alan and I found her. The same foreman was still there. He remembered the *Phosphorus*, and how my 1927 Morris always started first time on chilly mornings. He told me I looked twenty years younger than when he'd seen me fifteen years earlier. That was just after Alan had died. Life on the road was treating me well.

I took the train from Rickmansworth to Little Venice to join the *Beatty* as it chugged along Regent's Canal. The *Beatty* had once borne coal along that stretch. Now it carried my friends, a gorgeous black dog call Braunston, and Measham, a dear little kitten. We left Little Venice, went shopping in Camden Town, and returned to our very English setting on the canal to eat a tub of finger lickin' chicken. We continued down through the locks to

Regent's Basin, where the coal-loading piers and docks were still in evidence.

Robert Aickman was waiting to come aboard at the last lock before entering the Thames. He was the president of the Inland Waterways Association who had urged us to 'engage in pertinacious inquiry in outlying places' in our search for a narrow-boat. Aickman was a large man whose use of words like pertinacious tended to reinforce the image of a rather pompous person. The *Beatty* entered the Thames near Tower Bridge and we were soon passing the Houses of Parliament. It was a good feeling to be back on a narrow-boat — even if it wasn't the *Phosphorus*, and there was no Alan.

During that summer, I remembered vividly the intense cold of the previous winter when I was often holed up in my van in mountainous parts of France; and how I pushed an old jumper between me and my sleeping bag to prevent the zipper conducting the outside chill through to my body. I wanted to go somewhere warm. Spain, Portugal and Morocco sounded like attractive places to be. So, in November, I was heading across the channel again, this time for Dunkirk. It was the evening ferry and, after dinner, I went down into the hold and slept in the Dormobile. It was freezing outside.

I planned to drive to Arnhem to visit my cousin Marie who was in hospital, then across to Marseilles to a friend's place, then stick to the coast until I reached Spain. I dordled. Along the way I stopped overnight on the tarmacs of some French garages whose owners had befriended me the year before. I was driving south through the World War One battlefields and felt as miserable as the weather outside. It was not just bitingly cold but also foggy and wet. This was a countryside still crowded with the ghosts of the war dead and my mind was occupied with what it would have been like here during one of those deadly battles.

It was a considerable relief to move into Orléans, Joan of Arc country. I couldn't resist the temptation to park for the night under a heroic statue of Joan mounted on a fine horse. Floodlights cast a shadow of the statue onto a stone wall which had been built for just this purpose. The less romantic shadow of my camper, with a trunk on the roof rack, completed the display on the wall.

Next day I sat down to the first lunch I'd eaten alone in a restaurant in Europe. This was a grill where all sort of meats were barbecued. I wondered why I hadn't eaten at restaurants on my earlier travels, and decided it must have been a fear of being seen alone at places where previously I would have gone with my husband; and in some style. Also, I worried whether I could afford to eat out. This meal meant both fears were diminishing. Next lunchtime I went to an ordinary restaurant, the 'sort of place where people from shops and offices eat,' my diary notes.

AT 62 SHE'S A VERY HAPPY HIPPY

By HUGH SCHMITT

At an age when most women settle down to knit for their grandchildren, 62-year-old Cecile Dorward has happily donned the mantle of "the world's oldest female hippy".

In the past four years this cultured, wandering widow has made the world her adventurous oyster and travelled alone more than 70,000 miles around England, Europe, North Africa and South Africa in a converted van.

In Morocco she joined bands of hippies and adopted their lifestyle (minus marijuana) for nearly six months.

"They taught me the meaning of freedom," she says in a deep, resonant English voice. "I was a wanderer among the wanderers, a hippy among the hippies.

"The hippies used to tell me, 'I wish my mother would do what you're doing'."

But though Mrs Dorward dressed like a hippy and spent hours talking and eating with them, she had different motives for her wanderings.

"I wanted to divorce myself from the terrible fetish to which women of my age chain themselves — a humdrum, sheltered home life," she says.

Her second reason for getting out on the road was to study the art of as many countries as she could. "I love art and music, and I've visited art galleries and museums all over Europe."

She was 50 when she left her English home in Liverpool for Perth to teach occupational therapy at Royal Perth Hospital, where she heard travel stories from her students.

Eight years later, badly bitten by wanderlust, she flew to London where she bought a Bedford van with the idea of using it as a mobile home.

"I was pretty browned off with the accommodation in the van — virtually nothing — but at a London camping ground I met a young couple from Adelaide in a similar van which was well fitted out for the road.

"They advised me and helped to furnish my van but it took me years to

This is the only kind of housework Cecile Dorward doesn't mind.

get it like it is now."

(The van, somewhat battered from encounters with trees, posts and car bumpers, now contains a bed, foldaway stove, sink, refrigerator, cupboards, portable shower and a toilet. Around the walls are postcards of notable sculptures, paintings and ancient buildings.)

"I remember my first meal in the van," Mrs Dorward says. "I cooked bacon, tomato and eggs, and that meal made me realise I had something valuable. I felt like shouting to people driving by; 'I've just cooked myself a meal in the great outdoors'."

She didn't realise then that the meal would be the start of four years of travel in that van.

After a holiday in North Wales she decided to venture overseas, and took the van to France.

Long before then, Cecile Dorward had adopted Australia as her home, her 50 years of life in England notwithstanding, and with a bequest from her grandfather, she had bought a big home in Mosman Park overlooking the Indian Ocean, seven miles from Perth. The rent from this house financed her wanderings.

In Europe, the adventurous widow carried an Australian flag on the back of the van and told people that she was Australian — notwithstanding her English birth and the van's British number plates.

On this trip, Mrs Dorward often wore a brown wig while driving. "It took years off me," she laughs. "When men passed me they waved and smiled — and I was weak from laughter. How easy it is to take men in!"

She drove down through France to the French and Italian Rivieras, saw Italy right down to the "toe", returned up through Florence and drove through blizzards in the Italian Alps and up along the Rhine River to Holland from which she returned — temporarily — to England.

Her first sortie into Europe had taken six months. She immediately made plans for her second trip.

The following winter, like a migrating swallow, she again drove on to a ferry and into France, from which she drove south through Spain and crossed over to Morocco. There, she met groups of hippies who befriended her when they saw she was alone.

"I met a lot of wonderful hippies in Marrakesh, many of them Aussies. We used to sit around the town square, eating exotic food and swapping stories of our travels.

"They offered me a smoke of their pot, but I declined."

She did, however, buy hippy beads and found the long hippy dresses comfortable to wear when travelling.

Six months later, the wandering widow was back in England for the summer, after which a third European trip took her to Scandinavia, Germany, Italy, Greece and many other countries. By the time she returned to London, she had logged 60,000 miles on her European journeys.

By this time, Cecile Dorward had realised that she had seen a lot of Europe but really hadn't seen much of her adopted land, Australia. So she decided to see it the way she had seen Europe and North Africa — and

Cecile Dorward calls herself "the world's oldest female hippy".

to have a look at South Africa on the way.

For nine months Mrs Dorward drove around South Africa, clocking another 10,000 miles in her battered Bedford. Then she and her van took ship for Perth. "I'd been away four years but I was more convinced than ever that Australia is the best country to live in."

When *Woman's Day* interviewed her in the house whose rent financed her gypsy wanderings, she was preparing for a trip around the south-west of Western Australia. Next will come a journey around Australia to Queensland and back.

Hanging on the walls of Cecile Dorward's lounge-room are several original paintings.

One, called "String Bags", typifies the type of women the mobile 62-year-old doesn't ever want to be.

It depicts an elderly woman with a haughty, pinched face, a string of beads around her neck, clad in a stylish suit and clutching a string bag full of groceries.

"I just had to buy that," she says, "to make sure I never finish up like that. I can't be hemmed in. It's the hippy life for me."

An article by Hugh Schmitt in Woman's Day, *1972.*

Life Seven
The World's Oldest Hippy

Into Africa

At the beginning of December, as planned, I drove into Spain. I passed through Barcelona, with scarcely a sideways glance at the fanciful art nouveau architecture of Antonio Gaudi. I was determined not to be sidetracked. I had been bitten by the Moroccan travel bug and wanted to get close to North Africa quickly. But it was also an ambiguous urge. I was fearful about being a woman travelling alone in a country so different from the places to which I had become accustomed. Friends, who hadn't been to Morocco either, talked about the risks I was taking. A French friend warned that I would get my throat cut there; but he added sardonically, it would only happen once. Others said that at best I would be very lonely: they didn't realise that, increasingly, I liked being by myself.

I thought of a few reasons of my own why I should delay travelling alone in Morocco, having grown up with stories of terrifying men wearing strange clothes and swinging fearsome scimitars. My anxiety was broadening, and I began to worry about my safety in Spain. As I parked in a town square well beyond Barcelona, I drew my curtains. I seemed to be surrounded by university buildings, but they didn't interest me. I wanted to know whether Spanish girls walked alone in the streets. I peered though the curtains: yes, they did. In fact, everyone seemed to behave normally. So I went to bed and was soon asleep.

I liked the Spanish. Despite the continuing oppression of twenty-five years of Franco's rule, they remained extroverted, theatrical and proud — a bit like me, perhaps. They were also very helpful. As I made my way to Tarragona, then to Reus, people wanted to show me the way. They even accompanied me around corners to make sure I followed directions correctly. Around Almostair old men stopped their mules or donkeys to direct me up to villages hidden in the folds of the mountains, which I would not have found otherwise. Later, when I was in Granada, a young Spaniard chivalrously walked ahead to direct me and my van to an *electrica mecanica*, so that my windscreen wiper could be fixed. There was assistance available everywhere for me. It was assistance with a touch of grandeur.

Still cautious, I delayed my entry into Morocco by taking a diversion into Portugal. There I found the Portugese were quite as intense as the Spaniards, but they had brought melancholia to a high art form. They went about on their overloaded animals looking distinctly sad. Occasionally I saw younger women dressed in brilliant but often violently clashing colours, carrying large wine jars on their heads, but they were an exception in this dour and dark land. Portugal didn't suit my personality. I was pleased to cross the Chanza River back into Spain on a ramshackle car ferry that was just wide enough to accommodate my van.

It was good to be back. I watched fascinated as two blinkered donkeys — yes, the blinkers were embroidered — went by me as I finished my washing up on my first morning back at the side of a major country road. The dark and handsome middle-aged man who was leading them half-smiled at me as I looked up from my sink. I watched as he took the donkeys to the curve in the road. They stood there waiting. I thought to myself: now get ready, move across quickly. No. They were not going to run. The man knew he would have to wait until his donkeys could amble across. Time would have to wait. Meanwhile, just across the valley, dozens of large blocks of flats were being erected. I was not romantic when it came to the rows of old hovels I often passed through. I noted in my diary how lucky new countries like Canada and Australia were 'not to have these old village slums to contend with.'

Part of the excitement for a woman travelling alone in a van and needing to save her money comes towards evening when she doesn't know whether she'll find a safe place to camp that night. To have everything planned would be safer but also as dull as travelling by bus. Driving between Seville and Cadiz one evening I found my options were running out fast. Fences enclosed the baked red earth, just as in much of Australia. There weren't even the occasional openings where I could sneak off the road. I had that feeling which says: serves you right, you should have planned this better; now you'll have to drive all night.

Just then I came to a bright patch of light. It was a bodega, surrounded by trucks and a few cars. I thought I might be allowed to park overnight, as I imagined the drivers slept there in the cabs of their trucks.

In I went and, by chance, began talking with a young Spaniard and his wife. They had lived for a time in Glasgow and could speak English, with interesting Scottish and Spanish intonations. They asked the barman. He listened, looked me over, then nodded his head. All was well. I ordered coffee and smoked meat on bread which seemed to be the speciality of this bodega. Next morning I left before the truckies, before the sun rose, wearing my nightdress and a striped dressing-gown. Suddenly, a pair of headlights was coming directly at me — and very close. I snapped to attention as I moved to the other side of the road. I had been driving on the left, the British side. I wondered what thoughts might have occured to the rescue crew had they been forced to pull me from the wreckage still in my night gear.

I arrived at the historic port of Cadiz, on the Atlantic, and spent several days driving through narrow alleys, and visiting a church which I knew housed a Goya painting but which always seemed to be shut. On New Year's day its doors were still bolted. I eased my frustration by walking out along a pier which extended into the Atlantic. I gulped in the cold, fresh air. The spray from the waves showered down and soaked me. Then, without waiting to dry, I headed east for the Mediterranean coast and, in the process, edged a little closer to Morocco.

I parked on an area of elevated ground, from which I could see the Straits of Gibraltar and the town of Ceuta, a Spanish protectorate which was my closest entry point into North Africa. It was all very exciting. I also looked over Algeciras and found the place where I'd catch the ferry to Morocco. All of this exploration was really a diversion while I tried to generate the courage to cross the Straits and enter a different world.

I met a young Dutch couple. I told them I wanted to drive into Morocco, and of my fears that I might be murdered. The young man, who was named Vermeer and was a descendant of the seventeenth-century genre painter, said he wanted to return there for a brief stay and offered to travel with me. He also said he knew just the person to be my Arab servant, bodyguard and guide, all of whom he felt I needed.

This seemed a good plan. In January 1971 I drove with Vermeer as a passenger on to the midday ferry at Algeciras, had a first-class brandy and some second-class spaghetti, then a brief rest in my van ready for my arrival in North Africa. Well, not quite ready. I couldn't take my eyes off the colourful people swirling before me. They had assembled from near and far to meet the ferry, and to do some commerce. Strange men in wonderful striped robes; a sheep tied to a lamp post with only a motorcycle for company; kerb sitters selling flat bread and mutton rissoles which lay on the dirty footpath; fezed people and turbaned people; women with their faces half covered, with rags in some cases, with elaborately embroidered cloths in others; mules and donkeys trotting and dropping their faeces everywhere; women displaying stiletto heels under their long robes. These hooded robes of vegetable-dyed wool or cotton made the flowing robes of the multitude of western hippies flooding into Morocco from Europe and India look ordinary. I knew then that I would have to procure a djellaba, and began to look for a tailor.

Confronted with this exotic tableau of people, costumes, animals and foods, in Ceuta and later in Tangier, I realised that it was finally unnecessary to play the game I had delighted in since my childhood — that of filling surrounding spaces with people from the past, often the Middle Ages. 'This is where one wants to come for atmosphere of the Middle Ages,' I wrote. No leaps of the imagination were necessary here. I couldn't quite believe that what I was seeing so vividly was real.

When we arrived in Tangier, Vermeer went to the markets to look for a protector for me. He turned out to be an attractive young Berber with experience of service in Sweden. He had a pleasant manner, and was named Bookair. I suppose I had to find him admirable, as he'd be costing me close to ten shillings a day, plus his main midday meal, and accommodation in a cheap hotel each night.

That afternoon Bookair took us to the Hercules cave where wild seas broke over rocks and sprayed across the cave entrance, rendering it dark and rather primeval. After this I returned to the camp site high above the Atlantic Ocean. It had been raining much of the afternoon and the approach road was a continuing stream of mud. I turned back to drop my two male helpers in the city so they could eat and find somewhere to stay. I didn't want to have to do this later, and risk being bogged in the mud, alone and in the dark, when I returned to the camp site. A taxi to take them to the city would have been beyond my budget. So on return to the camp site, instead of eating spiced meat dishes, I opened a tin of baked beans — they were tasty.

Vermeer went home suddenly after we had been in Tangier for only two days. At this point I could have called off the deal with Bookair as well. I was getting more confident that I would come to no harm in Morocco, even in Tangier which had an odious reputation as a centre for every sort of dubious activity. But I still feared that everyone would rob me if they could. They didn't look honest. 'I appreciate the tremendous impact that Christianity has had on Western Europe when compared with these benighted places which believe in an eye for an eye and a tooth for a tooth. I'm almost starting to believe in it,' I recorded.

It seemed sensible to have Bookair around, particularly in case my van broke down in these parts. I still had little idea of what happened under the bonnets of cars. He also kept the beggars away when we walked through the crowded entrances of the *souks*. He had the added advantage of speaking no English; if I wanted to speak to him I had to do so in French. This limited my flow considerably, which it seemed was a blessing all round.

It was pleasant to relax in the Tangier camping area while Bookair washed my clothes, cleaned my car inside and out, and generally made a fuss of me. It was rather funny: me with a servant, while living in a van. The joke was lost on many of my fellow campers. 'Look at Lady Mary over there with her servant,' I heard said, without irony. I imagine others thought he must have been more than just a servant.

According to my diary I 'travelled alone' (ie., with Bookair) towards Rabat, the capital of modern Morocco, where the king had lived since 1956, the year when independence was won from the French. We went along the coast road where the rollers from the Atlantic soaked us with spray whenever we took a break from the van. It felt good to be travelling 'alone'. At Rabat I wrote of Bookair: 'I'm very glad I've got him. Otherwise, I would have to travel in convoy, and be at the beck and call of others. They mightn't want me tagging along.' I'd just discovered a group of 'friends' from the camping area had gone off to see King Hassan II progress from his palace to the mosque. It was an event of some significance, and I was annoyed they hadn't told me. Then Bookair arrived and said he'd learned the previous night that the king would not be going to the mosque that day. I went to the palace just the same, and made a point of strolling over to the group of campers waiting enthusiastically for the king. 'The king? Oh, it's no show today,' I said. I couldn't help feeling rather pleased with myself.

After that triumph I headed for Marrakesh, still travelling 'alone'. I was excited to be leaving the coast and heading over three hundred kilometres inland. In due course, the Atlas Mountains appeared on the horizon. A precise layer of cloud split the snow-covered peaks from the rest. They reflected a brilliant white then, later, shades of pink in the rays of the setting sun. There were date palms and camels. The tilling of the poor farming land was under way, the ploughs often drawn by an unlikely team of a camel and a mule, in harness. I'd seen pictures of such rural scenes but the reality was far more vivid. More vivid yes; but I still couldn't quite believe what I was seeing.

We passed — very slowly — through a teeming *souk* which was in full swing. The road for the last mile was crammed with carts drawn by two or sometimes three mules; or a single horse might be pulling a cart on which twenty robed figures were crowded on top of all their baggage. There were people on bikes, and on donkeys; people walking alongside heavily laden donkeys; and occasionally barefoot people. I was continually held up: there was no right of way for vans when there was a market to be got to. All I could do was wait for the next cart to pass, then hurriedly squeeze by before the next, and the next … Bookair tried to wave the carts aside to allow me to pass, but with little success.

The final kilometre or so took an hour before I could discover the cause of all this chaotic activity. In the centre of the market were sheep and goats galore, tents, and food stalls; and rubbish and dirt everywhere. What a mess! I had to pass a similar crush of carts and people coming and going as we emerged from the other side. Turbans, beards, long robes and hoods, half-covered faces, poverty and dirt. 'No wonder they said cleanliness is next to godliness. It certainly makes people look more honest if they are clean, but I suppose these people don't particularly want to look honest,' I wrote that night.

On the Edge of the Desert

I don't know what I expected to see when I drove into Marrakesh that afternoon — probably something romantic in the manner of Beau Geste or a city resonating with international intrigue. Instead, I saw mud red buildings and red granite buildings set along very wide streets; dual carriageways separated by vast desert-like median strips, apparently awaiting an oil-fuelled boom when they would be filled with large cars perhaps. In the meantime it looked rather desolate.

The camp site was neglected. It was a vast space of sandy soil with about fifty caravans dotted among trees. Some Americans I'd met earlier in Portugal were there and a group of Australians. We quickly made friends, and next day we were all heading for the hustling markets of Marrakesh. Bookair came too. Every form of craft, clothing, fruit and vegetables, pickles and preserves was for sale, on platforms on which the vendors also squatted. It was lunchtime. We were drawn through the labyrinth of alleyways by the marvellous aroma of roasting lamb, frequently juxtaposed with the less enchanting smell of donkey droppings.

Eventually, we found the charcoal-fired ovens where six or seven lambs were roasting whole, coated with herbs and spices, and filled with vegetables. It was noon, and the first lamb was being taken from the oven. The cooks sat, cross-legged, almost on top of their ovens, and cut up the meat on greasy pine tables. They wrapped the portions of meat in newspaper and passed them to their milling customers. No one seemed to worry about cleanliness.

We bought about one and a half kilos of lamb and two long flat loaves from one of the many women who sat with their backs against a wall and their bread on the footpath. At a nearby cafe we went at the meat with our fingers. There was a crumpled sheet of paper on the table, sprinkled with spicy salt into which we dipped the lamb. It was wonderfully tender and tasty; so tasty that we almost fought over a remnant of skin. We washed it all down with sweet mint tea, a perfect complement for the lamb.

By 12.30 only six charred lamb heads remained on the cooks' tables and children were gathering to scavenge for the scraps. At the cafe, we were given a pot of water and a piece of none-too-clean cloth with which to wipe our fingers. Fortunately, like all good campers, our pockets were stuffed with lavatory paper, useful for all sorts of purposes.

We ate other memorable meals in Marrakesh, usually in Djemaa el-Fna, a vast square in the old part of town, where most things seemed to happen. Portable food stalls opened there towards evening. Men arrived with barrows, stacked almost nine feet high with tables and chairs, grillers and steamers, the stock of food perched at the top of the pile. The stall holder would set up his cooker, his tables and chairs, and be in business selling his speciality in a few minutes. The *tajine* chicken — chicken stew — was cooked in a special pot called a *tajine,* and took on a wonderful variety of tastes during its slow cooking. It came with those Moroccan staples, chick peas and almonds. I tasted many variants of couscous, the Moroccan national dish, from these stalls: the fine semolina, light and fluffy, with meat, chicken and vegetables arranged on top, and a spicy broth poured over it all.

Meanwhile, in fine hotels where the *tajines* were of shining brass rather than rough cast iron, more elaborate dishes were prepared and large bills accumulated. I had neither the desire nor the money to eat in such restaurants. I had been thinking about making myself more comfortable financially by selling a Sheraton table which Alan and I had bought when we were at Percy Street. But no amount of money would have lured me into restaurants in the four and five star hotels. They were much too posh, and much too expensive.

Djemaa el-Fna was also a place of itinerant entertainers, the home of popular drama. I spent an increasing amount of my time watching performers there. One afternoon I found myself in the front row as a crowd encircled the stage to watch a spontaneous slapstick play, with men taking the women's roles. I thought of Shakespeare and the Globe Theatre, as the crowd jostled for positions closer to the action and joined in some rowdy audience participation.

The play featured a prospective bride in an elegant *djellaba* and purple headdress, her parents, and a lot of arguments between a large number of suitors. These developed whenever the bride performed an obviously provocative dance directed towards a particular suitor. One of the suitors wanted to show he'd had enough, and turned into a donkey with a flat fur face. He trotted off and made straight for my section of the crowd, and nuzzled me. I drew back in horror, but was reassured by nearby women who patted me on the shoulder. I had my part to play in the drama and the crowd seemed to love it.

One of my favourite articles of clothing was a pair of jeans I had found in a litter bin near Newmarket in England. I often wondered who could have thrown away a brand new pair of jeans. Perhaps they thought some old tramp would be glad of them. Well, the old tramp was me.

But despite the delight I took in my jeans, I still coveted the *djellabas*, which enveloped their lucky owners in a swirl of hand-dyed colour. One afternoon the perfect *djellaba* passed me. I'd admired many, some with ornate decoration, but this one was special. It was a very rich brown with broad cream and narrow green stripes. I pursued its owner through the alleyways of the market, dodged between the donkeys, and eventually accosted him when he paused to talk with friends. I asked him, with some difficulty, if he'd take me to his tailor. He'd be delighted, he seemed to say. Despite my fears, Moroccan men treated me well — in our admittedly limited encounters.

We went together to the textile *souk* where he introduced me to his tailor who sat on one of the benches which defined the perimeter of his stall. He agreed to make me a *djellaba* from similar material, measured me, and said it would be ready in a week. I could collect it then. This proved easier said than done. The next week I went up the alley where I remembered his stall being. He wasn't there, nor in the next, nor in the one after that. All the alleys and the hundreds of stalls began to look the same and after a ninety-minute search I was starting to panic. Unfortunately, I'd left Bookair back at the camp site. Then I finally found my tailor and became the very pleased owner of my very own *djellaba*.

I had been in Marrakesh for more than a week now, and had taken to life in the dry dusty camp 'like a fish to water'. Something about me — possibly my deep voice or my height — seemed to attract attention. Everyone wanted to talk with me, particularly the many young men and women who had recently been dubbed 'hippies'. They came to Morocco, and particularly Marrakesh, for its exotic lifestyle and, I imagine, the ready supply of cheap hashish. They came in vans and in cars, carrying tents, or hitching rides. They said they wished their parents were like me, and called me the 'Queen of all Hippies'. I thought, if I'd had a family I'd be too worn out to travel now, in my sixties. At first, they thought I was English, then they'd say: 'But you can't be, because the English are such a stand-offish lot.' Too true, I'd say, I'm Australian. This attention was very flattering.

The hippies taught me something about freedom: if I were to

be like them I'd never become a String Bag chained to a (non-mobile) home, I reassured myself frequently. I began to wear long dresses which were well-suited to travelling, and even beads, a long and chaotic set rather than the prim single strand around the neck of the subject of *String Bags*. I seemed to be completely accepted, a wanderer among wanderers. I spent hours sitting on the ground, talking and eating. If I was offered some pot I politely refused. It was not something which ever interested me. Also, I had just given up smoking to save money and I didn't want to take on another expense.

One young man, with his long curls tied back, asked: 'Excuse me. Do you have a clothes brush?' I thought of my mother's silver-backed brush which, funnily enough, I had with me in the van, then decided that was not what he needed. I realised he had no idea about how to clean his dusty clothes. I told him I banged mine first then washed them. He thanked me rather solemnly for this very basic advice. Later, I saw him standing inexpertly at the wash trough. He had obviously not been there before. He'd had a worn-out mum to do that.

I was becoming a connoisseur of campervans and camping sites. I noted the arrival of the VW kombi as the van-of-choice for many travellers, and creative refinements to the basic van when I was invited to visit others in the camping areas. One was fully carpeted; another had paintings hanging on the walls. I rated camp sites according to the quality of the toilets, their showers, and the quantity of shade trees. Except for the trees, Marrakesh did not rate well. But then nor did the Crystal Palace Harbour, where my Dormobile life began.

The unisex lavatories in Marrakesh were the stand-up or crouch types, which I liked. There were no dirty seats. Apparently, there is an Australian expression — 'to kangaroo the loo' — which refers to squatting over toilet seats to avoid lurking bacteria. Here things were more basic. A forty-four-gallon drum filled with rather dirty water, and a number of metal buckets for flushing, completed the lavatory system.

These lavatories were clogged when I arrived from Rabat, and the smell was not pleasant. I'd had my experience fixing rudimentary toilets in Fiji so I asked a young man to pass me a long piece of bamboo lying on the ground near him. I told him he could help me clear the blockage by bringing a bucket of water and flushing it down the hole. I saw he was a touch revolted by the prospect so I told him to look away and just pour. He did, but nothing happened. A second probe with the bamboo and a second flush did the trick. We were both delighted with the results of our joint endeavour.

Everyone at the camp site seemed to like Bookair. This was not surprising. After he finished fussing over me he did other campers' washing. I'd just lie on my folding bed and watch the chores being done: he would be upset if I tried to do them. My fellow campers were curious. I explained how I needed a bodyguard for travelling alone here; it was the price of being old. When we walked in the streets and the *souks* I wondered what people thought about us: that I had a jet black husband and Bookair was the offspring? That I had adopted him? Or that he was my Moroccan gigolo? Then I acknowledged that they probably didn't care who he was.

Eventually, after travelling with Bookair for a fortnight, I felt I could manage alone and I paid him off. He'd cost me a pretty penny; twenty-five pounds in fact. The total cost hurt, but I rationalised that at my age I was lucky to be able to come to Morocco at all; that I would have been too frightened on those first few days without him.

I dropped him off at the station with money for his ticket back to Tangier. He seemed sorry to be leaving me; for my part, he had done his job well. I could send him home when I no longer needed him.

On the way back to the camp, I stopped at Marrakesh airport and opened the van doors to take in the warm sun and a broad view of the Atlas Mountains. I had coffee and relished the civilised ladies' room with its hot-air hand drier. Luxury. I felt I would be happier now that I was really travelling alone.

I left Marrakesh alone — really alone — and happy, and headed south towards Tafraoute, feeling very confident. I even stopped the van to ask two young men the way. They answered most politely in French. I felt no threat.

The scenery along the way was the most stunning I had ever seen. A rosy red coloured the mountains which later reflected shades of pink and grey. The almond flowers were mostly white but sometimes pink with darker centres. There were tall date palms and the ground was covered with yellow daisies. As I ascended, the small villages of mud houses revealed themselves in folds of the mountains. Then I came to a spot where the road had been washed out, and had to take a track which led through a beautiful valley. I stopped the van and walked for a while so that I could appreciate my surroundings. I found a large well with an almond tree flourishing inside it. At the bend of a now-dry riverbed I saw the remnants of brick walls from what must have been a substantial village. A field of self-sown wheat grew nearby. What had happened? My imagination took over. A surprise attack ... the men killed ... the women and children taken ... the houses put to the torch. A few kilometres down the road I came upon a fairly new and prosperous village with plastered walls and windows decorated with ironwork. Perhaps the villagers just decided to move on and build afresh ...

I was by now so confident that I did what all the travel manuals told me not to do — picked up a hitchhiker. She was an attractive young woman from Sydney, and had been travelling for almost three years. In this time she had worked as a waitress on the freighter *New Endeavour*, crewed a yacht out of Bali, and spent three months in India, often sleeping in railway luggage racks, before reaching Europe and then Morocco. As we passed through the stunning mountain scenery she told me amusing stories of how she had spent a great deal of her time having to repulse men. I noted there were no descriptions of encounters with males who were not rebuffed. Perhaps she thought that, at my advanced age, I would be easily shocked. We parked under some gum trees, and watched the rapid changes of colour as the sun set on the mountains. Later a full moon provided us light for as long as we cared to keep awake.

Apart from her story telling, my hitchhiker had not gone out of her way to be an agreeable travelling companion. On the second night she complained that there was not enough room in the van for her to do her yoga exercises. I decided I could stand her no longer and made it clear she could find another ride the next morning. I was tempted to add that perhaps she would find a sufficiently large van.

We parted amicably enough after attending a camel *souk* on a huge enclosure of stony desert outside Goulimime, which calls itself the gateway to the Sahara. When we arrived at eight-thirty in the morning the market was half over but there were still several hundred camels waiting to be sold. I hadn't seen camels in herds before and their impact on me was marked. I began to think about camels, and on consecutive nights I dreamt about wearing my *djellaba* while riding camels. I considered taking a camel trek deep into the Sahara to Timbuktu, but common sense prevailed: fifty-two bottom-jarring days might be a bit much for someone accustomed to breakfast in bed.

After eighty kilometres along a road which reminded me of the old unsealed Nullarbor track, I reached Mahmid — and the edge of the desert. It was a *souk* day there too, and the camels and donkeys were coming in across the desert from early in the morning. I watched from my folding chair in the shade of an old earthen wall. I think from the smell this was the place used by old men for peeing purposes, so I suppose they had to find another wall. With my binoculars I could pick up small groups approaching from a distance, the men in their robes and turbans leading the camels; one carried a goat across his shoulders. The thing with binoculars was that I could stare to my heart's content without being seen.

The donkeys at the *souk* were not allowed to copulate. The keepers rushed up and beat any that started to get amorous. (Apparently special arrangements were made for donkeys to mate — and old donkeys were not allowed to do it.) Some camels sat and some lay down and the donkeys all ee-awed like mad. Otherwise, the old men greeted each other warmly, and the market sold its oranges and vegetables, grains, and sheep and goats. I was fascinated.

Driving back to Tangier I stopped in the camping ground at Fez. Four robed men came and stood beside my van. Four weeks ago I would have been frightened, would have imagined they were plotting to attack me and steal my belongings. Now I could watch them with interest while continuing with my breakfast: egg and bacon, naturally. One of the men bent down and picked up a large stone. Earlier I would have seen this as a sinister step which could represent the end of me. Now I saw four faces, each bearing a pleasant expression. The men laughed among themselves then slowly moved away.

I turned sixty and became an old age pensioner in heavy rain helping two young Americans on the road outside Fez. Their old van had broken down. I had met them the previous day at a camp site washing area and they had heard I was a connoisseur of campers and invited me to see theirs. It was completely lined with Middle-Eastern rugs and bookcases made from well-polished wooden crates. They had been in the United States army and one was a cook. He made a chicken lunch which we enjoyed, then they left for Tangier.

On that cold rainy day I was resting in my van and mid-afternoon when a tired face appeared at my window. It was the cook and he carried an empty petrol can. He told me he had obtained a lift back part of the thirty kilometres and walked the rest. He thought he wouldn't get a lift back at night so he'd come to ask if I could take him with some petrol back to the van. I did but the trouble was rather more serious than a lack of petrol. I left the pair, promising to return with expert help the next day, my birthday. I came back with a mechanic, a boy assistant, some tools and a towrope. The mechanic could do little with the van at the roadside so they towed it back to their workshop. I waited in Fez until the van was fixed, then loaned the young men some money to pay for the repairs.

I did not expect to get my money back despite our arrangement to meet for that purpose in Madrid on Easter Sunday. But as I hadn't been robbed or lost any money on my travels, I felt I owed the Fates a little in return, and took the chance. How wrong I was anyway. We did met as arranged on Easter Sunday and they also presented me with a necklace and another chicken dinner.

I returned to Britain, having again backed away from plans to take the overland route through India to Perth. A friend, noting my disappointment, suggested I return home via South Africa.

Soon my van was being hoisted from the dock at Liverpool onto the deck of the SS *Vergelegen*, bound for Cape Town. As the van was travelling as deck cargo I could sit in it, writing letters or just taking in the sun which streamed through the windscreen.

I stayed in South Africa for twelve months, sleeping anywhere. Often I did not stay at camp sites but slept wild along the small tracks used by black South Africans. Why did they want to take on the boring lives of the white people? I asked myself constantly. No answer made sense — to me at least.

Bowling along merrily, taking in the beautiful scenery and thinking how marvellous the van was, I'd just arrived at a town east of Johannesburg, called Ermelo, when there was a thumping noise, which sounded like a dysfunctional antique sewing machine. I drove straight to a large garage. 'You're in BIG trouble,' said the old man, who seemed to be the foreman. 'One of the pistons is shot but it's no good replacing just one of them. You should do the lot. And while you're about it there are other things you should have done.' This was going to take some time and a lot of money.

For the next few days I would have a van with no engine. That was a problem because I refused to sleep in hotels, so I asked if I could stay in the yard at the back of the garage, which extended down to the river. I could use the ladies' room which had hot water. The foreman wasn't keen on the idea. Instead, he offered to tow my engineless van the ten kilometres back to the caravan park, and back again when the engine was ready. Each day I got a lift into town and dropped in to inspect the progress on the invalid's engine.

I had intended driving up to the Victoria Falls but some people had just been shot there. It was said they had been spying. So when the engine was running again I decided not to take the chance of getting myself into trouble: I maintained my philosophy of not squeezing the very last drop from the sponge.

Over the next two months I travelled up and down the east coast, hoping to find a suitable ship to take me home. Suitable ship meant small ship, but that proved impossible. Eventually, I had to sail with eleven hundred others on the *Galileo*. This time my van, now with seventy thousand kilometres on the clock plus a few bruises from encounters with trees and car bumpers after four years' travel, was not on the deck but deep in the hold. I couldn't use it as a place from which to hide from the crowd. As a result I hated the trip but was pleased to get home.

In Training

No sooner had I arrived back in Perth in 1974 than my Dormobile was on the train heading for Alice Springs. This was to be the start of some travel around Australia. I had crossed the Nullarbor in my early days in Australia, when the road was unsealed and a known wrecker of cars. More recently, I had grown fond of the Dormobile and did not wish to see it wrecked, or even damaged. The RAC advised me to send the van off a week before I travelled as there were occasional delays with cargo. The first stop would be Port Pirie where the van would be transferred to the Ghan train, named after the camel drivers from Afghanistan who provided the only transport in the area early in the century.

When I followed on the train a week later I was expecting to join up with the van in Alice Springs. However, on arriving at Port Pirie to join the Ghan, I was told there had been floods and the Alice Springs railway line was under water.

I jumped back on the train and went on to Adelaide, then flew to Alice. From the air I could see the huge expanse of turquoise-coloured water that was Lake Eyre. In Alice Springs I climbed onto a bus, assuming it would pass the railway station where I hoped my Dormobile would be waiting for me. The bus driver told me he went only as far as the post office, so I got off with my luggage. Before I had time to call a taxi, however, he was back. 'Get in,' he called, 'I've got to go past the station to pick up another driver.' This seemed like a good omen for my trip.

Cécile and the Dormobile on arrival back home at Hamersley Lodge.

The first thing I saw when the bus pulled up at the station was my van waiting in the goods yard. I was delighted — it was like meeting an old friend, even if we had only been apart for a week. I got in and the Dormobile started immediately. I drove up to the railways office with the papers. A young man said: 'You'll be lucky if your van arrives in a week.' I pointed theatrically at the van and said in my loud voice, which meant the whole office could hear, 'You don't know what a good railway you have.' Everyone laughed.

Next I found a camp site. The people who ran it also had an Aboriginal art gallery. I did not know much about Aboriginal art. It was the first time I had seen such a collection apart from the works held in the old Art Gallery of WA in Beaufort Street. The owners took me around the collection but my knowledge remained rudimentary.

I stayed in Alice a few days while I accustomed myself to being in neither Europe nor Perth.

After the first thirty kilometres out of the Alice, the roads were all gravel or dirt, and the petrol stations few and far between. When I pulled into one of these rare stations to fill my tank, I discovered the proprietor was out of petrol and was waiting for the tanker to arrive. I too had to wait. I spent the night there parked behind the pub which was attached to the petrol station.

When I next stopped it was to buy fruit and vegetables at what was a station owner's store which also traded with passers-by. I left the Dormobile at the gate and walked up the red earth track to the shop. As I left with my provisions, travellers from a tourist bus were walking up the same track. I heard someone say: 'There she is!' I looked to see who the celebrated 'she' might be — but there was no one but me. To my amazement the passengers knew of my travels from their driver, who had read about me in articles by Hugh Schmitt in *Woman's Day*. They shook hands and congratulated me.

I went on to Ayers Rock (now called Uluru) but did not climb to the top. Ropes were installed to make the task easier, and it no longer seemed a challenge. Also, I did not feel altogether comfortable. I didn't belong there.

I returned to Perth convinced that I needed a vehicle more powerful and robust than my Dormobile before I could think seriously about making the overland crossing to Britain. The Land Rover stood out as the best choice from the restricted range of four-wheel drive vehicles available. However, new ones were too expensive for me, and they also needed what my diary calls 'expensive fitments' to convert them into a camper.

One evening I rang Faulls Brothers, the local Land Rover dealer, to check if they had any second-hand vehicles. They hadn't, but suggested I should try first thing tomorrow. Next morning I was told to come to the showrooms in Subiaco at two o'clock. I did as instructed and there, waiting, was my home for much of the next nineteen years. It had just been traded in. The former owners had converted it, and clocked a substantial sixty thousand kilometres, much of that on the London to Fremantle trip I had been planning before the Pakistan war broke out. It had a comfortable bed with good vision through the back doors, a two-burner cooker, a nine gallon capacity water tank, a small kero fridge, and a folding table. It only awaited such refinements as pictures on the walls and a book case.

My next task was to build up some experience at the wheel, and some practice at living in the van. The north of Western Australia was to be my training ground. On these trips I did not care too much about the route by which I might reach my destination. This meant that sometimes I did not know quite where I was, except in the most general sense. It did not seem all that important. Travelling was the important thing. Once I was 'somewhere beyond Kununurra' and about to pull off the road for the night when I heard on my radio that a tourist had thumbed a lift then shot dead the obliging driver. The dead man had been left on the side of the road while his murderer drove away in my general direction.

That night I sought a spot where the Land Rover couldn't be seen from the road. I found just the place — a large gravel pit. Part of it was under water but that didn't worry me too much as the surface seemed firm enough. As I crossed the 'firm surface', however, I had the familiar sensation of wheels sinking into soft ground then spinning. Oh God, now I've done it, I thought. I got out and found that, luckily, only one wheel had spun itself deep into the pit. But that one was stuck down to the axle.

Don't get excited I told myself: have a drink first. I had my drink and my dinner. Then, by moonlight, I found myself marching back to the road. Standing there in the darkness, the ludicrousness of my situation struck me. What am I doing, standing on this isolated road? For whom am I waiting? Mightn't my 'helper' be just the person from whom I'm hiding? I acknowledged that I had put myself into this mess and I had to get myself out. So I went back to the van, got out my overworked shovel, and started to jack up then clear around the bogged wheel. Next I packed rocks under it to provide some traction. After an hour's work the van roared free and I felt very pleased with myself. I thought that I didn't need to depend on anyone any more. Well, that wasn't quite true, although my vehicles did seem to understand how little I knew about their internal operations, and took the trouble to go wrong only when I was close to help.

On the trip north I shared camping sites with groups of Aborigines outside Mount Magnet, at Roebourne and at Darwin. I could see their campfires burning and I had no fear. This may evoke shades of Daisy Bates, the eccentric English journalist who camped in the outback and observed the Aborigines. However, she wore fine Edwardian clothing, I wore pants. I never took the trouble to walk across to meet them which may seem strange given my interest in the groups sharing camp sites with me in Europe. But the camp sites were much larger here, and I was more isolated from my fellow campers.

In Darwin I swam every day in the warm waters of Vestey's Bay, often with Lillian who was employed there as a social worker. Her problems — particularly the ambiguity concerning her sexual identity — were largely under control. She told me she was planning to marry Stephen, a computer programmer, early in 1975. She had kept all the letters I had written to her from Europe and Africa, and whenever she felt she needed to be more of a *real tiger*, she'd read an appropriate passage from them.

Back at twenty-seven Deane Street, I woke on Christmas morning 1974 to the news that Darwin had been destroyed by Cyclone Tracy. I spent the day listening to the radio for news of Lillian, the daughter I didn't have. I first heard she was safe when she rang to say she was heading for Perth with Stephen and a number of her friends. Her wedding plans were in disarray. She moved into a flat near number twenty-seven, while some of her Darwin friends moved into Hamersley Lodge. It was decided to hold the wedding reception in my garden. However, at three o'clock the following morning, I was woken by Lillian and Stephen, complaining they hadn't been able to sleep because their flat had 'a bad atmosphere'. I was furious to be woken at this time with an excuse like that. I imagine their friends in

Hamersley Lodge were not impressed either as we arranged sofas and chairs so that the wedding couple had somewhere to settle.

Later in 1975 a phone call revived my hopes of taking the overland route to Britain — through India, Pakistan, Afghanistan, Iran and Turkey. The caller had been at one of the many talks I had given to groups around Perth on my travels. She said she, her husband Frank, and their four children ranging in age from fourteen down to six, wanted to return to Britain by the overland route the following year. They had a jeep, and were willing to go in convoy.

I quickly realised I needed further training with my new vehicle. I got this on a drive north, in August, 1975. My diary indicates things went well:

> Oh wot a super day — beyond Wubin [two hundred and sixty-eight kilometres from Perth in the north-eastern wheatbelt]. Had a partial cold shower. Lovely sunset; stars galore; no traffic; no flies; no mozzies. Slept well.

I can't imagine now what my partial cold shower might have been like.

Next day my diary asked rhetorically: 'Why does no one praise the dawn?' I drove on to the Murchison town of Cue, four hundred and eighty kilometres north-east of Perth. Then on to another old gold mining town, Meekatharra, where I lived it up with a two-dollar counter lunch at the pub accompanied by a beer, compliments of the publican. My diary said the performance of the Land Rover matched the excellent weather: 'Everything works well, especially the flap-down table.'

The Overland Route

Preparations for my great travel adventure included purchasing tinned food and a bucket of peanut butter, tissues and toilet paper, and maps of half the world. I needed a box of emergency spare parts, which were assembled with the help of a mechanic at Faulls.

We were ready in January 1976, apart from endless farewell parties and lunches. At last my Land Rover and Frank and Norma's jeep were loaded on to the *Centaur* at Fremantle. Stewart came too, accompanying us only as far as Penang. The great adventure was under way. We disembarked in Singapore where Stewart went straight to a hotel. I stayed in the van in the garden of the YWCA hostel and used Stewart's hotel shower and lavatory, and Frank and Norma and family slept inside the hostel.

We crossed the causeway to Jahore Bahru to begin the trip through Malaysia. Some of the family wanted to go back to shop for radios and electrical goods in Singapore, but I wanted to push on and two of the children came with me. After a month we were in Penang and there was the first sign of tension between us. Frank and Norma thought the camping site I'd discovered on a beautiful beach was too sandy — and too expensive. This was, of course, ironic, since I was normally so thrifty, but the beach was exquisite. I was, anyway, too excited about the next phase of the trip to take much notice. Meanwhile, Stewart was installed in his hotel, where I used the hotel showers and lavatory.

At Penang Stewart flew home while the rest of us sailed to Madras. While the vehicles were being unloaded at Madras, five Indian customs men knocked at my cabin. I was half-asleep so I let them take over. They shoved all the things I hadn't packed into my zip-bag, then glued a piece of paper across the zip and said that it needn't be examined again. The seal was loose and I could have repacked the bag but, as inside there was a bottle of brandy three-quarters full, I was happy enough with the arrangement. When I emerged from my cabin our vans were sitting on the wharf, the jeep with a damaged spring, having been dropped over the last metre onto the dock.

There were thousands of Indians on the wharf as we assembled beside our respective transports. A polite official took over the paperwork and we waited while he raced from office to office exchanging documents. I rested in my van then actually dozed off, despite the high level of background noise. Later, I prepared Ryvita biscuits with peanut butter and vegemite and passed them around while we waited. The snacks were well received.

With formalities completed, we drove into Madras. I was very excited. Almost sixty years earlier Miss Haycock had told us about India, British India, of course. I could see Madras was quite a modern city, noisy, very crowded, and a major centre of transportation of all kinds. It was not a particularly attractive city although there were some fine buildings, remnants of the India Miss Haycock had taught us about.

We headed straight for Adyar House, the headquarters of the Theosophical Society. Bob, the husband of my artist-tenant Leoné Ferrier, had suggested this might be an interesting place for us to stay. An American woman of about my vintage received us graciously in a fine old building with high ceilings, set in twenty-seven acres of serene garden. The garden included a grove of mango trees, and a spreading banyan which we were told was one of the oldest trees in the world. I sat underneath and looked up and saw no reason to doubt the claim. We soon discovered, however, that the theosophists, who were dedicated to service and the improvement of society, embraced abstinence from meat and alcohol (and sex, although that was not an issue, for me at least). We decided to move to a youth hostel they recommended, which was more accommodating in these matters. It was run by a retired British Army colonel and his wife, Subadrah.

I reorganised my van for land travel, unpacking my books and paintings and setting them up, then went to the market to buy a rolling pin and a board. I wanted to experiment with the tricks of chapatti making which I'd gleaned from watching a street vendor at work that morning. I had also tested dosas, the thin crispy pancakes wrapped around a potato and onion mixture which are a speciality of Tamil Nadu. Delicious.

We left Madras on a Sunday. There was noticeably less motorised transport than usual but many more people, bikes and animals. I loved the way the cows and the odd buffalo ambled across the road, or just stopped and stared so I had to go around them. Waiting at traffic lights on the edge of the city, I saw two poor bullocks break into a run, apparently so as not to hold up the traffic too much. In the background were the large concrete buildings of the modern city.

We headed for Bangalore. Even in 1976 it was still possible to see why it had been called the Garden City of India, and chosen as the locale of E M Forster's novel, *A Passage to India*. Soon it would become the centre of technological development, India's Silicon Valley. There was no evidence of this when we arrived. Frank in his jeep and I with my van went searching to buy bottled gas for our cooking. It was a hopeless quest. Finally, I bought a kerosene stove.

On the way back I tried to squeeze the Land Rover out of a car park when there just wasn't enough room. I knocked over a bike which upturned an urn from which a street vendor was serving sweet coffee. The urn knocked down three motorcycles — one, two, three. A crowd gathered immediately but was fairly friendly; many laughed when they saw what had been done, and who had done it. I escaped with a small payment for damage to the urn. I didn't leave the van during negotiations. I knew I'd been very careless and was lucky to have got out of it so cheaply. When I met the jeep at the next traffic lights as arranged, I said nothing about my contretemps.

We set off from Bangalore for a traveller's hostel some fifty kilometres away. There were no vacancies so we drove on, passing through villages which were lit, sometimes by electric light, sometimes by pressure lamps placed on food stalls. It was both stimulating and nerve-wracking, driving among people, bullocks and donkeys, looking for somewhere to stop for the night. The high-pitched horn on the Land Rover was an essential part of my driving. Then a miracle. We were directed to a 'special place', just out of town and beside a dam. We ate on the verandah and later a car with four Indian men and a woman arrived. They too dined on the verandah and drank beer and whisky — the area was particularly relaxed about the consumption of alcohol. I asked them about the condition of the roads and they convinced us to head up the middle of India through Hyderabad to Nepal, rather than to go to Goa and up the coast.

One of the group said he owned a silk printing plant and we were invited to see it the next day. As a block printer from my occupational therapy days, this was an offer I could not refuse. Sari lengths of fine silk were spread over long tables, and printed using a succession of carved wooden blocks. Firstly the base design was printed then the different colours. I bought a length of printed silk, then ate lunch in the factory: rice cakes with a hot paste and yoghurt, and curry balls made from potatoes, spinach and rice. Meanwhile my silk was being ironed.

After this spicy lunch I watched the batik printing, which was housed in a room with high ceilings. Three girls worked on each length of silk, expertly painting in wax. In the next room girls with thick brushes were filling in spaces with colour; first the light, then the dark shades. I came away with five block-printed scarves plus my length of batik silk, which in total cost me more than five hundred rupees. I wondered how much these labour-intensive products would have cost to produce in Australia. Obviously, too much.

The tenuous camaraderie of our convoy gradually fell into disarray as we headed north for Hyderabad. Frank had decided I needed to be protected, despite the fact that I was really the only experienced traveller, and Norma naturally objected to the lack of attention she was receiving. I thought I detected Stewart's well-meaning but fumbling hands in all of this. Before he left us in Malaysia he must have asked Frank to take care of me, instead of suggesting that I could be of help to them.

Most mornings I was kept waiting for the others to be ready as we set off on long trips up the centre of India. Then one morning I relaxed, and was not ready when the family decided uncharacteristically to leave early. They gave me only five minutes notice of their departure. I said I'd be able to leave with them but that I needed ten minutes within the next hour in which to do my hair, etc. They agreed to this.

As we drove that day, I noted the similarity between the flat countryside and that along the Roebourne to Onslow road in Western Australia's north. We travelled rapidly and by mid-morning were in Hyderabad. But that didn't do us much good as it was impossible to find anything for which we might be looking. So I paid a young man to act as guide. He took us to the tourist office where a very respectful Indian man told me I should meet the Minister for the Export of Hand-woven Materials. It sounded rather impressive but I suspect the minister only wanted to sell me something. The official said we could stay in the city under a corrugated iron shelter which was part of a large building being constructed. There was also free use of taps and an Asian lavatory.

My companions complained about the dirt and the fact that there was a noisy construction site next door. I pointed out how lucky we were to be staying without charge in the centre of Hyderabad with all our requirements provided, and suggested that the building methods were interesting to view close-up. I hoped to inspire them with my joie de vivre, which they were rapidly destroying. I failed miserably. The family was becoming increasingly self-sufficient, and I felt I was one too many. I considered turning off to Bombay and taking a ship to Europe; or perhaps to Fremantle and home. 'It is sad to be made to feel my age — but perhaps salutary,' I recorded in my diary. I was about to turn sixty-five.

At our camp beside the building site, I liked to watch women carrying baskets of small stones on their heads to feed into the cement mixer. These upright women walked barefooted in a slurry of water, stones and concrete. Some of them were living in nearby straw huts with their children and their chickens. At night I could see them cooking. The scene changed on Sunday when their men were not working. I noticed the families were bathing themselves: a woman scrubbed a man with a brush and poured water over him as he crouched on the path.

We left Hyderabad one afternoon and stopped to camp wild at a very good spot, on a track with a view of water. The atmosphere was again pleasant with all of us offering things around, accompanied by lots of thanking. When I woke next morning there were four men and a child standing not far from my van, just watching. They saw that I had no one else in the van and said, 'No Master?' Then they placed their hands together. I did the same and they walked on.

Next morning I left early with the intention of waiting for the others at Nagpur, the geographic centre of India. Mark, the eldest of the four children, came with me and we were speeding along happily until I pulled out to pass a bullock cart. Just at this moment, the bullock turned sharply in front of the van. I could either kill the bullock, and probably those riding on the cart, or go down the steep embankment. Reflexively, I swerved to the right and went down the embankment. The Land Rover ended up propped against a tree at an angle of forty-five degrees. Mark and I inquired of each other whether we were okay and both agreed we were. I was less confident about the state of the van as we clambered out to inspect it. However, apart from a broken exterior rear-vision mirror and an extraordinary shambles inside, things looked all right. I pulled a small tree trunk from under the van and went up to the road and waved my arms at a large truck going past. It stopped, as did the new chassis of a bus, both of which I had overtaken a little earlier.

The truck driver produced a length of heavy rope and linked both the truck and the chassis to the rear of my van. They then combined to pull me back on to the road. But would the van start? It did, first time. I gave the drivers twenty rupees to share, then Mark and I resumed our journey as if nothing had happened. 'You've got nerves of steel,' the fourteen-year-old told me. I liked that.

We went straight on to Nagpur where we found a first class restaurant. We went in and had a blow-out lunch. Then the rest of the family in the jeep caught up, noticed my Land Rover and came in. The next day was my sixty-fifth birthday so I celebrated early by having everyone to lunch. I hadn't been too sure how my offer would be received in view of the recent tensions between us. But they accepted it with apparent enthusiasm — and even thanked me.

As we came out of the restaurant a wedding procession was coming up the street. I joined in, dancing with the band.

By evening I was admitted to hospital with severe laryngitis, and was treated by Dr Mukerjee and Dr Clatterbridge. The family brought me a flask of coffee. Later an old man sold me sweet coffee and spicy food but my throat was too sore to enjoy it. After three days I was out of hospital but still feeling weak.

For the next seven days I stayed in hotel or hostel rooms and just ate rice while I recovered my strength. Then I went back to my usual routine of cooking and sleeping in the van.

Varanasi, the holy city of the Hindus, was our next destination. We drove in twelve- and thirteen-hour stretches with only minimal breaks. It was tiring for me, but I pushed ahead because I wanted to see the unique concentration of temples and the related ceremonies performed along this stretch of the Ganges. Also, I didn't want to seem to be weaker than the rest.

Just before dawn two small boys took us in a slender rowing boat past thousands of people preparing themselves for immersion, which they believed would wash away their sins. In my diary entry I noted: 'The men go in wearing only a loin cloth, and soap themselves all over. The women enter the water in their saris which cling to their bottoms and bosoms in an unflattering way.' Shades of my censorious mother, again.

The boys paddled us past areas reserved for the ceremonial washing and drying of clothes; then past a pile of smoking ashes — a funeral pyre. Stretching up the steep slope of the riverbank were row upon row of temples, embellished with carvings in red and gold. Across the kilometre-wide stretch of water the other bank was starting to shimmer in the early morning sun. It was misty but hundreds of boats and thousands of people were gathering for other ceremonies. As we glided by, the curve of the river was accentuated by the great flights of steps and landing places which lined the bank for several kilometres. I thought of the Thames and the Arno in Florence and the Tiber in Rome: how minuscule they were by comparison. Just beyond the site of all this symbolic ritual, a dead dog was being consumed by a flock of vultures.

We left Varanasi next morning. It had been an enthralling experience but I could not have taken much more of it. The Hindu festival was getting too close for comfort. I could feel the rising excitement. Mrs Gandhi's arrival later that day would add to it. Worshippers were marking their faces — and everyone else's — with red and green dye powders. I didn't like the intense atmosphere, or the smell of the dyes, and I quickly wiped them off.

It was with relief that we headed northwards, and now we were getting so close to the mountainous scenery of Nepal I was not prepared to let anything delay our arrival. Repairs to the Land Rover would have to wait.

However, relations between me and the family were getting worse. I was finding that I often needed a break to keep up my energy after two hours at the wheel, and became cleverer at achieving it, with a number of excuses for stopping. There were occasions, however, on the long drives when I was the one who wanted to go on, while the others begged for a rest. I didn't fail to draw attention to that.

Frank and Norma were undecided about what to do next. I was in no doubt, and had already contacted David, a young American, who wanted to come with me to Kathmandu. He was one of a number of young hitchhikers I'd met earlier and seemed like reliable company. In the end, the family arrived at a decision, and I was pleased to take Frank and the two eldest children to the start of their Himalayan trek. Frank leaned forward to kiss me goodbye. I recoiled and said: 'Please don't.' I couldn't bear the emptiness of such behaviour. It reminded me of the cheek-kissing in my childhood.

Back at the camp site I said goodbye to Norma and the other children. I was free again. I realised how constrained a life I had been living with the family — just driving, eating and sleeping. I should have made the break long ago. I also knew that I needed a companion or two to travel with me at least as far as Teheran so I went to find David, who was waiting at the camp site, as we'd arranged some days earlier.

I drove for the first hour, then David took over. I liked that because we were passing through the most spectacular mountainous scenery of the whole trip. I wanted to be free to enjoy it. Then we actually stopped for lunch. Wonderful. We sat down at a village stall and ate chicken curry and rice which David paid for. Even more wonderful. What a change after the drives extending from dawn to dusk, many of which I didn't record because my enthusiasm for writing fell away as the tensions increased. Even my urticaria, the skin rash which often erupted after days of stress and resentment, did not appear that night.

When we arrived in Kathmandu, David took me to a guest house where I found a very pleasant room in the garden with a hot water shower and a crouch lav. I thanked him and he went on his way.

At the guest house I met Mrs Harrison from New Zealand, who was about my age. She was on an overland bus trip to Europe with twenty-four other passengers. The bus had crashed in Bali, putting her in hospital for a few days. Now all the passengers had been flown to Kathmandu and were waiting for another bus to take them on to London.

We went to dinner that evening at a restaurant called Aunt Jane's Place — up a dirty stairway but moderately clean when we got inside. The food was good — roast buffalo with veg. On a notice-board at the restaurant there was a sign which read: 'American couple want ride to Delhi, Agra, and Kashmir.' I wrote my name and hotel number on the contact sheet. This seemed a good schedule for me to follow. It had not been unusual for me, when asked by a hitcher where I was going, to reply: 'Where are you going?' The final destination was important but not the fine detail about getting there.

Mrs Harrison and I made a number of trips to get good views of the big mountains — but did not succeed. We were forced to agree the Himalayas were for trekkers and climbers. I made another attempt when I left with a group in a Land Rover for Nagakot, from which on a clear day the sun can be seen rising over Mount Everest. We stayed the night in a comfortable cabin just below the peak. Next morning we were driven to the peak before dawn. Alas, it was too cloudy. We saw the sun break through a heavy mist which did not disperse.

Next morning at six I was up and driving myself and saw the Annapurna range against a blue sky with wisps of cloud which gradually disappeared. The tips of the snow mountains tantalised me; I wanted to get close. But I was told there was a fourteen-day trek between me and the snow. Instead, Mrs Harrison and I went to a Kathmandu museum. In the doorway was a carving of a mythical beast about to copulate with a distinctly receptive lady — a recurring image at the entrances to the many art galleries and museums. I regretted that our western inhibitions in sexual matters had been allowed to deny us (and particularly me) such delight. Mrs Harrison gave no indication that she had even noticed the carving.

One of the guest house workers pointed out the Kathmandu garage which serviced Land Rovers, information which was filed for later reference. He then guided me to the Monkey Temple with its glistening gold dome on a large hilltop to the west of the city. I parked the van then walked up a steep slope and some steps to get a better view of the deep valley surrounded by tall hills. Above and behind were the snow-topped giants again — very beautiful, very clear, but not very near.

I went to lunch with two Australian girls I'd just met, and then we drove up a valley and into the hills. The track wound through fields and past small settlements of little brick houses with thatched roofs on the ridges and tops of hills. The snow mountains lay always just beyond reach. I suggested this whole area must be inhabited by Hobbits. One of the Australian girls replied that Tolkien had lived nearby. I hadn't heard that but saw no reason to disagree. All the people we passed on these tracks were carrying something — sticks, bricks, fabrics — in baskets on their backs, with a strap over their foreheads to steady the load. Those who looked at us smiled, with big beaming brown eyes.

On one trip out of Kathmandu my gearbox failed and it was only after a hazardous downhill run that I could engage second gear. I drove slowly back to town. When I contacted the Land Rover people they told me their gear and clutch expert would not be available until the next day — in the meantime to keep driving in second. 'If you can drive down the hill and up here in second then you can drive back to your hotel,' a mechanic told me. Next morning there was another problem. The repair firm did not have the crucial part. I remembered my emergency box of tricks. The necessary spare was there, not one but two of them.

I spent a profitable day in the rear of the van reading, writing aerograms and cards — and guarding the contents, while the mechanics worked on the clutch and gearbox. I tipped them and gave an extra two rupees to an old caretaker because he had sculpted the low green bushes which he pruned frequently so they read as LAND ROVER and ROVER.

I had hurried towards Kathmandu for a number of reasons. One was to meet a Mr Lamichhane, as I carried a letter of introduction from Peggy Buckingham of the Spinners and Weavers Guild of Western Australia. I asked the manager of the Land Rover garage if he knew Mr Lamichhane. 'Yes,' he said, 'we were at college together. I can send my man with you to show you where he lives.' Mrs Lamichhane was home when I called. Mr L came a little later and showed me a photograph taken at a conference of weavers, called the Sydney Summit. Peggy and many of my spinning and weaving friends were featured in it. During dinner I was invited to spend the night in my Land Rover parked in their garden.

So That Was the Khyber Pass

I had a particular personal reason for wanting to reach Nepal. This was as close to Tibet as I was ever likely to get. My father had always spoken of my gipsy heritage which he claimed came through my Hungarian grandmother. I was told of gipsy tribes coming into Europe from Tibet, and that this explained my brother Raymond's slightly sloping eyes. Dink, predictably, had every confidence in the accuracy of his claim, although those who would be better informed had their doubts.

I observed some Tibetan culture when I drove with the two Australian girls to Patan, an older city than Kathmandu with as many temples and a number of Tibetan monasteries. Stupendous. But more interesting for me were the beautiful knotted carpets made at the Tibetan refugee village. I went to find the factory, which looked like a large cow shed, but by then it was 11.55 am and lunch was from twelve to one. So I crossed the road and went to a dirty looking place with the sign RESTAURANT outside. It was full of flies so I backed off and ate cheese and biscuits and tangerines in the van.

I frequently came across the same hitchhikers in different towns, particularly around Nepal. For instance, when David left me I drove out of Nepal with Vincent, the engaging son of a Welsh farmer who was returning to help with the harvest, and his girlfriend Bev. I can't remember where I picked them up on the first occasion, or the second. I met them again at Kathmandu. They travelled with me over the next few weeks, with Vincent and Bev staying in cheap hotels and me sleeping in the car park outside.

En route to Pakistan, we drove through Delhi, Lucknow and Agra. Suitable camp sites or parking areas were becoming difficult to find and I had to park in the streets, sometimes in the main street. Luckily I usually managed this without attracting unwelcome attention. The Land Rover looked official and male and I called it The Protector: my protector that is. From time to time I could see the large carved wheels of the buffalo carts grinding past my side window. They were so large I could see only a small segment at a time.

While in bed eating my breakfast I'd watch the shops open. First, up would go the shutters which covered the top half of the entrance; out would come a head. Then down would come two or three boards and the shopkeeper would step into the street. Trestles were erected and the boarding from the shop front became the table top. Soon it was covered with food or goods.

In Delhi I was fascinated by some of the remnants of the British Raj. I went to a *son et lumiére* at the Red Fort which was, as my diary put it, 'a little anti-British which annoyed me.' My good mood returned later when I came across a large iron pillar which seemed to be attracting a number of Indians to it. They told me to put my arms behind my back, and reach around the pillar, and make my fingers meet. That I could do this was apparently most unusual. My arms were considerably longer than most. The crowd cheered and seemed to agree that I'd be a lucky woman.

We moved on to Chandigarh, which had been designed by Le Corbusier with wide roads and spacious roundabouts. But few residents had cars and there was little public transport. It had been designed as a symbol of Nehru's modern optimistic India but it looked unkempt and forlorn when I was there. Despite this the city had a strong fan in Gordon Stephenson who called it Le Corbusier's great masterpiece of town design. Then to Lucknow, and Agra where I became engrossed with the Taj Mahal and made several visits. I wrote a great deal after these visits but it was not possible to capture the scope and elegance of the shimmering edifice itself.

We were heading for Srinagar, the capital of Kashmir. The last day of my drive there extended from seven in the morning to six at night, but I wasn't tired. The prospect of staying there ruled out exhaustion. We — Vincent and Bev were still with me — were caught up in an Indian army convoy in this troubled part of the land, then further delayed at a point where the road had subsided, leaving a chillingly long drop down the face of the mountain. But next morning I was up at six and drove around the lake at Srinagar to take in the panorama of the snow mountains in the morning sun. I went back to bed for my breakfast, and to watch the reflections in the dimly lit lake.

A few fishermen in elegantly shaped boats were breaking the surface here and there with their circular nets. One boat put ashore near where I was parked. A young woman with a healthy round face and dark eyes came up to me and held out a rather dirty baby. The child reached out for the one rupee note which I passed across unwillingly. 'You are making a beggar of the boy,' I told the mother, quite unintelligibly of course. I decided I had no right to say this. I went back to bed to eat my breakfast and consider how lucky I was to be doing what I liked to do so much.

I said goodbye to India at Wagah on the border with Pakistan. I looked back on two months of conflicting impressions. I'd been horrified by dirty children and fly-ridden restaurants yet relished spicy curries and breads purchased from grubby village stalls. My diaries carried on about a lack of hygiene and general disorder while I made straight for the chaotic market areas of any city I visited. I had objected to the way the Indians stared at me while I studied them through my binoculars at a greater distance.

The picture was not all paradox. I had also seen a lot of Indian art in galleries and museums, though I lacked the knowledge or experience to appreciate it. I did, however, delight in the frank celebration of sex displayed in the carvings in temples and galleries, although again, I lacked the first-hand experience to appreciate some of the finer detail.

In Lahore we found a hotel for Vincent and Bev while I stayed in the hubbub of the car park: horses trotting, carts being pushed, people going by. But no one disturbed me or the van. I had decided at this point that there was no use being upset at not being able to do a great deal of sight-seeing. Vincent was in a hurry to get home and help get the crop in and I needed company as far as Teheran so I had to put up with it. At least we stopped for meals, so I didn't get too hungry or tired. Anyway, I told myself, I was becoming sated after the spectacular scenery of the previous weeks.

In Rawalpindi I needed to find the Afghan Embassy so that I could get a visa for the next stage of the trip. We were taken there by a young Malaysian student who came to our assistance when we were obviously lost among the booths and stalls and winding, crowded alleyways.

We stopped at a youth hostel set in a beautiful garden of roses and snapdragons. Among the flowers I met a super man. He was very handsome with extraordinarily dark eyes, separated by a long and slender nose. His hat was quite marvellous: soft camel-hair with a rolled brim. He lived on the Khyber Pass and my sense of an oncoming adventure flared when I discovered that he made guns to sell to warring groups. He carried a watch which seemed to say the hours and something like 'Allahhhhhh Hail Mary,' but probably didn't. He had come to see his friend the gardener, who was by contrast an unkempt man. The super man said it was time for prayers and chanted continuously something like 'Allah … OOOOH,' while he began to mesmerise me, pleasantly.

Sadly, it was the gardener not 'superman' who came to my van later, and gently placed his hands on my head. While he held it — quite nicely it must be said — he kept saying, 'One hour in the sun will make your head ache.' Or something like that. I thanked him for his attention, placed a one rupee note in his hand, and said sharply, 'Now buzz off! Goodbye!' This was a technique I'd perfected in Naples.

In Peshawar, I woke early and breakfasted surrounded by antirrhinum of all colours. In bed, with the van doors open, I felt as if I was sleeping in the garden itself. The breakfast and washing up routine I had developed into a fine art, and could do it comfortably while remaining in bed. Then I spread some Pears soap over my face and rinsed it off, combed my hair and put it up, and applied a little make-up. I was then ready to set off with Vincent and Bev for the north-west frontier, full of excitement mixed with a touch of fear.

We had gone only fifteen kilometres when we were stopped at a rope stretched across the road at the fort of Jamrud. Behind the rope were Pakistani soldiers carrying rifles. Go back, we were told by a pleasant enough soldier, try again tomorrow. It would be over by then. He did not say what 'it' might have been and we did not find out. Next day we travelled the stony plains again, in convoy now, with Dutch, Swedish and French groups in vans, along with the family in their jeep who had accompanied me on the earlier legs of the trip. There was no rope to stop us this time.

We started climbing on a very good road which wound up around limestone and shale cliffs then came down steeply in a series of zigzags until the road ran beside a racing river. I still couldn't help feeling that this was very wild territory, particularly when I saw the forts, perforated with slits from which I could imagine rifles pointing, along the commanding heights above the roadway. I almost expected to hear shots. About fifty kilometres along there was a sign in English saying we were coming to the narrowest point on the Pass, where there was only a four-metre gap between the cliff walls. A little further on cars, vans and buses waited to be signed out of Pakistan. I talked with three men who were travelling to Europe in a double-decker bus and it was only then that I realised I had come through the Khyber Pass. I was flabbergasted. So *that* was *it*? I had expected to climb far higher, on far more precarious roads. We travelled the remaining two hundred and forty kilometres to Kabul on a wide Russian-built road bordered by sheoaks, and trees resembling bottlebrushes and gums — a beautiful stretch of country quite unlike the rough, dangerous journey I had anticipated.

Along the way we passed patched nomad tents pitched in the more open areas. There were women in colourful dresses, sheep, and children standing half in and half out of the tents. The camels sat and waited. I couldn't help staring at the women and their children and tried to imagine what their lives might be like. Through the opening of some of the tents I could see bundles of clothing or bedding piled as though they were ready to be thrown up on a camel's back at a moment's notice. That gave me a clue: these were not settled housewives like my woman in *String Bags*.

I drove to the Kabul Land Rover repair centre early the next morning for a service, and enjoyed being the only woman among all those handsome Afghan men. The one who wrote up the job cards was particularly good looking, with appealing touches of silver grey at the temples, and wearing a red polo-neck sweater. I rested in the back to keep an eye on my possessions, indulged myself in a little fantasy and wrote letters while the mechanics completed their tasks.

During a week in Kabul, I ate steak in a restaurant which had been the king's palace; went to colourful rug markets; made a number of visits to Paghman now crumbling and covered with weeds but once the king's symbol of his efforts to Europeanise his country; and stopped frequently to gaze at the stone-coloured houses clinging to the steep rocky hills. What would it be like to live up there, I wondered, and used my binoculars to get some idea. There seemed to be electricity but I wondered about drainage. I had no indication of the turmoil which would follow in this country.

After a week Kabul was losing its appeal. I felt the urge to keep on travelling, with Kandahar, five hundred kilometres away, the next stop. We arrived there in the evening after having stopped to assist another Land Rover with a wobbling wheel, loaning them one of my spares.

'Kathmandu, Kashmir, Kabul, and Kandahar,' I wrote to Lillian and Stephen, in an alliterative moment. 'All places which sounded so far away and so exciting. Now, not only have I seen them, but have driven my own Land Rover to them and have passed through the most beautiful scenery on the way. Every day seems better than the one before.'

Vincent, Bev and I had a marvellous farewell dinner in a tent at Herat on the Afghan border, before they left on a bus. They decided we were travelling too slowly. This was good. Now I felt free to explore the amazing mosques, minarets, and mud houses in this quite unmodernised city.

As I left, I again ignored the wisdom of the road, and picked up Paul and Joyce. Paul soon showed himself to be a talented cook, with a particular skill with vegetables bought from stalls. He excelled himself with the first dinner in his tent. The conversation turned out to be as rich as the meal — Rembrandt, Dali, gawkers in galleries, and the defining characteristics of bad art.

We were now driving towards the Caspian Sea through mountainous country which gradually gave way to thickly wooded hills and fertile valleys. The flat-topped mud houses were replaced by cottages with trees around them. The shops in towns had glass windows, rather than being open stalls. Women were still enveloped in their sheet-like garments, but now their faces were showing. And, beneath the full length robes, smart shoes and trousers could sometimes be glimpsed. This was no longer traditional Asia.

We had planned to celebrate our arrival at the Caspian Sea by camping on the beach, taking in the sun and with a special meal in the evening. Instead, it was grey, raining, and cold. We searched in the rain for a hotel where Paul and Joyce might stay and were eventually directed to a quite grand place where, amazingly, we were given permission to cook the vegetables in the room on the Primus cooker. I cooked the meat in my van

Cécile with fellow travellers.

and brought it in when ready. However, the Iranian hotel-keeper was worried about an older woman sleeping in a van in his hotel car park on a cold and rainy night, and relaxed only after I'd taken him to see the van and inspect its furnishings.

On departing Paul insisted on driving. The fact that it was my van and he was a hitcher didn't seem to worry him or, surprisingly, me. His aim was to cover the distance quickly. He brought the van over the hills, through the spectacular entrance into Teheran, and continued driving in the heavy traffic there. I realised days later that my not driving was bad for me. I had become afraid of the traffic, in large part because Paul drove like most men — with the constant necessity of passing everything and demanding the right of way. I began to have dreams, prompted I think by this continued nerve-wracking driving, which combined many of the most scary elements of my travels in the mountains. Chased by a buffalo and dray, I drove onto a bridge to escape. But the bridge had a hole in the decking. Half the van was suspended over the hole. I was in that half: my sister and my cousin were in the other. I shouted to them to save me as I felt I was about to fall into the seemingly bottomless ravine.

The Dangerous Turk

When we reached Ankara in Turkey, Paul and Joyce took a bus. Alone and free again, I celebrated by driving all over the city for most of the day. I felt all right again: not at all fearful at the wheel, despite the chaotic traffic. That night I met Barbara, who worked in the Australian Embassy, at a party at the Aussie Club. I had been thinking I might park outside the embassy. Barbara said it would be better to park outside her flat and use her facilities. I was pleased to have such a good offer.

Lunching the next day with an embassy official and his wife I met their nephew Nicholas and his companion Eve, who had hitched from Scotland and were looking for a ride back. I went out with them and we ate goat-meat kebabs and discussed rules — like no smoking in the van. They travelled light, with only one rucksack between them, and told me they slept out on the ground and in caves and didn't eat much. Lest there be any misunderstanding, I told them I was not responsible for food or shelter, only the ride. I was becoming wary of my young passengers. I didn't want to lose control of my van or spend time arguing. So I arranged a short trip to see if we were too incompatible: it didn't seem so, and we left for Goreme the following day.

My companions must have been in their early twenties. They had been travelling together since leaving school about five years earlier. It seemed to me they had run out of conversation over their time together — apart from arguments. They talked to me at length, separately, about their problems. When they were together they combined to tell me how to behave and how not be behave, how to shop with more cunning bargaining, and generally gave the impression they thought I was daft. I was prepared to concede on the final point.

We stopped at the vividly painted churches carved out of the soft rock at Goreme, and the Buried City where, apparently, some two thousand people had lived underground in a complex arrangement of chambers, spread over several levels. These caves were dug during a time of religious persecution, and I tried to imagine where the excavated stone might have been hidden. I couldn't imagine. Later, camping wild in a muddy lane, two young men came by and gave us cherries. I would have been frightened if I'd been alone as I had developed a stereotype of the Dangerous Turk which was not unlike my earlier view of the Dangerous Moroccan.

Nicholas and Eve sometimes slept on a groundsheet, half way under the van to avoid the dew. Other times I could hear men and horses break stride when my passengers bedded down across one of the narrow lanes. Sometimes they slept in building sites, in partially completed apartments that occasionally had working bathrooms, which I also used.

We went over the mountains and the weather grew warmer. It was June and suddenly it was summer. I celebrated by replacing my jersey with a blouse. We couldn't be far now from the Mediterranean and my excitement was growing. What a journey! It was almost done now, and I had done it. I realised how important it was to know what I wanted, to make careful preparations, and to grasp every opportunity to achieve such a goal. The preparation of the past four years, of living on the breadline, of camping free wherever possible, even the decision to travel in convoy with the family, for all the arguments, had brought me here.

And then the clear azure sea, glinting in the sunlight, came into view: the Mediterranean, the cradle of my civilisation. I found a camp site on the beach and went for a swim. We slowly made our way around the lovely coast with its succession of promontories and small bays. My beloved breakfasts in bed camped beneath pines or olive trees, rear doors open and listening to the waves; midday swims and, once, hours spent lying on the beach in what my diary coyly calls 'my nuddlings'. There seemed to be no one around except lizards and they were fully occupied catching flies. Nicholas and Eve had walked to a nearby village to buy bread and would be away for much of the day: a relief, since they were annoying me again with their indications that I was so daft that I couldn't read the dials on the instrument panel of the Land Rover which I had driven half-way around the world. But we continued to be civil.

At Aspendos we inspected a beautiful old Roman theatre, the tiers of which rose up in a most visually satisfying way. Each row started close to the next then opened out like a fan. Nicholas and Eve and I sat in different sections and drank in the scene. They slept in the theatre and offered to carry my bed in so that I could too. I declined and remained in my van, outside. At Side I spent days on the beach with a backdrop of huge fallen stones from Greek and then Roman buildings: great lovely arches with the cut stones still in position and, within, a large open area with fluted columns and shaped alcoves still standing. I couldn't help looking about for a piece small enough to steal but they were all too big. I observed, somewhat obliquely, in my diary: 'No wonder Lord Elgin took the stones of the Parthenon frieze away. They were probably all lying around neglected and broken and likely to be burnt for lime ...'

These were weeks of camping wild on rural tracks where a tractor might pass by with the driver wondering at our presence; on beaches where flocks of sheep or goats might pass on their way home. Then there were the Turkish baths at Bursa, the lovely town built on the foothills of Mount Olympus of Mysia. The women's baths here were very large and very hot, and a number of rituals were apparently taking place. I had my hair washed by a fellow naked bather, while a bride-to-be was being closely examined by representatives of her family and that of her fiancé to check, I presume, that her virginity was intact.

Taking a shower, on the road.

At Bergama, the Roman part of the old city of Pergamon, I explored alone. Nicholas and Eve had gone to visit a friend. I examined the ancient theatre which was partially covered with earth. Climbing the steps of the temple I found two small pieces of marble which I studied with a view to theft. But they had not been carved so I replaced them. I went on to the Aesculapion, the old Roman therapeutic centre with its ruins of hot baths, sacred pools and waterways. Exhausted by my explorations I sat under an olive tree, ate my lunch, and went to sleep.

When I woke I was still alone. I walked up an ancient walled street which had been exposed in an archaeological dig and I was examining the base of a marble column when a young man in an orange shirt hurried towards me. He said furtively, 'Fish, fish, Turkish cure,' or something like that. It dawned on me, more slowly than it should have, that I was in a fix. He forced me against a wall, and pushed my legs apart. In a few moments of (his) fevered activity he'd had his satisfaction, without penetration I happily note. My would-be rapist then helped me up and dusted me off. In his hand was a number of bank notes which he was obviously offering me: naturally I refused. Then he left with his head bowed and apparently bewildered. I was too. At sixty-five I was still oblivious of sexual details like premature ejaculation. When Nicholas and Eve met me later I said nothing about the assault. I thought I'd been lucky again — and left it at that.

In Istanbul we were immersed in wonderful mosques, castles

and palaces. The blue tiles on the walls which give the Blue Mosque its name went straight to my head. It was the same with the blue and white china in the palace. The courtyard of the palace also provided me with a peaceful parking space, with no fees. I would never have known that I could camp here if a policeman who pulled in next to me hadn't passed on the tip.

I was there the next night as well after a concert in a Byzantine church and dinner with a group from Hamburg who wanted to tell me that I could look like a statue which had come to life. They had seen me at Ephesus when I was walking with a sunshade, in a long dress with sleeves. Using the sunshade, I had hidden my face from the tourists bustling about there. It was a considerable coincidence that at that very time they had seen me striding

Cécile, 'like a statue'.

along, I was in fact thinking I *was* a statue. The Germans took me to a fish restaurant on the Bosphorus where the deliciously fresh fish was grilled on a rocking boat.

Our last days of five interesting weeks in Turkey were spent at a camping site fifteen kilometres from the city. The site was full of tents belonging to Turkish families who seemed to have settled in for the summer, complete with cupboards, tables and comfortable chairs. We left these impressive

Turkish families and drove across the Bosphorus and into Greece. It was a significant moment. I was back in Europe and my journey was virtually over. I wanted to stop on the bridge and drop to my knees to thank the guardian powers for having looked after me. I can't deny that I also rather admired myself for succeeding. The rest of the way would be easy. I knew Europe and travelling had become almost routine.

In Thessalonika I began looking for a Professor Minopoulis who I hoped would unlock for me the secret of bronze casting which had intrigued me since my first trip to Delphi. Where did the legs of the statue end and the solid mass begin? Or was it all solid? An American approaching from the other side had similar questions, but no answer. I found Professor Minopoulis but he spoke no English and I no Greek, and we had to get a young woman to interpret. I examined some of the professor's casts and he gave me the address of a foundry in Athens where they poured bronze, and told me where I could take a short course in casting. I noted that on my increasing list of things I'd like to do in the future. And the answer to the question? It depends ...

We crossed into Yugoslavia and decided to risk stopping the night in a remote parking area. Pine-covered mountain slopes were lit by a full moon; slight wisps of mist floating in the valley turned silver in the moonlight and glow worms added their contribution to the light show. We camped undisturbed then drove through further majesty until we reached the Adriatic at Petrovac. For the next two nights we chose camp sites near groves of trees or on small coves, flagrantly ignoring the NO CAMPING signs. We were sent packing from both sites after visits by police at three in the morning. On the second visit I used extensive sign language to convince the elder policeman not to be mean and wake Nicholas and Eve, who were sleeping, wrapped in my Galashiels rugs, half under the van. I pointed to my watch, indicating we'd be moving on shortly and he relented but returned an hour later just to make sure we were on our way. We'd had our last free camping spot.

Cécile in a sculpture park.

At Split, Nicholas and Eve went into the village and, as I half thought and half hoped, they discovered there was a bus next morning which would take them north where they would have a better chance of hitching than here on the Adriatic coast. Their hippy, patched and grubby appearance did not seem to go down well in Yugoslavia. So we had a pleasant evening meal and a good bottle of wine to terminate our five, sometimes turbulent, weeks travelling together.

It was a relief to be on the road and alone again; to depart or stay as I wished. I did not need to cover the ground quickly. The Protector and I could stop, and I would pour myself a gin and tonic while frying my dinner of onions, cucumber, smoked bacon and beans. Then another gin and tonic while I consumed what I thought was my delicious cooking before sleeping.

Next morning I passed men and women, solo and in pairs, hitching. I resisted the temptation to stop and pick them up: it was so wonderful being alone. Then a black-bearded man of about twenty-five held his hands up in supplication. Had there been an easy place to stop I would have relented, and so I did soon after when I stopped for another man of about the same age. We talked a great deal. He came from a family of ten and was a teacher of the handicapped. He and a friend had started a special school in an old house with a single pupil. They now had forty pupils. We had lunch together, then an evening meal in a field dotted with beehives, and drank a bottle of white wine.

Next day we stopped at a castle on the Austrian border, thick with atmosphere. With permission this time, I parked beside an old and very large tree. While I slept in the van the teacher rugged up under the tree. Next morning there was a bus load of 'oldies' to view the castle, but firstly to shake my hand and study my bed, fridge and cooker.

In Holland visiting my cousin, I also went to Gouda to call on British Leyland to have the van oil changed. They said that I'd have to take it to Rotterdam. They made the booking for me, explaining over the phone that I'd come overland from Australia, that I'd last had a check at Izmir in Turkey, and that I was over sixty-five and travelling alone. Could they do it that day? The question was never answered.

A young man presented himself and said he was 'Publicity'. He'd heard the phone call and would I mind being photographed with my Land Rover for the company magazine. He took me up to his office. It was all very grand and there I was in my dirty trousers and my sheepskin jersey, not very clean at all. While I was telling him of my travels the Land Rover was driven around the back for an instant oil change and inspection. Then the publicity man asked if I'd mind talking to a reporter from the *Daily Telegraf*. The reporter arrived and during the interview and the taking of photographs, a luncheon of very fine sandwiches appeared. Sadly I was so busy talking that I couldn't eat much, but the rest went into a bag for my dinner.

The resulting story appeared under the headline:

RESPECT FOR GREY HAIRS TAKES AN ELDERLY LADY SAFELY AROUND THE WORLD.

Well, half-way around. The story called me an 'adventurous English lady' and said:

> The Land Rover is her hotel because she lives, eats and sleeps in the car which has been specially modified for this purpose. In her travels Mrs Dorward is not often alone as she enjoys picking up hitch hikers, who sometimes do the cooking for her. She does her shopping along the way whenever she passes a market.

On 17 August 1976 I arrived at the car ferry at Dunkirk. I had just enough money for my ticket. The past seven months began to seem like a dream In fact it had seemed like that since I crossed the Bosphorus.

Life Eight
Acting My Age!

A Landholder in Provence

Driving became tiring as my total mileage and my age increased while visiting friends, galleries, and just dordling. I thought about this when in 1983 I was walking along a Moroccan beach at Essauoira, about three hundred and fifty kilometres north of Marrakesh. A board rider surfed ashore almost next to me. 'You're Cécile aren't you?' the young man inquired. I agreed I was, then asked who he was. 'I met you in Afghanistan,' he said. We talked and I mentioned that I was thinking of cutting back on my travelling. At seventy-two it was becoming something of an endurance test. I wondered if I should buy a smaller van and restrict my travels, or whether I could afford to get power steering fitted.

The surfer told me of a lovely part of Provence called the Domaine des Canebières, and suggested it would be a good resting place for me between trips. The French use the word *domaine* as we use estate: this seemed not to be the usual housing estate, however, but a vast camping estate.

A year or so later I was there to see for myself. I found a large spread of wooded country stretching over four hills, between Le Muy and Fréjus on the French Riviera. Views across the forest of pines were stunning. Halfway down the steep hill was a tiny 'ant trail' — the road which led to Ste Maxime and the Mediterranean, just twelve kilometres away. Beyond the trees I could see the Massif des Maurés and Estérel mountain ranges. What a wonderful place, I

At the Domaine des Canebières, with a gin and tonic.

thought; then, more particularly, what a wonderful place to drink a gin and tonic, sitting alone among the trees. I tried it and it was. I was not alone, however. There were hundreds of similar small plots with unobtrusive portable dwellings on them. The land had been so sensitively divided that only an occasional tip of a roof could be seen.

This was an area with an exciting recent history which centred on Freddie Brown, the cavalier son of a Quebecan trapper with Scottish origins. Before World War Two Freddie Brown was running a small radio shop in Algiers and building a number of covert radio stations in Provence which, he thought, 'may come in handy some time.' Which they did; and quickly. With the fall of France, Freddie Brown became 'Tommy 20' and made more than twenty daring parachute jumps into the area around the Domaine to support the French Resistance fighters. The Gestapo put a very large price on his head but, with some help from Freddie, they placed the wrong head on the 'wanted dead-or-alive' ads. As a gesture of gratitude for this dangerous wartime work, a French countess who had also been a member of the Resistance gave Freddie five hundred hectares of the hill country in Provence, into which he had jumped so many times. Freddie divided his land in a way which allowed people to have a relatively cheap plot of land, but disallowed any development which might destroy the area's wonderful sense of isolation.

On my first visit to the Domaine des Canebières, I met Harry Poole, a retired defence scientist, originally from Perth, who owned a number of plots. He and his wife Mariel had been students at the University of Western Australia in the twenties when that institution had been housed in a collection of corrugated iron and weatherboard buildings in the centre of Perth. The Pooles invited me to park on one of their plots which had an old caravan on it. It was just a short walk from the Pooles' place to 'Piccadilly Circus', so-called because of the number of English people living close by.

I bought quite cheaply lot number 597. This would be much better than renting a flat in Greece during the coldest months, in the years I didn't fly back to Perth. There was more to my purchase, however, than an enchantment with the view and the associated peace and quiet. There was an economic imperative: I was short of money. I'd never had much while travelling but things were really tight now. Because I was constantly moving, I had never received an Australian pension although I'd paid Australian taxes. My British pension was only five pounds a week, and my tenants at twenty-seven Deane Street were impecunious artists and students so I charged them only half the going rent. After a successful exhibition, my artist friend Cliff Jones, on behalf of all the tenants, wrote to say they wanted to pay more rent. The gesture, while touching, did not make a big difference. I needed a proper pension and the only way someone continually on the move — like me — could qualify for a full pension was to own a property in an EEC country. The plot on the Domaine was my opportunity, and I took it eagerly.

I was intrigued when I found that each plot featured the wonderfully French *cabinet sanitaire*. It was a curious forerunner of the corrugated concrete public toilets of today: just an S-shaped sheet of corrugated fibreglass with a small WC in one curve and a shower in the other. There were two doors. The plumbing was basic and self-contained: a hose connected to a tap with a link to a gas bottle. I didn't ask about the drainage.

Life was simple and very enjoyable. There was a permanent holiday atmosphere, with people coming and going. There was also a feeling of remoteness — which must have been a major attraction for a wartime flier wanting to land unnoticed. The nearest town to the Domaine was Le Muy, situated unspoilt on the plains between the nearby mountain chains and happily clear of the motorway which runs along the back of the French Riviera.

Le Muy had a lovely atmosphere with its crumbling old stonework, peeling paint and rusting ironwork, its sixteenth century church and fifteenth century birdcage bell tower. I could visit the church when I came to withdraw money from my bank which was down a narrow lane opposite. The bank had a dark glass door set in the ancient stone wall, which provided access only as far as the lobby. It was necessary for one of the tellers to release the lock on the inner door before I could enter the banking chamber. Once inside I was welcomed like an old friend, which over the years I became. I got to know about their children as the bank staff did not change frequently, as they seem to in Australia.

Le Muy had the usual French village square with the mandatory plane trees, dappled light and a beautiful statue. It lacked the variety of colour and texture of my favourite Italian villages but it was a pleasant place in which to wait for the completion of the washing cycle at the laundrette; or for Toto, the jovial, stereotypically French mechanic with black hair and a substantial drooping moustache, to service my Land Rover.

On Thursdays and Sundays the village square became a colourful, noisy market, selling foods, crafts and clothes. It specialised in locally produced vegetables — tomatoes, aubergines, courgettes, squash, peas and beans, onions and leeks, potatoes, mushrooms, and even truffles; also small crisp apples, small dried figs and delicious black cherries which grew on the hillsides.

This was an area where the residents showed an extraordinary interest in growing, cooking, eating, and talking very earnestly about food which was both elegant and rich in taste. I liked eating good food but I was not a cook, even after buying from a second-hand bookshop a cheap copy of the nineteenth century classic, *Larousse Gastronomique*. My diary has entries like: 'Fried two fresh fish with potatoes and onions, in the van. Delicious' or 'Restaurants closed so opened some tins. Tasty.' They demonstrate my fairly prosaic approach to food preparation.

Not so at the impressive La Bastide des Moins where my friends and I arrived one lunchtime in the European summer of 1987 after a short trip to the coast from the Domaine. We were famished — but not properly dressed. This was a restaurant where hotel guests ate, and everyone dressed accordingly. We had been down at the beach. Still, the waiters sat us down without hesitation, then tried to explain the menu. The point was that there was no menu, but we took some time to grasp this. Everything to do with eating in France is so organised that we expected to see a highly detailed menu as we stepped through the door. After a time of indecision we decided to help ourselves from the extraordinary collection of hors d'oeuvres spread along ten metres of counter — salads, *saucissons*, pickled vegetables, various olives, anchovies, squid, octopus, oysters, and lots more.

We were still feasting when a couple came over to our table. They had noticed our difficulty with the notion of a no-menu-menu and wanted to be sure we understood the system. They were French but had lived in Canada, and confirmed in English that we had stumbled on the correct protocol. A second course — we gasped — would be sliced from a herbed lamb, roasting on a spit behind a screen, and served with small French beans and fungi from the forest. We also discovered we could help ourselves to as much wine as we liked from what looked like beer taps spaced along the counter.

By now the whole restaurant was part of the event — my poor hearing meant that any conversation had to be conducted at a high decibel level — and everyone became very friendly. Then in walked the archetypal French chef, huge and smiling, but with a presence which hinted that he would stand for no nonsense. The place broke up with cries of 'Oo-la-la' etc. While we celebrated, everyone around us wanted to talk. So much fun and quite unplanned!

The restaurant served bulk wines only slightly superior to those which I could purchase for day-to-day use. I'd go to the *caves* (cellars), where the cooperative winemaker for our district operated. I'd fill my five-litre plastic jerry cans with red, white or pink, depending on the prevailing temperatures. It came from pumps, just like getting petrol for the van. While I was filling my containers, a local farmer might arrive on an old and spluttering tractor, hauling a trailer fitted with a rusty wire cage filled with grapes. The farmers knew which variety, or rather colour of grape, would be accepted on a particular day. Occasionally, the tractor would be shiny and the driver neatly dressed, which signified a businessman-farmer from Nice or St Tropez. Either way, the grapes would go straight into the crusher.

I'd take back these inexpensive but excellent table wines which I'd decant into my collection of empties, which would have included a number of gin bottles. This wine provided the catalyst for many an afternoon spent in the sun, sitting with friends and neighbours at a laminex table outside my demountable home. The table, as with much of my furniture, came courtesy of the Le Muy rubbish tip.

The Domaine was a convenient starting point for visits to friends or galleries throughout Europe and Britain; or just to head off almost at

Cécile and a young friend outside her demountable home on the Domaine.

random. I could for example visit Paris. Paris didn't attract me as the French provinces did, but I still loved parking free outside the Louvre during weekends. I'd race in to see if *La Victoire* was still on the Grand Stairway: she was the sister of Nike, one of my Olympian friends. After that I'd sleep outside in the van, with the 'kitchen window' open for ventilation.

One Saturday night I woke after midnight to the sound of the mozzie net over the kitchen window being pulled away. A pale face was peering in, and a hand was reaching for my kettle. I roared like a lion and the intruder disappeared with the sound of rapidly retreating footsteps. I secured the window and went back to sleep.

In 1989 when I was seventy-eight, I went to meet Lillian and Stephen for a sailing holiday in Greece. I went the long way, via Taunton in Somerset where I stayed for two weeks with my old interior decorating colleague Hilary, who was now totally blind. We went for walks, arm in arm as we used to do on the ice rink fifty years earlier.

In Greece I met up with my friends, the Lawsons, who owned five or six hire yachts. The aim of the trip was to sail the whole flotilla around the Greek islands for a fortnight, stopping at a different island each night. Before we started there was a brief

ceremony when my van was awarded the status of 'honorary boat' by the Lawsons. It was an acknowledgement that the Land Rover had for me assumed the role previously filled by the *Phosphorus*, although I hadn't thought of it that way before.

The plan was that during the day we'd

land on any island we wished, have picnic lunches, and swim in the navy blue water when we were sufficiently far out not to need bathers. Each evening we would end up at a taverna on some island designated beforehand.

Lillian and Stephen joined us at Aegina. I was so excited I could scarcely move towards them let alone speak. I had been working on this sailing holiday for years. We went with the Lawsons to a taverna, where everyone but us was Greek, and had a wonderful meal — grilled octopus with salad and chips. Back at our yacht, we prepared to leave the next day. I slept in the forward bunk while Lillian and Stephen slept in the body of the yacht. In the mornings they would bring me my breakfast in bed. On the first afternoon we had sailed no more than halfway to Poros before a gale struck. We had to lower the sail and motor the rest of the way — cold, wet and exhilarating. Thereafter it was clear seas and blue skies, enthusiastic talking and eating and drinking. It was everything a yachting holiday should be.

Back Home

When the snow fell on the mountains and the gales hit the Riviera and the nineteen eighties became the nineties I often flew home, initially to twenty-seven Deane Street, to hot weather, and the sea breeze blowing through my front door (which incidentally was at the side of the house). I was always delighted to see that my garden still attracted a considerable range of birds; particularly the fig and mulberry trees which were heavy with fruit.

Sometimes I would find, installed in Hamersley Lodge, a traveller I'd met somewhere around the world. I was accustomed to giving notes to people on the road asking Cliff Jones to 'Please accommodate David (or whomever) in HL if possible. Twenty dollars a week for power and water, if possible.'

Flora Stephenson had died in 1979 and through the eighties Gordon would call to take me swimming most mornings while I was at Deane Street. My first swim of an Australian summer, out past the Cottesloe pylon, was always an exciting event. Once in the deeper water I slipped out of my bathers and slung them over my arm, feeling more at ease than I ever had overseas. I came away from visits to the beach with Gordon feeling rejuvenated, as if I'd absorbed some of his excess of energy. With Stewart I felt the opposite, as though I was being drained.

Into the mid-eighties I used a lot of energy vacillating between wanting to sell and to keep number twenty-seven. Such indecision was unusual for me: I often acted rapidly and on impulse. The decision largely rested on my future health, about which I could know nothing. How long would I remain sufficiently healthy to enjoy the active lifestyle I led from number twenty-seven? And, if I sold it now, would I have enough money to buy a unit where care was available *and* still keep travelling? It was costing me about the equivalent of a hundred and fifty to two hundred dollars a week in today's value to travel, and I could afford that for only three more years without selling the house. These were muddling questions with too many unknowns. I tried not to think about them. However, I disapproved of older people who had not prepared for this stage of their life. That's the one thing about Stewart I admired: years earlier he had moved into a unit at the Salvation Army Village in a Perth suburb.

It was Stewart who advised me to put number twenty-seven on the market. I hesitated because this was a time of demolition and the building of units. Twenty-seven with its large block looked a likely target for the bulldozer. This was a time of turmoil for me and my tenants. None of them wanted twenty-seven to be sold. There were bitter arguments among the 'family' there. In the midst of these arguments I wrote to Cliff from Hamersley Lodge, thirty metres from the main house:

> I realise only too well how venomous I am when angry.
> It makes me ill. And it probably makes other people ill.
> I hate myself for this behaviour and am ready to be told
> to keep away altogether.

I stopped vacillating and sold the house in 1985. I bought my

Stewart with a young friend.

present home, a small unit at the base of a limestone hill in nearby Mosman Park. The wrench was painful, particularly the loss of Hamersley Lodge. It meant, however, that I had the funds for another ten years travelling — until I was ninety-four.

During my time of indecision, Stewart suffered a stroke which left him unable to speak and with muscular weakness down one side of his body. I was in Greece at the time, and Cliff wrote to provide the gist of the sad story. Stewart was becoming frustrated when he could not communicate and threw frequent tantrums. A major outburst followed the arrival of my letter stating that I would not be returning for some time. Both Cliff and Leoné advised me to stay away. They said that if I were to return all Stewart's friends would leave his care to me.

Stewart had been a burden to me since Alan died thirty years before and he had followed me to Perth. Whenever I was away Stewart moved easily with my friends at social functions, and was very friendly with a woman of about my age. He still saw himself as attractive to women. Once I was back however, he'd direct his attention to me. Likewise, while I was travelling Stewart would just as likely turn up somewhere along the track. He wanted to help but he drove me mad in his gentle, well-meaning sort of way. It was a tragic way as well. He could remind me of the feelings I'd had for Alan on which normally I kept a protective lid.

When I returned to Perth, Stewart was recovering physically.

He was working at re-establishing his verbal skills by writing down the simple words he could recall but not articulate. It was also sad that Stewart, the careful dresser, now had to be dressed. He was angry that he couldn't look after himself, although from another perspective he had never been able to do this.

I took Stewart back to twenty-seven for lunch each Sunday and out for drives. Once he walked into the kitchen and said 'Hello'. That sounded like an improvement. But he was looking straight at Cliff's cat and the word was probably a reflex rather than conversation. I had seen this earlier, whenever I arrived in Britian and visited Marjorie Holford, my friend who painted my portrait at the start of World War II. She was living in Brighton when she suffered a stroke, but had recovered sufficiently to travel in my van to visit Hilary. She looked marvellously well but her problem, like Stewart's, was with language. She'd start a sentence in full flight but before reaching the crucial part it had gone. Her look of horror followed by general frustration used to break my heart.

Eventually I followed the advice being given to me by my friends and went back to Europe. I was in Rome when I heard that Stewart had died on 1 June 1985, aged ninety-one. My emotions were mixed. I was sad because Stewart had been a good man who wanted to help even when I didn't want his help. I was angry because he had plagued me for so long. And I was relieved for a whole range of reasons, mostly concerned with Alan.

What I did next is still difficult for me to comprehend because, apart from my search for free camping sites, I had avoided thinking about money whenever possible. I walked into the first hotel I passed, and ordered a good dinner and a room for the night.

Stewart had often told me I would be a beneficiary of his estate. However, when the executors sought his will, the only one which could be found was in a bank safe deposit box and had been torn up. Consequently, it was not legally binding. I had no

291

idea who did the tearing, or why. What was clear was that, since I was not a blood relative, I would receive nothing. Even the possession of personal treasures like Alan's desk was in danger. For the next ten years the legal battle went on. I became angry and possibly quite vicious with my friends while legal costs consumed my funds.

The Land Rover remained at the Domaine over many winters. Meanwhile I had journeys to make as I sought to know more about Australia, so I bought a cheap VW camper. On a number of occasions I drove north to see Lillian in Darwin; shorter forays took me to the forest areas of the south-west of Western Australia where I was always entranced by the tall clean trunks of the karri.

I was still setting what I called in one letter 'a cracking pace' when I flew back to Europe in 1988. In three months I covered 12,000 kilometres while visiting one hundred friends. I classed it as 'a super trip'. And my luck with the vehicle held. No sooner had I pulled up the steep hill and parked on my plot at the Domaine to close the trip than the petrol pump packed up and I had to get Toto up from Le Muy to replace it. The vehicle seemed to know when it was safe to break down. Or was someone up there watching over me?

When I returned to Perth in 1991 I wanted a break from driving. I bought a Circle Oz ticket and travelled by train and bus around Australia for six months. I stayed in Baffle Creek in Queensland's north with Fred and

Providing a bit of publicity for Land Rover and Cécile's insurance company.

Audrey Green, friends who had sailed their yacht, *Coorong*, around the world. I'd last seen them in Greece. Or was it Italy? Or Cyprus? I went by bus to Port Douglas in tropical Queensland, with its long beach and rain forests. Lillian and Stephen had planned to move there, and I was playing with the idea myself. More than playing: it was difficult to resist the warm weather, the tropical rain forest and clear ocean currents.

In Europe, I was making less tiring and shorter trips from the Domaine to the beaches on the Mediterranean. These resembled my trips from Perth to Yanchep when I began my travels while working at Royal Perth Hospital. At one of these beaches, Les Issambres, I had a friend who hired a cruising yacht. Groups from the Domaine would sail up the coast. We'd stop for a swim once we were discreetly distant from prying eyes. Then we'd come ashore and eat lunch in a ramshackle cafe run by an English couple and erected right on the beach. We'd select from anchovies, sardines, octopus, mussels and other seafood, which sizzled over a bed of glowing coals, and drink local wines. We had to visit in season because at the end of it the building was unbolted and taken away, beyond the reach of the winter storms which seemed to target this section of coast.

I also liked to take my various guests for gentle drives down the coast, around the spectacular Estérel Peninsula, and through the poetic villages of the Riviera. Other times we would go down what seemed like an ants' trial when viewed from the Domaine, to Ste Maxime, to St Tropez, then to the stunning drive around Cape Camarat, and come back through forests of pines, cork oaks and sweet horse-chestnuts.

But trips of any length became increasingly rare. I was getting lazy and mostly drove to the sea for a swim. I wrote to a friend:

> I have just had in the van, lunch of croissants and farm butter, French cheese and wine and olives. The door of the van is open. The ocean is an amazing blue.

I still wondered about my future, as legal fees ate up both my funds and my patience. Two of Alan's cousins, who referred to themselves as 'very elderly ladies', tried to speed up the legal process. They wrote to the lawyers, probably overstating my situation a little:

> This poor lady is presently living in a caravan in France as she is so distressed at the long drawn out state of affairs she cannot bear to go back to Perth, WA, until it is all finalised.

They passed across their share of Stewart's estate but other family members remained recalcitrant.

I thought life would be more comfortable and cheaper if I used some of Stewart's money which had been passed across by the 'elderly ladies' to add a front verandah to my demountable home on the Domaine. This would allow me to stay put during the chilly months rather than flying home.

I was very taken with the heated pool at Draguignan in winter. It was here that I became friendly with a number of the locals. One of the swimmers, who called himself the Dyed-in-the-wool Frog, spoke good English and was continually asking about Australia. He took me to meet his wife who did not share his passion for swimming. They took me out to restaurants, and for picnics and walks in the hills. They were considerably younger than I was, and sometimes I rested in their van if I became too tired to walk as far as they did. Bit by bit I almost became a relation, and met their relations, and their friends and their relations. They would make leaving more difficult.

In September 1992, my zest for long distance travel returned. One morning I just climbed into the Land Rover and turned the key. I was off through the Canabières, Vidauban and Brignoles before driving inland on to the autoroute and spending the night on the roadside outside Montelimar. I visited the friend of a friend for an hour at Crest. Then on to Lyon and almost to Macon for my second night. As I was about to leave Macon, two young men in a BMW asked me where I was from. I told them, 'Perth, Western Australia.' One of them asked if he could take a photo of me (needless to say I didn't refuse). He said he worked for a magazine and asked me a lot of questions, and took more photos. I gave him an address to which he could send the photos. All of this pleased me no end. This is still the life, I thought. After only two days at the wheel I was feeling more like my old travelling self. Mind you, without the Land Rover which I'd been thinking of selling, the young men wouldn't have spoken to me. I couldn't imagine having an ordinary car: I'd be nothing.

The road from Macon to Bourges was ideal for me and my van. We could take the steep downhill stretches at a good speed so that we went up the other side like a bird. I loved hearing the engine pulling uphill in top gear, or even overdrive. The sound reminded me of driving to Scotland in my old two-seater Morris with the hood down. I stopped the third night on the outskirts of Bourges. I saw a quiet spot and asked the householder if I could stay there. She invited me into the house and offered me meat and bread and water. I assured the lady, who was leaning over a wooden gate, that I had everything I needed; but thanked her warmly.

The fourth night was spent under a fine big tree in the yard of a little cafe. Then I headed for Dinan, in north-eastern France, near where my family used to holiday; but not before ringing a friend, who had been an exchange student at Liverpool University fifty-six years before, to warn her that I was on my way. I arrived on her doorstep just at dusk with the makings for gin and tonic with lemon in my hands to mark three interesting days and four comfortable nights on the road, including two on the autoroute. My friend and I then further celebrated with a fine roast chicken, home-grown vegetables, and wines and liqueurs. Next morning I was on my way, speeding back towards the Domaine.

A few months later some of this enthusiasm for travel had waned. It was 1993, I was eighty-four and in the process of changing my mind again about where my permanent home should be. I wrote to Cliff Jones:

> I must let you know I am seriously thinking of returning to Perth next year — in fact before the 30th May which is the end of the three-year permit for being allowed back. At first I thought of coming back for two months. Then it struck me. If I did that, and came back here after another year or so, they might not let me back in again. If only I'd had the sense to become an Australian citizen while I was working I would not have had this problem. As it is, I don't want to run the risk of not ending my days in Aussieland! Unless I drop dead soon!!

I'd be broken-hearted to leave the Domaine. It would be nearly as bad as when I left Hamersley Lodge seven years earlier after selling Deane Street. I had always hoped that Cliff, Lillian and Stephen, and Leoné and Bob would come for one great summer and make 597 their base as we all moved through Europe. The Domaine hadn't been the magnet for my Perth friends that I'd expected. The only ones to visit had been Colin and Linda Andrews, Libby Baily, and Roger Dawkins, who turned up in 1992.

I then thought of hiring a really big camper in which to tour Italy and Greece with Lillian and Stephen. Then a letter from Lillian devastated me. She was to have an operation for bowel cancer. She told me she'd be okay: the cancer would not recur. But it did. She seemed to have recovered from the second major operation — but was not yet ready for travelling. Perhaps next year, she suggested. But that would be too late for me. I felt I had to be thankful for the travelling life I'd had, and to start preparing myself for yet another new life. But not quite yet.

Two months later I was driving from Montefiascone back to the Domaine along a beautiful road in central Italy which crossed and re-crossed the Tiber. I spent a night at Lucca then drove north on the autoroute for Palma, Piacenza, Alessandia, around Turin and west to Draguignan. Then Hey Ho to the Domaine 597. Travelling still excited me but I wanted this to be my last view of the mountains. 'I think it is most unlikely I'll come back to Europe. Life when I'm really old might be better in Australia,' I wrote to a friend.

I passed in my Land Rover to Toto and, just in case I should change my mind, I bought a camper version of the Renault van called the Gitane. The Renault was much easier to drive and the name Gitane (French = gipsy) naturally appealed to me.

After spending summer in Perth in 1995 I flew back to Rome. The flight exhausted me and it took me several weeks to recover. I stayed at Montefiascone near Rome with my friends Anthea and David. They drove me back through Pisa to the Domaine des Canebières. It was very restful. By June I'd changed my mind again. I wrote to Cliff:

> I am back in Provence admiring the view of five or six wooded hills and of course the valleys between them. There's scarcely a building in sight. All the same, I do not feel that I want to stay here forever. I actually want to get back to Perth. It's great to know that I prefer Perth and am looking forward to returning.

The friends I had in Perth, the closeness to the sea, and the fact that a winter in Perth was like a European autumn had persuaded me. There was also the question of language. I'd never been absolutely fluent in French.

At the Domaine I drove up and down the steep hills in my Gitane and waited for the weather to be warm enough for swimming. Swimming made me feel better but I still wanted to go home. I set off for Montefiascone where Anthea and David would care for my van — just in case I changed my mind again — and drive me to Rome for my flight.

I was about thirty-five kilometres from my destination when I rounded a corner with green fields on both sides of the road. A big truck keeping to the middle of the road forced me wide. That would never have happened had I been in the more substantial Land Rover: the truck driver would have moved over. As it was I went over the kerb then slid on the wet grass. The Renault careered down the hill until it came to a stop against a little wooden bridge. I got out unhurt, and the audience which gathered quickly helped me to a nearby pub to celebrate my deliverance. There I was able to ring Anthea — and have a glass of wine. Anthea came to collect me.

Soon I was flying back to Perth, probably for the last time. My back was extremely sore and it got worse sitting in the plane seat. A flight attendant wheeled me from the plane and into the passenger lounge in a wheelchair, right past my waiting friends, who failed to recognise me as an invalid. Then someone did and they all came running after me. It was great to be back.

Life Nine
The Anxious Author

Not Lying Down

I still felt full of beans as I resumed living in Perth and began my eighth life: that of the aged, anxious and often angry author. I bought a third-hand Mitsubishi van for some restricted travelling and occasional sleeping, and a friend loaned me her computer so that I could get on with my story.

I saw a lot of Gordon Stephenson. I'd known him since 1932 when he had just been recruited by the University of Liverpool's School of Architecture, and Flora Stephenson was one of the first wives on whom I'd called as the fledgling professor's wife. Our paths had crossed as Gordon's reputation as a modern planner and my infatuation with travel brought us to the same places at the same time. He and Flora had encouraged me to come to Perth in 1962.

In the mid-nineties, when I was in my mid-eighties and Gordon was three years older, I settled permanently into my unit at Mosman Park. I'd owned it for nearly a decade but hadn't lived in it very much. Gordon began to call every Sunday evening. I liked talking with this forceful man who was, I must say, considerably taller than I was. I liked doing the things he liked to do, like swimming and going to concerts and galleries —

but not watching cricket. I particularly liked the attention he paid me. I was also intrigued by his family background which was so different from my own. He often told me of his youth in Liverpool where his policeman-father had been sacked after the nation-wide police strike of 1919, and how he had to advance his education by way of scholarships. These took him to the Liverpool Institute High School which, he liked to relate, the Beatles Paul McCartney and George Harrison attended many years later.

Surprisingly, I came to enjoy cooking for Gordon. My menu was always the same: microwaved frozen whiting, potatoes and peas. He brought a bottle of wine. Sometimes we travelled to the south-west, to the picturesque timber town of Pemberton, and once or twice stayed in adjacent rooms at the hotel. These dinners and our occasional travels generated talk of wedding bells among Gordon's family and my friends. But I had no wish to be married again. I didn't want to be tied down. There were still distant places I wished to visit, even if it seemed most unlikely that I ever would. Besides, Gordon never actually asked me. He came closest when he invited me to go with him to inspect a unit in a retirement village. I thought I was there as a mere spectator but, during the inspection, he asked me whether I'd like to share the unit with him. The sales representative seemed interested in me and my answer, which wasn't surprising. By an extraordinary coincidence, she had been present years before when Stewart sprang the same question on me in similar circumstances.

I declined Gordon's offer as I had Stewart's. He seemed miffed and asked me why. I reminded him that years earlier he had rebuffed my suggestion that he should stay in my demountable house on the Domaine. I knew at the time he would have enjoyed living in France. He'd spent a year, 1927, on the Left Bank in Paris, and in the thirties he'd worked with Le Corbusier in the rue de Sèvres. But Gordon had declined my offer because he felt a need to be closer to his family and friends — and to cricket.

During his visits to Mosman Park, Gordon would glance over the bundles of paper packed in boxes around the unit — letters, diaries, photographs, postcards, receipts, and newspaper cuttings of almost a lifetime. He'd stare censoriously at my computer sitting there unmastered. Then he'd tell me I should be working on my book: I'd reply that my hands were so painful with arthritis that I couldn't operate the computer keyboard; that I had to use a pair of pliers to turn the key in the front door. He just said, in a way which encouraged no rebuttal, that he'd take me to his publisher.

Gordon had published his last book, *On a Human Scale*, in 1992; and soon we were on our way to the Fremantle Arts Centre Press. As always he knew the ropes. I followed his instructions and took with me the transcript of an extensive interview I'd done with Barbara Blackman from the Australian National Library. Barbara had been returning from Britain in 1987 when she began talking with my friend Colin Andrews who happened to be in the next seat on the plane. She told him of her interesting occupation: how she specialised in interviewing artists, scientists, writers and eccentrics. Colin said he could provide an eccentric like no other. Barbara left the plane in Perth to visit friends, and she also interviewed me. The publisher read the interview and agreed that I'd had an interesting life, but also that I needed to find someone to shape it into a book. This was not going to be Gordon.

For much of forty years, whenever he was in Perth, Gordon had dined every Saturday at the Houghton Winery in the Swan Valley, or in the city. On Easter Saturday 1997 Gordon drove to lunch through a continuing rain storm. He lunched with Angela Mann, they watched a video of *The Third Man*, then he left. He stopped, as he always did, to do his weekly shopping.

The heavy rain made driving tiring. That evening as he stood under the shower Gordon collapsed with a massive stroke. He was dead when found next morning. My emotions on getting the news were mixed. I was devastated by the loss; I was angry that the coincidence of the rain storm and driving had left him stressed; but I was glad he hadn't clung to life as Stewart had done. He would have hated that. He was not a patient man.

Without Gordon's impetus any prospects of ever writing a book seemed to disappear.

Cécile, Gordon Stephenson (right) and friends.

My health had deteriorated markedly over the two years between eighty-four and eighty-six. My brain was not working well. I'd forget things and I'd forget words. I'd lose my keys and the names of those I'd met only a few hours before. I'd search everywhere for one of my hearing aids then find I was still wearing it. My hands were sore and my knuckles swollen. All of this made me mad; and getting mad made me even madder. I wondered whether I was getting like my father who became so angry in his last years that people avoided him. I moaned a lot about my situation, and ageing generally, to anyone who would listen.

Then I had an extraordinary experience. Fremantle Arts Centre Press had promised to try to find a suitable person to work with me but I became less and less optimistic as the months passed. In my state of health and mind I wouldn't be easy to work with. Then, one morning just before Christmas 1997, Ron Davidson arrived on my doorstep. The first thing I noticed (of course) was that he was taller than I was, which seemed like a good beginning. I asked if he was a publisher. He said he was a writer and a psychologist, that he had recently retired from the Department of Psychology at the University of Western Australia, and was looking for a project to keep himself amused.

The writer-psychologist combination seemed an appropriate one: I was clearly a bit of a lunatic. We talked. I told him about some of the more spectacular aspects of my life and elaborated on the Blackman interview. Ron said I seemed to have had not just one life but a series of them.

I was accustomed to dealing with artists, not writers. I was unsure what they had for morning tea, so I offered my prospective collaborator a substantial glass of port. He seemed surprised but drank it. I asked why the Press had sent him to me. He said he'd already written a successful book in close collaboration with an older woman, and was prepared to try it again.

Over the next week we met two or three times, with Ron being interested and encouraging but also a little wary. I began to wonder if he reminded me of Alan, but then decided that he reminded me of the feelings I'd had when Alan was with me. These were unique feelings because I had loved only one man. The feelings were not easy to recognise as I'd been repressing them for more than forty years. Initially, I'd needed to do this to avoid thinking of myself as Alan's widow as I tried to start a new life in Australia (my journalist friend Hugh Schmitt called me the 'wandering widow' in his articles in *Woman's Day*).

Working on a book was pleasant enough at first but it soon threatened to kill me, literally. I made my first mistake when I decided that, because Ron reminded me of Alan and the feelings I had for him, he should therefore be doing for me some of the things Alan had always done. Alan had provided me with financial security, guided my social behaviour, and protected me from some of life's rough edges. But he'd also made me confront some of those rough edges.

I was in for a jarring disappointment with my collaborator. Instead of protecting me from the past he kept uncovering aspects of it I'd never wanted him to discover. Some of these came from books and some from my own letters written at the time. But he also emailed some of Alan's colleagues asking about their former professor. At first I was unfussed: Alan was a very good man. Who could say anything but nice things about him? He always said nice things about others.

Ron was evasive — or possibly protective — when I asked him to show me the email replies he was receiving. He hadn't heard anything; his computer wasn't working; perhaps the email address was incorrect. Eventually he just handed across a reply. It said that Alan and a number of the older professors might have provided the model for a satirical character, Deadwood Dexter, who featured in a book called *The Red Brick University*. He was also known as a wise man who only spoke when he had something important to say.

The first part of the reply was bad enough, but there were further shocks. I had always imagined that few people knew that Alan was a drinker; or that our marriage lacked a vital ingredient — sex. Now the evidence was flooding in: many knew the things I had tried so hard to hide.

I began to realise that an honest book about oneself involved a great deal of pain, and that I had probably been two years too old when I started. My reaction to my situation was strange. I didn't try to stop the collection of the material which was hurting me so much, even though that would not have been an unreasonable thing to do. I tried to protect Alan and the memories of my marriage by shooting the messenger. My early warm feelings towards Ron were rapidly cooling. I became exasperated about what seemed like his inaccuracies. He knew I was born in 1911. How could he suggest that I was four at the start of World War One?

I wanted to punish him. I began by telling him that he'd written about Hampstead, where I lived in my first and second lives, in a way that was all wrong; that he'd made it resemble some part of the Australian outback. If he couldn't write accurately about Hampstead what could he write about? I felt he wasn't too happy about that observation, but his self-contained personality refused to give me the satisfaction of a dramatic rebuttal. Then I read one of his books, *High Jinks at the Hot Pool*, about a titillating little Perth newspaper called the *Mirror*. I became fearful that he would write about me in an inappropriate manner; possibly in the style he'd used to portray the city's *demi monde*. Ron would only say that he was a writer and could write in a variety of styles to match the subject of interest, but he didn't say where that left me. I was beginning to feel hostile and highly anxious. I wondered what my friends would think of me if I told the whole truth.

Next I complained that Ron didn't praise anything I wrote or did. He responded that I didn't like praise and had said that, on the road, people had given me too much of it. This was true, but if ever I needed praise it was now. Our relationship became strained even further. I worried that perhaps he'd lose patience and drop the project. Sometimes I felt I wanted it to end: the process was too revealing and too damaging. Yet I feared going to my letter box lest there be a note terminating our ambiguous collaboration. Whenever there was a letter from him I'd keep it for days before opening it — with trepidation. Each time I'd be relieved to find I hadn't been sacked.

Finally, at my eighty-seventh birthday party, I exploded. Ron came into the room where I was surrounded by friends and enjoying being the centre of attention. He looked very pleased with himself as he approached me with a bunch of orchids: 'Happy birthday, Cécile ... I discovered today that Alan was hit by a tram during the war.' Instantly I became extremely agitated and hostile. Just a few of my guests were aware something dramatic had happened but had no idea what it might have been. Even Ron, the catalyst of my outrage and the target of my hostility, looked bemused during a tense one-minute silence. I broke the silence with, 'I wish you hadn't said that. You've just made me recall the worst day of my life.' That was all I said but I imagine my manner said much, much more.

Alan's encounter with the tram had been the trigger which led to my breakdown more than fifty years ago, and I had no wish to relive that awful evening. It was also the last thing I wanted Ron to know. This was about genuine personality breakdown, not a passing eccentricity. (I discovered a few days later that Ron had chanced upon the information in a brief footnote in Olaf Stapledon's biography when the book happened to fall open at that page.)

The event passed by most of my guests without leaving any impression. But I knew that this was showdown time for the writing project — and a crisis for me personally. I also knew I'd been caught out attempting to hide a pivotal event in my life.

That night and for several nights after I had terrible dreams and cried a lot. I thought they were the tears I hadn't been able to shed when Alan died in 1956, as I clamped the lid on my memories. My explosion had blasted away that lid and left me unprotected. The desolate feelings about the lack of sex in my marriage returned after a forty-year absence. Memories of being abused for ten years by my cousin returned unrestrained into my consciousness after more than seventy years. Ron was to blame for my predicament. I chided him: he was a psychologist and should have provided me with more support. He said that to that point in our relationship I'd provided no clues about the dark secrets lurking deep inside me or given any hint that I'd accept help from him.

There was another problem. My birthday signalled a threat to my mobility. During the previous thirty-five years I had been living and sleeping and travelling and just being independent in my various vans. It was a lifestyle which had suited me. I'd accepted, rather sadly, that long-distance travelling was now beyond me. But I could still pause and rest in my van whenever I liked. It might be outside the art gallery, where I'd take a break between intensive viewing sessions. Sometimes it was at Greenplace, a magical clearing among the limestone cliffs abutting the Swan River, which had once been the site of an institution for alcoholics and the mentally ill. For me that seemed to increase its appeal. I liked to sleep there, or walk down to the beach for a picnic or a swim: the waves there would caress me, not knock me over, as they did at Cottelsoe. In earlier times Greenplace was where I would take my friends, the twins Meg and Bar Evans and their sister Rachel Cleland, to have breakfast offshore, in my aluminium runabout.

My birthday meant I had to be re-tested to retain my driver's licence, which I'd held for the previous sixty-one years. The chances were that I wouldn't get it as my eyes were becoming a problem. I failed. My van stayed in the carport, while I had to be fetched by my friends. Normally I like being fetched, but not *having* to be fetched. It was very hard. I couldn't survive without transport. The train station was too far away for me to walk there. The home I loved quickly became a prison, and I was very miserable. I said I wanted to die, and checked that my life membership of the Euthanasia Association was still in place.

I thought I should get the van off my plot so I wouldn't be reminded of my earlier freedom, or be tempted to try to drive it again. Renée, one of the artists who had been a tenant at Deane Street, bought the van and drove it away. It was a big wrench but it put money in my hand.

I decided to test a four-wheel electric Shoprider, and rang a company specialising in equipment for the ailing. The salesman who answered asked what sort of vehicle I wanted. 'Oh, the best you've got. I want the Rolls Royce of scooters,' I said rather grandly. And this was what arrived, on the back of a truck. It was finished in a rich red lacquer with black lacquer trims; multiple speed settings with a relatively high top speed; a cloth cover to protect me from the sun; and even headlights. I bought it on the spot. The salesman provided some quick driver-training on the road behind my unit, then I took myself shopping.

In thirty minutes my life changed. I was free again, although not as free as I'd been with a van. I was at ground level and moving much more slowly than before. It reminded me of driving my 1927 Morris with the hood down. I talked with more people than before and made many new friends. Outside my supermarket I met a young women who obviously thought I must have some culinary skills — I'd had long enough to develop them. 'Can I use spring onions when the recipe says shallots?' she asked while checking off items from a recipe she'd torn from a newspaper. 'I don't cook,' I replied with a fair degree of honesty. We became fast friends.

The store manager noticed my glistening electric chair approaching on the second day and invited me to bring it inside the shop. Sadly, the automatic door-opener was not adjusted for the speed of the scooter — and the plate glass came tumbling down and shattered. No one was hurt, and the store manager seemed almost apologetic that his doors were so slow.

Having mastered the supermarket circuit, I went further afield in exploring my neighbourhood which included the Indian Ocean less than five minutes away and the Swan River which was twenty minutes in the other direction. I visited Greenplace, admired the yachts passing by and wished I was in one; then I went over the railway line and down to the beach. My only problem was that the electric chair was slow and had a battery with a range of something less then forty kilometres. I'd run out of petrol before and had had to send kind people back to the nearest village to get some for me, but having to slip a charge back into the battery was rather more difficult. Nevertheless I plotted longer and longer trips: south across the Fremantle bridges and perhaps into the Port City itself, or north to Cottesloe and beyond.

During all this activity I'd scarcely given my old Land Rover, The Protector, a thought, except perhaps to note how much bigger and noisier and faster it had been than the scooter. Then I received a letter from Peter Head, a Scot living at Port Grimaud on the French south coast below the Domaine. He had purchased it from Toto and had found my name and address in the service booklet. He wrote to me:

The Land Rover is my pride and joy, but you would hardly recognise it now. Whenever I have time to spare I carry out a little restoration work, or a modification, but it will be well into next year before it is completely finished (If it ever is!) ... Using parts from a Spanish built Land Rover I changed the bulkhead and windscreen, fitted left hand steering, changed the engine to diesel, and refitted the interior etc etc.

The front axle was rebuilt with disc brakes but I can't say that the braking has improved too much!

Anyway I use it daily when it's not being worked on — and am very pleased with it now. It was in a dreadful state when I bought it and the engine rattled like mad.

I was delighted to hear that my companion and protector had found a good home. But I wondered whether it was really the same vehicle after all those modifications. It was like the exam question Alan must have asked his philosophy students at one stage or another: 'Your bicycle has had three new wheels and a new frame. Is it the same bicycle?'

Other reminders of my past arrived at Christmas time. There was a letter from a couple who said I'd listened to them in the back of their van in Morocco, and others I helped in Rome and Nice. I couldn't remember them but they obviously remembered me. During my travelling life I had frequently helped other travellers, sometimes stopping for a month while their problems unravelled. We talked in the van. They seemed to get better, and that was sufficient reward for me. On those occasions I would leave the personal me outside the van door, rather than on the gatepost of my earlier life in occupational therapy.

Boxill, at ninety-two, made a Christmas call to me from her hostel in Kensington and we talked long and expensively about the joys of doing men's work. I told her about my book: she told me she had a photograph of the Women Decorators sitting on a plank between two ladders. It had been taken to be used in advertising and to be placed in the Women Decorators' window. She said she'd have the photograph copied and sent to me. I was excited at the prospect of seeing my old colleagues again — but nothing arrived. I phoned her but no answer. Eventually I phoned the hostel manager. She confirmed what I had begun to fear. Boxill had had a stroke soon after we'd spoken and died two days later. I was very sad. She was my oldest friend. Her nephew Roger had flown from New York and found the photograph. Soon I had a copy in my hand. Instantly I could run off all the names, most of which I'd forgotten over the years.

I also received an Inland Waterways calendar for the year 2000 sent as a present by a boating friend. Obviously the canals had been saved and would move into the new millennium as a major tourist and recreational activity. I thought of Conn, who had called the *Phosphorus* my 'seventy-two foot occupational therapy project', when her daughter Tregaye dropped in to see me on her way back to London from Sydney. I wondered what advice Conn would have given me about dealing with my miseries: 'Start some real occupational therapy on yourself,' I imagine. Real occupational therapy meaning an emphasis on occupation, not counselling.

So, I began a daily and extensive series of solo card games and my hands improved. I took my electric chair along a cycle track through the coastal dunes near my unit to a World War Two gun emplacement with a lookout. There I performed a daily regimen of one hundred steps. The lookout tower had twelve steps: that meant eight trips to the top of the tower, plus a few more to bring up the hundred. Then I would watch some rewarding Indian Ocean sunsets.

After this exertion I'd return to my patio and rest on the lilo. Gazing upwards, I would see only the overhanging branches of the sheoaks and gums, and the darkening sky. I could imagine I was camping in the Australian bush. There was no way I ever wanted to leave my home again though. I had once thought of finishing my days with my 'daughter' Lillian at Port Douglas in Northern Queensland. But Lillian had died of cancer, an event which left me utterly shattered. I'd always sent detailed descriptions of my travels in my letters to her and she had kept them. Her husband Stephen bundled then up and sent them to me. It was a long time before I could bear to read them or even look at them.

Over time I began to feel stronger, and the speed of my stepping increased. I could walk up the steep pathway from the beach at Greenplace to the parking area where the electric chair awaited me, with only an occasional pause. I was starting to show off to any passing walkers. This exercise was supplemented with daily doses of a Polynesian medicine which was based on a two-thousand-year-old recipe I procured after an advertisement was dropped in my letterbox. My doctor was treating me for a thyroid deficiency with thyroxin tablets which seemed to bring my body back to life in an amazing way. I became sexually aware in a way I hadn't been for many years. I wished it would go away. I was too old to be confronted with such feelings and decided to cut down on the number of tablets I was taking.

The need I'd felt to punish Ron disappeared as I began to write down a daily summary of my emotional experiences, as a sort of therapy. We worked together and treated each other like human beings. For the purposes of the book, Ron prepared many sheets of paper on which there were questions and spaces for my answers. I loved providing them. Earlier I'd have responded to some questions with bursts of hostility. Now I think both of us were coming to understand each other for the first time. I could write:

I now realise how much I owe you for having inadvertently opened the floodgates and cleared me of the dregs of my hidden sorrows. I can again enjoy my memories of Alan.

I thought of my time with Bill McRae and decided that Ron had done for me what I had done for Lillian. He'd offered himself as a dumping ground for the emotional residue — both positive and negative — from my marriage.

My dreams also became less threatening. One night I dreamt I was swimming in heavy seas off Cottesloe. A well-shaped wave picked me up. I looked down the chilling wall of green water. On earlier nights I would have been dumped, sucked up to the cusp of the wave, then dumped again. But this time I slid off the wave into a tranquil pool. Here I was safe.

Had things changed? Not completely. I still woke up crying. I decided it was my body not my psyche which was crying; crying because it had been denied its sexual needs when I was with Alan. Perhaps the thyroxin tablets were reminding my body of the problem. But I had to acknowledge to myself that no other man could have satisfied those needs as I had fallen in love with Alan and never fell out of love. I told Cliff and Leoné, who were becoming more and more like a son and daughter, my theories about the activation of particular hormonal pathways by my tablets. They laughed, but in an understanding way.

The developing book became an important part of my occupational therapy, especially after the tensions of the first year were resolved. I was reading drafts of the later chapters based on my travels. I loved reliving my journeys. I was in much safer territory emotionally. I also liked to do something I hadn't done before: like drop in some reinforcement for Ron. I could write 'Gorgeous. Thank you' beside a sentence which pleased me.

Another positive by-product of the book was quite unexpected and found me waiting at the Perth International Airport. I was there to greet Robert, Lord Balfour of Burleigh, and his wife Janet

Morgan. I hadn't seen Robert for about seventy years, when he was a two-year-old and I used to entertain him when I came to get work instructions from Bruce, who was his mother. We talked a great deal. Robert wanted to know more about his mother and how Bruce operated as a decorator from day-to-day. He also told me stories of his mother's early life, which astounded me.

By Christmas 1999 I had become a thoroughly experienced, (relatively) long distance scooter rider. I could comfortably reach several of my friends' houses to have lunch, and still have enough battery power to get home afterwards; sometimes just enough. Some of those at the lunches were older than I was. They could chat about the frequency and intensity of sex in relationships as though it was the most natural thing in the world: for instance that a friend in earlier times had expected an orgasm every morning before breakfast. I said nothing but I was reminded once more that mine had not been a normal marriage. I was starting to get some knowledge from my friends what a 'normal' marriage might be like. But, of course, for them that would have been some time ago. I wondered yet again whether Alan could have thought I preferred lesbian relationships — though I didn't have a clue about what they might involve. I still don't. But perhaps this, along with the additional problem of the effect of heavy drinking on the libido, was why he didn't pursue me in the way my luncheon friends seemed to consider normal.

There were other queries which came to mind. Should I have gone into Gordon's hotel room when we were travelling? Would he have welcomed that? We were both in our eighties. I still knew little and asked Ron about male expectations in such situations. He wasn't very helpful. He said he didn't know Gordon well and he wasn't in his late eighties. It was difficult to say. The same day I received a letter from a student I'd taught forty-five years earlier. She wrote: 'I used to watch your sad eyes in class and I knew that yours was not a normal marriage.'

Yet I knew I'd do it all again if given the chance.

Meanwhile I extend the range of scooter destinations. I cruise silently along a path which curves around the tops of the limestone cliffs overlooking the river where it runs deep approaching Fremantle Harbour. Large fish leap out of the water as they tear into a school of whitebait. I turn away because I am on my way to see a friend in North Fremantle, and worry that I might get lost and waste precious battery power getting back on course.

I stop to ask three old men who are chatting beside the path how I may reach the road where my friend lives. They all admire my scooter, then two of them drift away. I stay talking to the third man. He says he is only eighty-four years old, and he asks me for my telephone number. It is as if some button has been pushed. I astound myself by giving it to him ...

Selected Bibliography

This list focuses on those sources which were particularly important in the writing of this book.

PUBLISHED SOURCES

Bell, Quentin, *Bloomsbury* (London: Weidenfeld and Nicolson, 1986).

Brown, Andrew, *The Neutron and the Bomb: A biography of Sir James Chadwick* (Oxford: Oxford University Press, 1997).

Clark, Ronald, *J B S: The Life and Work J.B.S. Haldane* (London: Hodder and Stoughton, 1968).

Clark, Ronald, *The Life of Bertrand Russell* (New York: Knopf, 1976).

Cobban A, *A History of Modern France, Vol 2* (Harmondsworth: Penguin, 1967).

Dorward, Alan, *Bertrand Russell* (London: British Council, 1950).

Margaret Drabble (ed), *The Oxford Companion to English Literature* (Oxford: Oxford University Press, 1996).

Encyclopedia Brittanica Fourteenth Edition, Vol 12, Interior Decorating (London: The Encyclodedia Brittanica Company, 1929).

N Griffin (ed), *The Selected Letters of Bertrand Russell, Vol 1*, (Allen Lane, 1992).

Kelly, Thomas, *For the Advancement of Learning, University of Liverpool 1881-1981* (Liverpool: Liverpool University Press, 1981).

McNight, Hugh, *Canals, Locks and Canal Boats* (London: Ward Lock, 1974).

Mersey Dock and Harbour Board, *Port at War* (Liverpool: Mersey Dock and Harbour Board, 1946).

Mott, N F, *A Life in Science: Sir Nevill Mott* (London: Taylor and Francis, 1986).

Ray, John, *The Night Blitz: 1940–1941* (London: Arms & Armour Press, 1996).

Stephenson, G, *On a Human Scale* (Fremantle: Fremantle Arts Centre Press,1992).

Truscot, Bruce, *Red Brick University* (Harmondsworth: Penguin, 1951).

White, Alan, *G.E. Moore, A Critical Exposition* (Westport, Conn.: Greenwood,1979).

The Sphinx, University of Liverpool Students Magazine, Vol 14, 1, October 1906 (Work in the Settlements). 2

The Studio, Vol. XCV, 418, January 1928.

PRIVATE PAPERS AND ARCHIVAL MATERIAL

In possession of Cécile Dorward:

    Dorward, Alan, Journal on life at Cambridge, 1910-12

    Dorward, Cécile, Overseas letters 1958-1995, family letters, travel journals, canal journals.

    Dorward, Cécile, Personal diaries 1938-95

Liverpool University Archives:

    Report of the selection committee on the appointment of A.J. Dorward to the Chair of Philosophy at the University of Liverpool, University Report Book, vol 13.

Acknowledgements

Many friends helped in a variety of ways to get this book to the publisher. Barbara Blackman started the process with an interview for the National Library of Australia, and continued to provide support throughout. Thanks are also due to those who collected Cécile's letters from around the world and over fifty years, and returned them when we began work on the book. And to the many others who wrote letters to her over the same period.

Lord Balfour of Burleigh called in to Perth from Scotland and provided facts and insights about his remarkable mother, the twenties feminist, Dorothy Bruce, and photographic remnants of her time as a woman decorator. Janet Morgan (Lady Balfour of Burleigh) read an early draft with the critical and occasionally stern eye of the Oxford don.

The archivist at the University of Liverpool, Adrian Allan, gave us almost instant answers to a string of questions and provided primary information about Alan Dorward's life and times at the university. Barbara Milech advised on ways of writing an autobiography with two authors. Roger Boxill from New York flew to London and rescued the wonderful photograph of the Women Decorators on the job in the twenties, and sent it to us after finding it among his aunt's effects.

The photographs on pages 2, 311, 315 and 319 are by Victor France.

The article on page 224 is reproduced courtesy of *Woman's Day*. Unfortunately, efforts to identify the photographer whose work appears with the article have not been successful.

To Dianne, Emma and Jane Davidson, for their commentaries and corrections; likewise to Leoné Ferrier and Cliff Jones who helped so much.

There were many more.

Despite all this help, however, any shortcomings in the book are our responsibility.

The Authors

Cécile Dorward was born Cécile Marguerite Gabrielle Schmidt. In 1932 she married Alan Dorward, a Professor of Philosophy, and for a decade travelled the waterways of England, living in a canal boat. At the same time she worked as a pioneer in the fledgling occupational therapy profession. At fifty-eight she began touring the world solo in a campervan, travelling until she was eighty-four. Cécile now lives in Perth, Western Australia. *Anything But Ordinary* is her first book.

Ron Davidson was born into a newspaper family in Perth, Western Australia. He worked as a journalist in Australia and overseas and lectured in psychology at the University of Western Australia. He is currently an Adjunct Research Fellow at the Research Institute for Cultural Heritage at Curtin University. His works include *The Divided Kingdom,* with Connie Ellement (1987), *High Jinks at the Hot Pool* (1994) and a chapter on newspapers and propaganda in *On the Homefront* (1996).

First published 2000 by
FREMANTLE ARTS CENTRE PRESS
25 Quarry Street, Fremantle
(PO Box 158, North Fremantle 6159)
Western Australia.
www.facp.iinet.net.au

Consultant Editors Ray Coffey and Janet Blagg.
Production Coordinator Cate Sutherland.
Cover Designer Marion Duke.

Typeset by Fremantle Arts Centre Press
and printed by Lamb Print.

National Library of Australia
Cataloguing-in-publication data

Dorward, Cécile.
Anything but ordinary.

ISBN 1 86368 294 5.

1.Dorward, Cécile. 2. Women travellers - Biography. 3. Travellers - Biography. 4.
Occupational therapists - Biography. 5. Teachers - Biography. 6. College teachers' spouses
- Biography. I. Davidson, Ron, 1936- II.Title.

The State of Western Australia has made an investment in this project
through ArtsWA in association with the Lotteries Commission.

Publication of this title was assisted by the Commonwealth Government
through the Australia Council, its arts funding and advisory body.